One Man, Hurt

One Man, Hurt

by *Albert Martin*

MACMILLAN PUBLISHING CO., INC.

NEW YORK

Macmillan Publishing Co., Inc.
866 Third Avenue, New York, N.Y. 10022
Collier-Macmillan Canada Ltd.

Library of Congress Cataloging in Publication Data

Martin, Albert J 1929-
    One man, hurt.

    1. Marriage counseling—Personal narratives.
2. Divorce—Personal narratives.   3. Martin, Albert J.,
1929-   I. Title.
HQ10.M376   301.42′84′0924   75-4667
ISBN 0-02-580470-7

FIRST PRINTING 1975

Printed in the United States of America

TO OUR SONS,
who are what life is all about.

One Man, Hurt

ONE DAY LATE on a Saturday afternoon in February, 1972, my whole world suddenly exploded and was no more.

At the time, there was nothing further from my mind than disaster. I could not have wanted anything more than what I had: a wife I loved completely and exclusively; four fine sons who made life full and interesting; and a job I went to each day, looking forward to the work and feeling satisfaction when I got through. The home we lived in was perfect for us: comfortable, rambling, unpretentious, located in a lovely wooded area of a suburban Connecticut town.

As a man, a husband, and a father, I was at a point in life where I felt absolutely content with what was happening to me and with the direction in which I was heading. Most of the anxieties about what kind of life I could achieve were already behind me. Ahead were those situations which would only develop further what was well underway: making sure that Jim, Dan, Charley and Mark—strung out in ages from fifteen to five—got all the help my wife and I could give them in preparing to tackle their own lives; and, for Jean and me, using those middle years that were creeping up on us to deepen our own sense of fulfillment and enjoyment.

Half a lifetime of being married and knowing each other was a solid part of Jean and me as we both neared our forty-third birthdays, only a few months away in April. After eighteen years of a stable, untroubled marriage, I was convinced that there could be no big surprises in store nor any profound changes that had not happened by now. There was for me, in the way we lived each day, a deeply established sense of regularity and familiarity, an almost instinctive sureness that what we were doing was exactly right and appropriate for us. Jean and I had always worked out any differences over how to raise the kids, how to spend the money we had, and what to do next with our lives. More than being merely sexually compatible, we loved each other and sex was a continuing expression of this.

As I looked around at what life held for a man of my age, there seemed to me to be only a certain number of basic ingredients which could make him happy: the woman he loved and who loved him, children and a home, and a job that was challenging and satisfying. When you had those, there could be no imagining or faking the reality, you felt it in every fiber of your being.

I felt this wholeness completely and I knew deep down that I was content. And since nothing had come up to disturb the idea, I thought I had every reason to assume that my perfectly happy world would go right on the way it always had, right on until my old age, following the rhythm that six people leading normal, joyful lives together were producing.

That is why I was absolutely devastated when I came home from a short business trip that Saturday, February 5,

1972, and my wife told me that she did not love me any longer and wanted a divorce.

Wednesday, February 2, 1972

The night before I left on a short trip to Philadelphia was not particularly different from any other. Somehow, it should have contained some hint of impending disaster, but as I look back, I can't find any.

I had driven up our driveway, feeling the same relief to be home after the hour-and-a-half train trip from New York that I felt every night, and looked up contentedly at the big house set in the side of the hill, lights shining from it in the early evening dark of winter. The air was clean and cold. Someone nearby was burning a fire in his fireplace, and it smelled good; I hoped it was ours.

I climbed up the front stairs, felt the welcome warmth of Jean's hug and kiss, said hi to the kids, and went into our bedroom to shuck off the clothes and cares of the business world. With my around-the-house pants, shirt, and loafers on, I felt like a different man. I went to the refrigerator, took out a beer and sipped relaxedly while Jean and I caught up on the day's events. This was a nightly ritual which I looked forward to. While we talked, I usually set the table, unless one of the boys had done it already. Jean was easy to talk to; she had always been that way.

Suppers around our house were usually kind of noisy, and that night was no exception. Keeping four bouncy, exuberant boys under control around a dinner table is no easy matter. Jean and I were not insistent upon too many rules, but we had to have enough so that some order prevailed. For instance, no one was supposed to start eating till Jean sat down, and no one was to leave the table without being excused. But tonight Jim and Dan, the older boys, were in a hurry to get downstairs to our basement room for a jam session. Jim played bass guitar and Dan the drums in a rock group. Charley and Mark were trying to edge into the conversation to tell what happened to them at school. Amidst all that, Jean and I would like to have exchanged some information, but it was a bit difficult communicating over the din. Before scattering from the table, the boys had to answer my usual question: "Have you done your homework?" The answers came back: "yup," "none tonight," "did it in school," "did it."

As I began filling the sink to wash the dishes, Jean came by and gave me a kiss on her way out the door. She was going to a meeting at her church. We both went out to a lot of meetings. After leisurely doing the dishes, I packed my bag for the trip in the morning, watched some TV with the boys, and then put the younger kids to bed.

Just before going to sleep myself, I made the rounds of the boys' bedrooms, tucking in an arm here, picking up a toy there, covering a kid, giving the younger boys a goodnight kiss as they slept, exchanging a few words with the older boys, who were still awake. If there was one daily routine above all others that I deeply loved, this was it. After making the rounds of the boys' rooms, I would normally go to the day's final peaceful moments with Jean. On that night, she was still out at a meeting when I climbed into bed, so I was asleep when she got home. To my surprise and delight, she woke me up as she got in bed and we made love.

Going away on that short trip wasn't unusual. I had gone away scores of times over the years but I never bunched the trips too closely together or stayed away for too long. Jean and I were acutely aware of the problems caused by absentee fathers, especially in our area of town, where it was common. Besides, I knew what distance and separation from the family did to me, personally. The moment I liked best about a trip was coming home. Every time I came back, we picked up very naturally from where we had left off; the flow continued.

In the morning Jean made breakfast and drove me down to the railroad station so my car would not have to be parked there while I was away in Philadelphia. The conversation going to the train was so inconsequential, I can't recall it. As the train approached, I scooped up my things and started to leave. Jean moved over to the car window to kiss me goodbye. She looked the same as she always did: same delicate face, blue eyes, prominent brow, brownish hair, trim figure, still a size 5 dress after four children. I am much bigger (just under 6 feet and 185 pounds) than she is, so I had to lean far over to kiss her goodbye.

Saturday afternoon, February 5, 1972

I hopped off the train in late afternoon, hurried over to the waiting car, and slid across the front seat to give Jean a kiss. Her return kiss was only a dry peck. I looked at her in surprise, but she was already beginning to wheel the car away from the station.

I couldn't imagine what was wrong. She didn't look at me, just kept her eyes straight ahead on the road. After a few minutes she said, "Al, I want to go home to Texas." I was startled. A trip like that cost a lot of money, which we really didn't have. Besides, in the middle of a school year, someone would have to get the kids off to classes and be there when they got home; all kinds of complicated problems and involved housekeeping arrangements presented themselves.

I began to feel an uneasiness creeping over me. I sensed something was very wrong, but I didn't know what. Jean was different. She had never acted this way before, never. There was no warmth reaching out from her. She had never met my questioning looks so coldly, evenly, unansweringly.

"Maybe we ought to stop somewhere and talk before we go home," I said.

"Good idea" was her reply.

We drove to a park that was on the way home. As we pulled into the park, I remembered the many picnics, outings, and softball games I'd enjoyed there as a kid growing up.

Jean turned the ignition key off, paused for a moment, and said, "Al, I don't love you any more. I want a divorce."

I couldn't believe my ears. A divorce! I searched her eyes frantically for some hint she was kidding. It would have been totally out of character for her to do that because we never played games like this with one another, but what she had said was so staggering I wanted desperately to find some sign she was fooling. But I saw she was deadly serious. Her eyes were cold and set. I felt a falling sensation inside, as if the world had been yanked out from under me. My mind was spinning. Everything was a jumble, fragmentary images of what we were and what Jean was saying. This couldn't be. This couldn't be the same Jean, the Jean I had known and loved all those years. I couldn't find words to answer immediately. My mind and my voice were in two different places. Finally, I half cried and half choked, "You can't mean that. Why? What for? What about us? What about the kids?"

"Don't worry about the kids, they're tough, they're resilient. They'll get by. We can't stay married just for them. Al, I don't love you any more. I've got to get out. I've got to have freedom. I've got to find myself, become me."

"But why can't you do it with me?"

"I want spontaneity, life in my relationship. Ours is dead, flat. I just don't love you any more."

For a few moments neither of us said anything. My mind was filled with thoughts of me alone, in a strange room, surrounded by drabness, emptiness, loneliness. I remembered some divorced men I knew and pictured the kind of life they led: grabbing happiness in quick, makeshift relationships, visiting their kids on weekends for a few hours, trying to cram into a tiny interval the substitute for a whole lost life style. Some men liked this new freedom, their chance to get out and have fun. Very often it was their idea to split. But for me, Jean and the boys were the only things I wanted. Divorce was a rancid, distasteful, unnecessary, humiliating defeat for everything we stood for. How could I go on living my life without the people I loved? What would be the point of it?

I looked at Jean, but her eyes reflected no feeling for the enormity of what was happening. Little blotches of red showed just beneath the skin of her cheeks, so I knew she was excited. But any emotions she had were being held tightly inside, walled up there by sheer determination.

When Jean finally broke the silence, her words came out in measured spurts, precise phrases, as if she had been rehearsing what she wanted to say.

"I have been thinking about this for a long time, Al. The last few days gave me the space to make up my mind. I have been restless for months, troubled, awake at night."

I was shocked and surprised. This was the first I had heard of any of this. "Why didn't you tell me?"

"I tried, but I couldn't get it across. Remember our conversations late at night?" My mind raced back to them, and I remembered Jean saying that something was bothering her, but she didn't know what. She hadn't known how to explain it, except that something seemed wrong. We had talked about it on a couple of occasions, but she hadn't been able to come up with anything specific. I assumed she was just tired or working too hard and tried to comfort her by saying that she ought to take things easier and assuring her that everything would be all right. I remembered especially assuring her of my love because I thought she might be doubting it, might be worried about some middle-aged fling on my part, and I wanted her to be secure in my love. But I also remembered that she never mentioned any unhappiness with me, never made any complaints. The conversations had usually ended with Jean crying and me puzzled, trying to figure out how I could best be helpful.

I remembered that during those talks Jean had mentioned her religious conflict, and now I thought this might be the reason she wanted a divorce. Jean is Methodist and I'm Catholic. But during our life together religion had never divided us: I didn't want her to convert and she didn't want me to. We both accepted that we were different and helped each other practice the faith we believed. The children were being brought up Catholic, but that had been decided fifteen years ago and we'd never talked about it since. However, Jean's conflict had arisen recently because we both had become involved in a religious group called the Modern Liturgy. It was essentially Catholic, but also experimental; all the non-Catholic husbands and wives within the group were full partners and took an active role in all that we did. For the first time in our married life, Jean and I had been able to go to Communion together, plan the services, participate wholeheartedly, and enjoy the social gatherings together. Still, Jean did not want to leave her Methodist church, so she went to both. I thought this might be at the bottom of her unsettled feelings.

"Jeanie," I asked, "is it religion that's the problem?"

"No, that's not it. I want a simpler life, a new life, fresh beginnings. Al, I've got a different outlook, new values. This just doesn't make sense any more. I don't love you."

As I sat locked in my own despair, I suddenly remembered that same face twenty years ago, not taut and dead to me, as it was that instant, but alive and full of tenderness and love. Jean was a young ballet dancer when we first met; one critic had described her as a "tiny Dresden doll with a wide serene brow." She was a member of a newly-formed ballet company and I was a graduate student. I liked ballet, and during one performance I saw a petite dancer whose movements stood out in the corps as if she were dancing alone. The clean, precise way she moved her arms and legs caught my eye first. Then as I continued to watch her through rented binoculars I noticed the fragile, childlike face, the brunette hair pulled back in classic style, the clear blue eyes, the lovely brow. Her legs were long and graceful and her body dainty and elegant. She moved like a dream.

At subsequent performances, I found myself looking forward more to seeing her dance than to watching the ballets themselves. One night the curtain went up on Balanchine's *Concerto Barocco*, and I found she was doing a solo role. I quickly thumbed through the program to find her name. There it was: Jean Singleton.

I felt that I had to meet her, but it was more than a year before a high school friend joined the company and arranged a blind date with Jean for me. Waiting for her in the lobby of her apartment building one Saturday night in 1950, I thought that I was going to meet someone who was, like her stage presence, dignified and aloof—maybe even downright haughty in the flesh. When she emerged without her stage make-up on and without her toeshoes, she was even smaller than I imagined. She was wearing a wine-red velvet dress which made a stunning contrast with her light skin. But the biggest impression that hit me was of an extraordinarily friendly and open person, utterly un-pretentious.

From the moment that we met, there was a sparkle and wondrous quality about the night. We talked easily, comfortably, without any hesitations or pauses. When we got to the University Club, we glided out on the dance floor and held one another as if we had known each other for years. There was such an easy accessibility about Jean; she threw up no barriers, needed no defenses. She was just who she was, and that was that.

There was a strange, exciting feeling coming over me. I had never felt it about any other woman before. Until that night, I had dated a different girl almost every weekend of the fall; I had no desire to or intention of going steady with anyone. But this girl was different, a complete change of pace and personality from anyone I had been taking out.

Her Texas background might have explained part of this. Jean had the most delightful drawl and a charming, outgoing personality. But that wouldn't explain it all: I had gone out with girls from all over the country, Texas included. She was just extraordinary: direct, simple, friendly, intelligent, human, lovely.

I sat fascinated, listening to Jean tell me about growing up in Texas, a skinny, shy girl who didn't date much because she was so small. About her having begun ballet as a little girl, going through the rituals of recitals. And then about ballet gradually becoming so serious that she had to give up lots of things the other girls did—the after-school hanging out, weekend get-togethers. And about coming to New York at eighteen to study ballet seriously and being chosen to become a member of a New York ballet company that was just then being formed.

Jean was a wonderful listener, too; I had never met a person who seemed to listen so readily and to understand so accurately what I meant. Sipping her one whiskey sour, she looked up at me with lovely blue eyes I couldn't get enough of as I told her about growing up in Connecticut, a mailman's son who had wanted to go to college and someday be a reporter on the New York *Herald Tribune*. About my fulfilling this wish about college, doing well at college in activities like the school paper and being chosen president of a senior honor society, but never quite threatening Phi Beta Kappa with my marks.

By the time the night was over, I was completely captivated by this beautiful, disarming woman. She was a joy to be with. And she seemed to enjoy thoroughly and completely being with me. I knew something unprecedented was going on inside me. Never before, not even in my most romantic moments, had I imagined I was in love. But this night I was almost sure that I was.

For the next six months Jean and I carried on a classic stage-door-Johnny courtship. I would come down to the theater about 11:00 P.M. to pick up Jean after her performance. If it was a long program and she was still dancing, the doorman used to let me stand in the wings and watch the final ballet.

Because Jean was always one of the last girls to get

dressed and leave the dressing room, I had plenty of time to make friends. Many of the dancers I had admired became part of a nightly routine of greetings and conversation.

Jean may have looked tiny and fragile—she weighed only about ninety-two pounds then—but she had a tremendous appetite after performances. It took a big sandwich and some beer at the Carnegie Tavern to replenish the food she had danced off, and then we would go back to the apartment on the West Side where she had moved recently with two other girls from the ballet company. There we would talk, hug, kiss, revel in one another. It was a beautiful time and situation to be in love.

After my graduation in the spring of 1951, we reluctantly separated. I got drafted and was sent off by the Army to Japan. Jean went off to Europe with the company for a six-month tour. She and I had considered getting married before we parted, but decided to wait and do it right when I returned. Both of us felt absolutely confident that we would feel the same way in a year or so. While we were apart, there was plenty of time and opportunity for our romance to cool, for me to meet young women in Japan and Jean young men on the Continent. But nothing like that happened; instead, letters flowed between us daily, Jean's from Spain, Italy, Switzerland, France, Germany and England; mine, from Japan, had to be sent ahead of her schedule to be waiting when she arrived at each point. In Florence, she had nineteen letters waiting—and was the envy of the company. Neither of us had ever even thought about wavering from our intention of getting married; time and distance did nothing to the feelings we had for each other.

At long last, on August 29, 1953, a nervous young priest performing one of his first weddings married us in a Catholic church in Texas. That night, having known each other for almost three years and having been in love all that time, we made love for the first time. It had not been easy to wait, because we shared a healthy, active appreciation for sex. But this was a value we both shared and agreed upon. Our religious beliefs, the kind of standards instilled in us by our parents, and the morals of the time were all part of why we waited. But sex within marriage was part of the sense of commitment and responsibility we brought to our relationship, and we continued to live that commitment through the years—*until that day.*

But now, on that day, sitting side by side in our car, there was a different reality, and I came back to it painfully. I began to cry. I begged. I pleaded with Jean for what we had meant to each other for so long, for the children, for our parents. I asked her what had been wrong, what could I do—we do—to change it? I said I didn't know I had been hurting her—I never meant to—but now, for God's sake, couldn't we go on from here? We had so much to live together for. So many lives depended on what we did. This was something we had to, and could, work through.

All I wanted at this point was some sign that we could change this, that we could work together. But nothing I did or said got that kind of a reaction from Jean. When I looked at her, I was shocked and horrified to see that she gave no indication she was touched by what was happening to me. She was like marble. I couldn't reach her. There were no connections. She had become a stranger.

The stranger was telling me that my marriage was over. That she and I were through as a couple, and that the family we had built was now finished as a unit. That from now on, we would never touch each other, feel each other, have each other again. That children, parents, relatives, friends, love-making, parties, drinking, laughing, crying—everything we did together—didn't matter any more and were gone.

Dark, threatening clouds had been moving overhead slowly as we talked. It was chilly and damp. I sank further down into my topcoat, peering over the upturned collar so that I could look at Jean. She was watching me, waiting to see if there was anything more I wanted to say. Numbness, disbelief, shock, terror, confusion—all struggled within me. About half an hour had passed since we parked. It was beginning to get dark while we were still sitting there in the big blue Plymouth station wagon.

Jean turned the key in the ignition and started the motor. She had brought us there, said what she wanted to say, and then ended it. The ride home was a blur of trees, roads, cars. It was also a tunnel of despair tinged with the emergence of a new feeling, one I had never felt before—pain. Pain was located somewhere within me but not in any one place. It was an aching-all-over feeling I was to know almost without letup for the next year.

When we got home, I don't know which of the boys I saw first. I don't remember what I said, but I know how I felt inside: hollowed out, crushed, squashed into nothingness. And into that dreadful void, panic was creeping, a wild, desperate feeling that *my God, what has happened to my life? How can I live this nightmare? Something has to change this and make it go away. Jean wants a divorce! Oh, no!*

Saturday evening, February 5, 1972

The whole house was still standing as if nothing had happened; the furniture was in place, the walls were still

14

there, our children needed to be fed, the stereo was blasting, the kids were all talking, the cats and the dog were looking for food, nothing had stopped. I went to the phone and called Father Jack Connors, the priest who had worked with us in the Modern Liturgy and was very close to both of us. He was not home, so I left an urgent message for him to call.

In these first few hours of shock, I was already groping between two states of existence, my mind in one, my physical presence in another. Driving me relentlessly inside, pushing me for an answer, was the question: why? Meanwhile I went through the outward motions of eating, listening, talking, but my attention was focused on trying to reconcile those two worlds. Did Jean really say what I thought she did? Was that as real as my sitting there at that moment with activity going on all around me?

The rituals of the household continued, and I sank into them gratefully. One of the most satisfying from the standpoint of my being able to take time to think was washing the dishes. Over the years I had done some of my best thinking at that time. And that night, with the warm, soapy water swirling reassuringly around my hands, I set in motion the long process of trying to find out why.

I went back in my thoughts to those early years of our marriage in Texas, relived the feelings and searched them in the light of what had just happened that night. But what I recalled didn't lead in the direction of problems or post-wedding letdowns at all. The easy, comfortable relationship Jean and I had struck from the moment we met carried over into our marriage without a hitch. Living with one another only increased our happiness because we had each other full time. We discovered even more positive feelings as the pleasures of married love, of doing things for one another and with one another, took place daily.

Our differences of background and upbringing fed our interest and delight in each other. We both simply wouldn't have been happy with conventional, familiar types. Jean was not the kind of girl who would have married a Dallas insurance man, and I wasn't interested in a local stereotyped Catholic girl. Instead, we had reached far out for our choices, but they reflected the imaginative, ground-breaking way we felt about life. In choosing a career in ballet, Jean was departing from a proper WASP background of teachers and office workers. My going into journalism was a far cry from the manual labor that had been a part of my family in the generation before me. In each other, Jean and I found the excitement, challenge and fulfillment we had been looking for in a marriage partner.

Without any trouble whatsoever, Jean got a job teaching ballet at the school she had attended before going up to New York. Scores of pony-tailed little girls in leotards who had watched her in adulation while she took classes on vacation from the ballet company flocked to take her courses. Jean's return home was a triumph and wonderful fun for her.

Wherever we went, I liked being introduced as "Mister Singleton." I was proud of Jean and loved being her husband. While she taught, I frequently watched classes, admiring the grace and beauty of her movements.

Soon, the singular situation of being a Yankee in Texas with a New York City journalism degree landed me a job on a local paper. At long last, after all the years of preparing, I was finally a professional reporter at age twenty-four. In a short time I'd fulfilled the starting cub-reporter assignments and moved on to become a regular page-one byliner.

My job plunged us into the heartbeat of the city. Dinners, speeches, visiting celebrities, major meetings, feature stories put Jean and me where the news was.

Our circle of friends grew to include dancers and musicians and reporters and their wives who flopped on our living-room floor to drink beer and talk about art, argue politics or discuss world affairs. Jean and I were finding out the simple pleasures we liked best: enjoying the companionship of a few friends, talking, reading books, listening to ballets Jean had danced in. But above all, just being with each other.

As I looked back, I realized that this had to have been a testing time, too. Both of us were trying out new, basic roles in life. Jean was seeing whether she really was ready to leave the glamour of ballet to be a housewife. I was finding out whether I could make the grade as a reporter on a big-city daily. More importantly, we were testing whether I was really a husband and lover for Jean and not just a guy who wrote eloquently about those things from Tokyo; and whether Jean wanted these things and could make her own adjustment to her comparable roles. But it was all so enjoyable that it never seemed like a test or a challenge.

Thinking about Texas and feeling the mood of our years there, I was struck by an ironic recollection. Yes, Jean and I had talked about divorce! Over the years we used to kid each other about who would get Jean's parents if we split up because we both loved her parents so dearly. And as I searched through the dishwater now for one or two remaining forks, I thought that the one person I'd like to have been talking to just then, in this terrible crisis, was Jean's father.

Les Singleton was one of the most remarkable human beings I had ever met. Warm, friendly, understanding, very well-read, he was for me the kind of father I never had. He was also, I found out, an excellent dishwasher. He and I spent some of our finest hours in the kitchen, smoking our pipes and talking. One of our favorite topics was Jean. A mutual and noncompetitive love for her enabled us to talk for long periods about her, about our life together, about what we were doing, and what we intended to do.

Pap was short, trim, baldish, with glasses, and had a completely disarming way. He got along well with people, but not by using a patronizing or a hail-fellow-well-met approach; rather, he would peg people higher than they seemed to estimate themselves and in so doing draw them up to a higher level. He brought out the best in a person. He took substantially from everyone who passed his way in life, but he gave back something more, something which contained a lot of himself.

Pap and I enjoyed talking about politics, sports, religion, current affairs, Texas. On each he had observations which were finely intelligent and leavened with a sharp, playful wit. It was impossible to have a dull or unrewarding conversation with Pap.

There was another aspect of our relationship which was awfully important to me, too. Pap was not much impressed with making money or holding important positions just for the sake of doing so. What counted with him was doing something useful in life and enjoying it. He had made enough money as an accountant and office manager to provide comfortably for his wife and daughter. But it was the books that lined his library, the papers and magazines he took by the score, the conversations that grew out of knowledge and experience that were important to him.

Ruth Singleton was harder for me to get to know. She was by nature shy and bashful. Her childhood in the Southwest hadn't exposed her to people like me, Yankee and Eastern. It wasn't that she was afraid, but rather was too timid to reach out. She wanted to, just as I did, but something held us both back. Sometimes, though, on the screened porch in the evening, after we had been talking a while, we would hold hands for a moment.

Both parents were very much interested in what Jean and I were doing. They admired my newspaper work and followed Jean's dancing accomplishments closely. When we had our reporter friends or ballet dancers over, we enjoyed having Pap and Mamma with us. Pap especially liked the conversations he could get into with the young newsmen.

So as I looked back, all I had were good, positive memories of Texas. Whatever we'd expected from marriage, we found even more. There was no disillusionment, no planting of destructive seeds that I could find. Nowhere was there a hint of the answers I was desperately seeking.

As the evening wore on, I felt terribly alone and isolated. Nobody in the entire world knew what was happening to Jean and me: not her parents fifteen hundred miles away; not my parents a few miles down the road; not the people next door, whose lights I could barely see through the trees; not even the children, whose lives would be profoundly affected by what their mother had said to me just a few hours before. And not even Father Connors, whose help I wanted so desperately.

Jean had gone downstairs to the cellar and was putting a load of clothes in the washing machine. Without giving it a second thought, I started down after her. I wanted to be with her. I'd always done that. We would often chat while Jean sorted out clothes from the dryer or made sandwiches for the boys' lunches next day or sewed some torn pants.

Then I stopped short on the landing. The realization struck home: Jean didn't want me. She had said she wanted me out of her life. She didn't care to talk to me. The impact was hard. But what was I to do? I had to have some contact with her, we just couldn't cease to exist for one another. We couldn't throw away emotions and habits rooted in almost nineteen years of living together. We couldn't go into reverse gear at a moment's notice—at least, I couldn't.

I couldn't go away from her, so I continued down to the cellar. I picked up where we had left off a few hours ago, asking her to consider what she was doing to everyone. But Jean had a tough resignedness about her. "No, Al," she said, almost wearily, "it's no use talking about the same things again. I don't think that helps anything."

Rebuffed, I went upstairs to wait for Father Connors' call. Fortunately, the children were scattered throughout the house so that I didn't have to make conversation with anyone.

My mind again went back to the question "Why?" as if magnetized by it. Had there been any unhappy periods? I had to think hard. Yes, but we'd thought about them as strengthening us, not as being destructive or negative in any way.

One time was when we decided to leave Texas after two years there and move to New Jersey. There were a number of reasons why we did this: I wasn't making enough money as a reporter there, and prospects were very limited for the future. When a job offer of twenty dollars more a week came, we took it. We left Texas with genuine reluctance and happy memories, but we both felt eager to make the move.

Everything turned out to be wrong about Newark. The newspaper was the exact opposite of the Texas paper. Stories we covered were lurid and sensational—crime news, articles about freaks doing freakish things, the bizarre disguised as something of news value. The city room was cluttered and filthy; at night large rats hurried across the floor into dark corners. The atmosphere and the purpose of the paper contrasted completely with what I had known before.

Where Texas had seemed clean, modern, bursting with vitality and friendliness, New Jersey was tired, dirty and old; people seemed unhappy to be there. Jean and I knew no one and were able to make few friends.

And our apartment, a place we found after more than a week of looking, was a far cry from the cheerful Texas rooms. The walls had been painted over several times, cockroaches abounded in the kitchen, and the windows overlooked a bleak tarred parking lot. If there ever was a time for us to be recriminating, angry with one another, disillusioned, this was it.

But instead we drew closer. When I came home from work near midnight, Jean and I huddled together out of sheer relief and joy. We had each other. That was what counted. Instead of driving us apart, the miserable living conditions made us find new depths and new resources in one another. Just the presence of each other gave us strength. I couldn't imagine going through the experience with anyone else.

In a few years we got out of New Jersey. We had come East to be able to seize job opportunities in New York when they opened up, and one such chance came up at a network. I got the job and we moved to Connecticut as soon as we could.

The New Jersey years couldn't be, as I looked back on them, a time in our lives which foretold of trouble ahead. I thought about this some more and realized that there was only one other period of our lives I could describe as a tough time—a true emotional trial—but I couldn't call it unhappy.

My thoughts went back to a morning in May 1958 at the

local hospital. Our second boy, Dan, had just been born. As I waited nervously, the doctor came in to me with a frown on his face; I knew immediately something was wrong. "Don't worry," he said. "There's a problem, but everything will be all right. Come on, meet your son."

When the nurse held the tiny baby up for me to see, almost pressing him against the window of the nursery, my knees buckled. His tiny lips and mouth were laid open as if they had been hit with a meat cleaver. The doctor had mentioned something about a "cleft palate and lip," but I was too excited to register what he was saying. I felt myself get weak all over, reached for a doorjamb and sank down to a sitting position on a stair. The doctor told me to put my head between my knees.

When I went to see Jean, her eyes were red. She was a small mass of bedclothes, ether, cracked lips and tears. We cried together for a few moments without saying anything. Then I told her the doctor assured me Dan would be all right; in fact, we'd get going on the first operation, in New York, within a few days. We both smiled at that, reassured ourselves that everything would be all right and felt better.

And everything *did* turn out okay. Dan had four operations by the time he was eight, but he became a physically normal boy. The process wasn't easy for us or for him. We borrowed three thousand dollars from Pap to cover Dan's medical expenses for the first year, and paid it back within a year. I went on the network's overnight staff to make the extra money we needed. Dan went through lengthy speech therapy and orthodontics and came out of it physically perfect. At the same time he developed an inner strength and determination that have been an important part of him ever since. Jean and I had worked closely together during this "unhappy" time, and the experience strengthened all of us.

Now, as I finished the dishes and went into the living room, there was still no call from Father Connors. The housekeeper at the rectory had thought he would be back soon. It was about five o'clock when I'd called and it was seven-thirty now. I began to get worried that he had gone out for the night.

When I thought about Jack Connors calling, I realized how much I relied on him, even though we had known him only about two years. Jack (nobody in the group called him "Father Connors") didn't know us when Jean and I first moved to Connecticut, but that was our real formative period. That was when we bought our first home: a small, cheerful white house with a weeping willow in front and a wild cherry tree in the backyard, with boulders left by the builder dotting the area and giving it a natural look.

For the first time we felt like solid, substantial grownup people. We owned our own home, had our first-born son and were permanently sinking our roots in this community. What we did in that first home, as it turned out, affected a great deal what came after. That was where Jean began her role as mother, pouring into her care of Jim the creativity that she had previously put into church and dance and other activities. The first complications of parenthood —the disruptions in our freedom, the adjustments we had to make—took place in that first home. And we seemed to cope with them effortlessly and joyfully.

In the evenings I'd come home from work and take Jim out for a walk while Jean finished getting dinner ready. We both shared his feedings and diaper changes. When I first gave him a bath, I felt awe at the tininess of this little creature who embodied so much of our love. Our life centered on Jim during those early months. Moments talking together when he was asleep tended to drift around to what he had done or how he was coming along.

Home meant a great deal to Jean and me—it was our anchor—but we both felt our lives would be incomplete and too narrow if that was all we had to live for. Becoming active in the community in some way was part of what we thought our lives should contain. Commuting to work one day, I read a story in the paper about the need for active interracial groups within religious denominations. When I found out through a few phone calls that the Catholic church had nothing of that sort in our area, I began to form a Catholic Interracial Council.

The first meetings took place in our living room. Only a half-dozen or so people took part in the organization. From the start, Jean was part of our planning and organizing. We both felt strongly about the principles that lay behind such a group. She brought to our efforts the long experience she had gained in Methodist church committees. Jean and I worked well as a team; it was the first time we'd ever tried to do something together that wasn't directly related to our own family. While I was absorbed in trying to set the goals and directions of the group, she was very good at sensing how people were reacting, who would be good for certain jobs. After a meeting we would talk over what happened, and Jean would say, "Rose seemed really excited about a speakers' bureau. Why don't you see if she'll take it over?" Or, "Wynn is disturbed over the direction of that intergroup program. Do you know why she feels the way she does?"

Jean helped me in another important way. She gave me the confidence to do things I'd never done before. As a reporter, I had always watched others speak, act and relate to one another. Now, as a founder of this group, I was being called upon to be a public leader and spokesman. The first time a group called me to make a speech before their next meeting, I was petrified. I wanted to do anything to avoid having to get up in front of an audience and make a speech.

Jean began by giving me the assurance that I could do it. Then she worked with me on the speech, listening as I delivered it to her in our kitchen, making corrections, telling me how I was coming across. When I grumbled that I'd "never be able to do it," she wouldn't listen, but kept me busy working at it.

The night I was to give my first speech, I went down to the meeting shaking inside. As I waited to speak, I wanted desperately to be somewhere else. But finally the introduction was made, and I was on my feet. My eye caught a man who had been on our local draft board and I directed a remark to him, saying I'd never really had a chance to thank him for my trip to Japan. The chuckles that greeted my comment broke the tension, and I went into the speech which Jean and I had rehearsed. I'm sure the talk was no world-beater, but I *did* it; and afterwards she could say, "See, I told you you could do it."

As the two boys got past babyhood, Jean had a chance to get out and try things herself. She went to meetings of the League of Women Voters, started teaching ballet classes at the YWCA, took on more responsibilities in her church's Sunday school. And we both continued our involvement in the growing work of the Catholic Interracial Council.

Out of our enlarging number of activities came a whole new group of friends. We had naturally started with the people I grew up with as a youngster. Now we added friends from the interracial work, from Jean's ballet teaching, from the television world in New York. We always liked to be around people, to entertain small groups of friends for an informal evening, and we did more and more of this. We felt we had a perfect balance of serious, worthwhile effort and easy enjoyment of people.

And our family began to grow again. Charley came along, four years after Dan. That meant a temporary curtailment of Jean's activities. The children were growing up in an easy, pleasant atmosphere: kids swarmed all over our neighborhood, crossing from yard to yard in packs, spending the entire day outdoors, climbing trees, jumping off rocks, playing cowboys and Indians or Army. We were extremely, extremely happy, very much in love, and doing what we wanted with our lives.

Those were the years that had given us our choices, that had started us in directions leading right up to where we were that day. They had seemed sound, healthy patterns, ones leading to a solid relationship and family life that could withstand pressures.

My thoughts were suddenly interrupted by the ringing of a telephone.

I SNATCHED UP THE PHONE and Jack Connors' cheerful, booming voice was saying, "Well, Albert, what are you doing home on a Saturday night?"

I closed the kitchen door with one long swipe, gripped the phone tight to my ear, tried to steady my voice down low, and said, "Jack, something terrible has happened. Jean wants a divorce."

There was silence. A long pause. Then: "Are you kidding? Are you sure?"

"Oh God, yes. She told me just a little while ago. I've been trying to get you ever since." I began telling him what had happened in the park. As I started to talk, my voice broke and the tears choked me off. I put the phone down and cried. When I thought I could manage to talk again, I began, but it came out half sobbing, half talking.

For about ten minutes, I struggled along this way. Finally Jack had pieced enough together to realize the absolute seriousness of what had happened. "Why don't you and Jean come right on down," he urged.

Going to see Jack Connors—or having him come to our house—was such a normal thing to do that it caused no unusual reaction among the boys when we told them we were going there. Jim and Dan were instructed to stay home until we got back, then they could go to the coffeehouse at the church down the street.

As we got into the car, I was glad to be going somewhere with Jean. This was part of our normal world, exactly what we would be doing on a Saturday night—going out together —and it connected me with the rest of our life. My spirits lifted, too, because of the person we were going to see, Jack. I felt he was the one person we should be talking to right then. He was a friend, a clergyman, a man we both trusted and loved, and he was trained in handling personal crises. After all, Jack had seen people die, had been with them in their last moments. He would know how to handle an emergency like ours. Jean and I said little as we drove along; we were both wrapped in our own thoughts.

Jack's rectory was about twenty minutes away, and when we got there, he answered the door almost immediately. He was wearing a dark polo shirt and slacks; I could count on the fingers of one hand the number of times I'd seen him in a Roman collar. He looked at us both briefly, searchingly, and then led us into one of the parlors. Jean and I took seats on a sofa and Jack sat opposite us, behind a coffee table. His face wore a welcoming smile, but beneath it I could see worry and concern. His appearance was deceptive. He looked and sounded like a Boston Irish parish priest— affable and charming, but without much depth—but you had only to talk with him a few moments to discover that he was a perceptive, sensitive human being who perhaps sensed intuitively as much as he caught with his attentive eyes and ears. Although he was several years younger than I was, in his late thirties, I always felt he was older than me.

Jean looked at me as if to say, "Go ahead, you begin," so I repeated in greater detail what I had said over the phone.

After a few moments he said, "Okay, look, the best way for me to talk to you two is separately. First let me talk to Jean alone, Al, and then you. Why don't you go upstairs for a while and wait?"

That sounded fine to me, so I climbed up the stairs and walked past Jack's room, rumpled and book-strewn, down the hall to the big living room. I wandered into the empty room—none of the other priests were around—drifting aimlessly, taking books off the shelves, looking at them, putting them back; picking up magazines, flipping through them, putting them down; checking through rows of liquor bottles on a server, thinking I might make myself a drink, then deciding not to. Finally I sat down in a stuffed chair, lit up my pipe and tried to convince myself that I was relaxed and settled. I looked at my watch. Only five minutes had gone by.

What a strange sequence of events, so inappropriate to this night, had originally brought Jack, Jean and me together. Three years before, a group of us going to the same Catholic church had become dissatisfied with the kind of worship we had been experiencing each Sunday morning. Each of us had been looking for something more meaningful and expressive of ourselves. Gradually, just by talking to one another, we found a number of people who wanted to start something different.

The "something different" was at first a folk mass, the kind of less formal Catholic liturgy that was just becoming possible. But soon it evolved into much more. Working together, we created a whole new, warm, friendly atmosphere. The group was basically Catholic, but it was open and ecumenical in all respects. Everyone was invited to receive Communion; everyone was eligible to take positions of leadership; everyone helped plan and carry out the services. Jean had been feeling the same lack in her own personal worship, so she took part in the liturgies from the start, as did many other non-Catholic husbands and wives.

I remembered the pioneering, almost revolutionary, feeling of those first few weeks. Everything was in our hands. We planned the themes for the liturgies, selected readings, thought of ways to dramatize and illustrate the essential points. We dealt with loneliness, alienation, conscience, guilt, faith. Dramas, monologues, poetry readings, slides, movies, records—all were used to give color and impact. Dammed-up creativity burst forth in a torrent.

Our long-haired teenage kids dropped their cool and joined us. Soon a rock group with electric guitars, drums, trumpet and tambourines was thumping out music from *Hair* and *Jesus Christ Superstar* during our services. A teenage singing group led us in a combination of folk and spiritual selections.

Enthusiasm spilled out over every aspect of the service. Couples took turns standing at the door and greeting newcomers. An impromptu nursery took care of toddlers. And instead of sitting mutely in pews during our "dialogue sermons" the members of the congregation got to exchanging ideas among themselves and with the priest.

Going to church on Sunday, for the four hundred people who crowded into the pews every week, became something to look forward to eagerly. A coffee hour after each Sunday service loomed as a social highlight of the week; conversations between adults finding each other after years of stereotyped churchgoing went on for hours.

What was happening in between Sundays was just as important. Planning the services brought couples together and made deep, purposeful relationships flourish. Soon families began coming together, first for social events, then just to get to know one another better. The idea of a community or an extended family took hold. Nothing like this had ever happened to any of us before. We discovered mature human beings we wanted to be with who were not relatives, not people we grew up with, not business associates, but people from all parts of the country who came together out of spontaneous and mutual needs.

At the center of the whole experience were Jean and I and Jack. I had been elected chairman of the group; our home was the headquarters for frequent meetings, drop-in get-togethers, evenings for talking and having a drink. Jean was part of the liturgy planning group; Jim played guitar in the rock group; the whole family was involved. On some weekends five or six couples would go away together to Manresa, a huge Jesuit retreat house in Ridgefield. Together, with scores of children roaming the grounds and endless halls, we got to know one another, planned for the future of the community, ate, prayed, sat around fires in the massive fireplaces, experienced grownups to a degree unprecedented for us.

This gave Jean and me a chance to worship comfortably together in a "neutral" setting. She had come to my Catholic masses and I had gone occasionally to her Methodist services, but the Modern Liturgy—as our group was called —was something we were all evolving from the ground up.

Leading all of us, was Jack Connors. No clergymen in any of our backgrounds had ever played the role Jack was playing. He had dropped all barriers between us and him. He was simply part of the community: its priest and minister, but as a servant, not as an authoritarian leader. He moved among us as if we were all part of his family. Most times, he ate an evening meal at someone's home. Every kid in the community knew, welcomed and loved Father Connors. Jack knew all their names and knew them, too. Whatever we did as members of the group, Jack also did. He planned with us, argued with us, anguished with us, joined us on Saturday nights for parties. He became a confidant and close friend of scores of individuals, women and men. He was an integral part of all our lives; at that point he knew us better than our own parents.

That was why I had turned to Jack this night and why Jean had agreed to see him. I looked at my watch; it was now twenty minutes since he had started talking to Jean. Five minutes later I heard a door opening downstairs and then Jack's voice calling, "Hey, come on down." As I started down, Jean was coming up, her eyes held tight to the floor in front of her.

I looked anxiously at Jack as he closed the door behind me. I wanted his look to tell me that he had not found things as bad as I had thought. But what he said was "Look, I can't begin to counsel Jean and you. I'm not qualified to, and you're both too close to me. It takes someone who's an expert. I have a person in mind. Right now, the important thing is to give Jean some space. She wants to get away to Texas, and that's the first thing we have to take care of."

"What do you make of this?" I asked.

"I just don't know," he said, his voice serious. "I'm just as shocked as you are. I thought I knew Jean and you, and I never would have predicted this, never. I know how you feel. God, it's all over your face. But you can't tell yet. These things take time to work out. I know Jean's in a big turmoil now, and we have to let that settle down a bit. When she gets back, there's one guy I'd like you two to see, but he's awfully busy. There's lots of this stuff happening. I'll have to call him and see if he'll take you."

"Do it, Jack, please, for God's sake," I said. "Whatever he charges, we'll pay it somehow."

"Jean doesn't even want to talk about counseling now, and I don't think I should press it. She just wants to get away and that's what she needs most."

"Okay. But can you call the guy for me? I want to get going as soon as I can."

"I'll try. His name is Samuel Glazier. I'll call him tonight or tomorrow, whenever I can get him, and I'll let you know. Let's call Jean back now."

When Jean came back into the room, my eyes went to hers immediately, hopefully. She ignored me, brushed me aside; I tried, but couldn't attract her eyes to mine. Instead, she fixed her gaze on Jack and waited for him to say something. I felt the coldness and harshness of the rejection.

"Okay, so I think we're agreed, Jean, that you ought to get away to Texas as soon as possible. How soon do you think that can be?"

"I'll call home tonight and see. I'll have to make some arrangements about the kids while I'm gone. I'll take Mark with me. That will solve a lot of problems."

"Good. Now, there's one guy I'd like to see you both with."

"Jack, I'm not making any commitments about that yet."

"I know, Jean, but Al wants to get started and I think it would be good for him to do that if this fellow's available."

We talked for a little longer, about Jean's trip, about how other members of the Modern community could help me and the boys get along. Both Jean and I talked separately to Jack, not to each other. He seemed to offer a buffer between us, a protection against the strange new uncertainty of talking to one another.

Only the week before, all three of us had been together at a Saturday-night party, everything seemingly normal, nothing unusual. A little more than a month before that, the group had a New Year's Eve party, a gambling-casino affair in one family's huge living room, with roulette wheels, gaming tables, chips, prizes. When midnight struck, Jean and I found each other amidst the cheering and yelling, kissed and wished each other a happy new year, and added, as we always did, "I love you."

Now here was Jack this night, seeing us to the door of his rectory, Jean's and my life in pieces, and a whole new mood and relationship existing among the three of us. Jack showed his worry in the lack of bounce in his step, the preoccupied frown on his face. Even so, I felt a sense of confidence in him, as a friend and as a clergyman who had seen plenty of people in trouble and who knew what to do. And surely, I thought, he knows, as I do, all that Jean and I have going for us, what an unthinkable thing it would be to get a divorce; and he believes, as I do, that this is a temporary furor, inexplicable as it is, that we will survive it, that everything will be all right.

At the door Jean reached up and gave Jack a kiss, as she always did. I gave him a firm, lingering handshake, searching his face still for answers. But all he gave me was a quick smile and a simple "Good night."

When I took the boys to church the next morning, my appearance must have betrayed the terrible shock I had received barely eighteen hours before. I had slept fitfully and I felt drained, desolate, exhausted. Normally, being among these people I cared about so much and worshiping with them uplifted me and made me feel joyful and full of zest for the day. This morning it pained me just to be there. As I sat down and looked at Charley and Mark sitting next to me, and Jim and Dan off with a group of teenagers, I wanted to cry again. Losing the boys, being

34

torn away from them, was the greatest calamity I could imagine. Jean was not with us; she had gone to her church, and I missed her badly.

Nobody knew what had happened or how I felt inside. It was an incredible feeling. I was an absolutely smashed and shattered individual behind the mask of my face, but to all outward appearances I was still Al, of Al and Jean. A few friends detected something wrong and asked what was the matter. I gave a phony, superficial answer about "not feeling well this morning." When the service was over, I didn't linger for the coffee and conversation I usually looked forward to.

The rest of the day was a restless, disjointed blur of trying to live my two lives going on at once: the talking, hearing, seeing, doing that were measured by the ticking of the clock and the passing of hours; and the timeless, constant flow of questions, anxieties, fears and uncertainties going on inside me. Most Sundays, Charley, Mark, the little girls next door and I would go for a walk in the Arboretum or the Nature Center, both nearby. Or in the summer the family would go swimming in the lake; during the winter, if we had ice we'd go skating and play hockey. This had been a bad winter for skating; there wasn't any ice this day, so I drifted from thing to thing while the kids played out back.

I couldn't read the Sunday paper. Nothing took priority or was strong enough to distract me from the single subject that filled my mind: my relationship with Jean. She wasn't even around; she had gone to some affair at her church. All I could do was wait. At some point I called my brother Ralph in Vermont and blurted out the shocking news of Jean's announcement. He was very upset. I promised to keep in touch with him.

That night the short phone call I had been hoping for

came through. Jack called to tell me that he had reached Sam Glazier and that I had an appointment to see him at nine tomorrow night.

Early Monday morning, long before dawn, I became aware that I was awake. I had apparently been conscious for some time, but lying in a stupor, as if groping for the cause of my being awakened. It seemed as if a force, rather than a specific reason, had been working on me, edging me out of sleep and leaving me with vague feelings.

I sat up in bed and looked unbelievingly at Jean. She was sound asleep next to me. Her hair trailed across the delicate line of her shoulder as it always did; her face looked childlike and soft, as I was used to seeing it. She breathed with the same regularity; her warmth was just as comforting as ever. But she was not the same Jean; nothing was.

I began to sweat profusely and lay back trying to calm myself. But the more I tried, the tighter I got. I didn't want to awaken Jean—there were many more hours of sleep to go before daybreak—so I lay very still. The ghastly, riveting, inescapable reality of what had happened to my life grabbed me and I began to feel panicky and sick to my stomach. I told myself, "Get a grip on, don't panic, don't imagine the worst, everything will work out." Then I remembered my appointment that night with Sam Glazier, and the tight knot of my muscles, which had contracted throughout my entire body, relaxed a little. Sam would help; he had to.

For the rest of the dark and quiet hours until daylight, I lay there half asleep, half awake; half torn by fear, half assured by hope. My hand slid between Jean's thighs as it had throughout the years, and the warmth and familiarity of the feeling gave me comfort. In that position I dozed off briefly. Then the alarm went off.

36

On the train to New York, I held my newspaper in front of me, but my eyes were not reading it. I was still in a trance. I could see men all around me, scanning newpapers or working out of attaché cases or playing cards or sleeping. I suddenly felt a longing to be one of them, any one; to slip out of the trap of my skin and my identity. Over the years I had not felt particularly close to men such as these. The business world was alien to me; I felt awkward, off balance, out of place with men who absorbed that life so completely and took it in stride. I felt more at home with people doing more abstract things: writers, like myself, social workers, civil-rights supporters, artists, dancers.

But this morning, envy was the emotion crowding in on me. I looked at these men and saw in their solidity and conventionality an assurance that their lives, specifically their *home lives*, were just the same: set, regular, dependable, happy. And that I envied more than anything in the world just then.

When I got off the train in Grand Central, I headed for my office at Park Avenue and 52nd Street. Just the year before, I had left the network and taken a job as director of communications for a nonprofit organization in the human rights field.

One discipline I had acquired in my network days was the ability to concentrate. In network news I had to be able to write a story on any topic under any conditions: the assassination of a president, the launching of a rocket to the moon, the din and clatter of a crowded floor at a national political convention. So that morning, even though a large part of me had been shattered and my mind was going in many directions at once, I was able to pull myself together—once I sat down at the typewriter and put a piece of paper in it—and concentrate on work. It was not easy; all my training and conditioning was severely tried. But by and large I was able to keep going, to make phone calls, to check on the progress of materials in production, to function almost as well as I normally did. That was to be my professional salvation in the months to come.

As soon as I stepped out of that professional stance, however, I fell apart. Just before lunch I stopped for a breather, sat back, and let my feelings about the past few days flood back into me. I got up quickly, shut my office door and returned to my desk, shaken. I began to sob, harder and harder. I got up, trying to stop, trying to shake it off, but I couldn't; I ignored my secretary's buzzer, the telephone calls. For about fifteen minutes, I simply fell to pieces.

I had to talk to someone, tell someone what was happening. I looked at my watch. It was just before noon. Maybe Stu Robertson had not left for lunch.

I called his number. When Stu came on, I couldn't speak for a few seconds. Then I blurted out why I had called. He couldn't believe it. "Not you and Jean," he kept saying. But mostly he just listened. That was one of his remarkable traits; Stu listened as no one else did.

Stu and I had met through the Modern Liturgy. He was a toy salesman by profession, but he also wanted to be a writer. He had written many articles and even a few books, but so far nothing had been published. Stu also read widely in psychology and human behavior and seemed in a constant process of digesting and applying what he read. I felt closer to Stu than to any man except Jack Connors.

"Have you talked to Jack yet?" Stu asked.

"Jean and I saw him Saturday night."

"Does anyone else know?"

"No, not yet. I can't bring myself to talk about it to anyone. I can't believe it's happening."

More silence. I cried during the pauses. But I began to

feel better. I was reaching out with this terrible burden of information to someone else.

"Stu, can I call you if I need someone to talk to?"

"Of course. Anytime. I'm here."

The way he said it was reassuring, and I knew I could count on Stu.

When I hung up, I felt spent and used. The effort of holding in my emotions all morning, of struggling to keep working, the turmoil and anxiety of the hours since Saturday—all this had drained me of more than I realized. Now I slumped back in my chair and looked out the window. It was a drab, dreary day and the backs of buildings only increased the darkness. Somehow I had to get through the afternoon. And that night I would have my appointment with Sam Glazier.

When the train pulled out of Grand Central, I felt a strange kind of elation. For the first time since my world fell apart forty-eight hours before, I was now going to tell someone who was trained to listen about this catastrophe, an expert in such problems who would be able to see what was wrong and help Jean and me make it right again.

As the train emerged from the tunnel and clacked along toward the 125th Street station, I had already settled into its rhythm and begun a dialogue with a marriage counselor I hadn't even met yet. I didn't have to know him, I felt, because no matter who he was, there were certain things that had to be true. Undoubtedly he regularly counseled people who had been snarling and chewing at each other for years, people who had bad marriages and stormy relationships and who came to him to try to reverse a whole pattern of destructiveness and unhappiness. Jean and I would be a refreshing change, for we had none of these problems. In fact, I thought to myself, if Jean and I wound up with a divorce, then no one was safe. Because happy, dedicated, responsible people like us didn't get divorces. Our marriage was basically sound, I was positive of that; it was just a question of putting everything into proper perspective.

And after all, a marriage counselor was an expert on saving marriages; that's what he was in business for. We weren't going to a divorce counselor; we were going to a guy who by definition dedicated himself to preserving marriages and families. It stood to reason: if you were sick, you went to see a doctor; if you had emotional problems, you got yourself a psychiatrist; if you had marriage problems, you went where I was going. None of these specialists were against what they specialized in. What kind of psychiatrist would drive people crazy? Who else could help us?

The thought came to me—and grew more appealing as I mulled it over—that all I had to do was take the counselor by the hand and show him how we lived and what we were; then he would understand and agree that it was the most insane and senseless thing in the world for Jean to think of getting a divorce. Right now, in the dead of winter, he would be able to see the little kids sleigh-riding down the slope by our house, dodging in and out of trees as they went, and coasting to a long, level glide onto the ball field. That was the ball field, I would explain, where Dan and Jim first, as little boys of eight and nine, had learned to hit pitches I threw to them. He could walk through the woods beyond with me and see the clearings the boys had made, where they'd camped out or made huts or slung rope swings between trees. The counselor would know this yard and these boys suited each other perfectly; that was one of the main reasons Jean had picked it out eight years before. We'd been delighted the yard fit into the boys' pattern of growing up.

Across the street was a lake, and I chuckled at the thought of the counselor slipping around on the ice where we all skated and the boys and I played hockey against the neighborhood kids.

From our living room he could look out, as we often did, and see seasons change, the bright mass of green in the trees giving way to dark, naked limbs which reached up high into the changing sky. I thought he would feel with us a sense of completeness, of being a part of a separate and special way of life. On the big round oak coffee table in the living room, Charley and Mark would play with us at night, games like Monopoly or Scribbage or Rummy. Almost every winter night a fire crackled companionably in the fireplace.

Downstairs, in the basement game room, Jim and Dan and their friends would very likely be jamming. If it was a weekend night, a score of teenagers would be gathered for the rock session, sprawled on the carpeting, a layer of blue jeans and long hair; the sound waves buffeted the sturdy construction of the basement walls. Frequently, some of the teenagers stayed over at the invitation of our boys; our house was a favorite place to spend a night. And Jean and I loved this: that was why we wanted a roomy, informal house, so we could all live in it and enjoy it.

Doing all of these things and making a healthy, happy home environment for our children were what mattered most to Jean and me. We both felt that the family was the most vital unit of society, being parents the most important role we played.

I would want the counselor to know, too, that Jean and I placed great emphasis on our own pleasure. This began with the simple fact of having each other. From the moment we met, talking was one of our major preoccupations and enjoyments. No event was complete for me until I had reported it to Jean and hashed it over with her. We had begun that in our letters two decades before, and it simply carried over. We talked about what had happened during the day, what we were worried about—people, politics, religion, our children, our hopes.

Jean was the center of my life. She was the warm, responsive woman who made everything fall in place. I was happy to be home with her; if we went out, I was absolutely sure she would charm and delight whomever we visited, and she did. We liked to listen to classical records on our stereo; we liked to go to the ballet in New York at least once a season; we liked going to movies; we liked parties given by friends who meant something to us; we liked to have the children with us at home, but we also liked to get away from them on occasional weekends in New York; and we liked making love and all the delights that being married made possible for two people.

With the train lulling me, and these thoughts making me glow, I settled back contentedly. Then I came to with a start: my God, what's wrong? I mean, something is horribly wrong or I wouldn't be going where I was going. What was it? How could I point all this bliss out to a marriage counselor and still say my wife wanted a divorce? What could I point to that was a problem?

One thing we differed about was how to handle Jim's turning off from school. During all his early grades, he'd been an honor student. Then in late junior high and high school, he'd gone into a nose dive. He was getting poor grades, not studying, not caring. My reaction was to look into putting him into a prep school where he could get the individual attention I felt he needed. Jean's was to let him "find himself," be patient, give him time. We were still giving him time and two years later he still hadn't changed. But even though we differed, we did work it out together.

What else? Jean was unhappy with the condition of our kitchen. She said it was old-fashioned and outdated and needed to be modernized. But when we got an estimate on the job, it came out to six thousand dollars, and I said we couldn't do it until we got the money. That had been a sore spot and a continuing difference.

And, of course, religion. But I had already gone into that with Jean and had to accept what she'd said, that religion wasn't the problem.

As I searched my mind for more, that was all I could honestly come up with by way of problems we had. And yet Jean had said our relationship was dead; we were through.

The only comfort I took from the moment was the trend of thinking I had done about the counselor and us. I felt sure that if a counselor could read my mind, could see what I had been thinking as if watching a television play, then he could certainly help Jean and me and we would soon be able to put the whole thing back together again. Nothing else seemed sensible or even possible.

It was nine-fifteen before we finally pulled into my station, twenty minutes late owing to brake trouble. I raced off the train and ran all three blocks to where I had parked my car. I sped through the streets, jumping red lights, driving faster than I ever had. I had to go to a neighboring community where the counselor's office was located. When I found the building, there were still lights on upstairs on the second floor. It was now nine thirty-five. I ran up to the front door and yanked. It didn't open. It was locked!

I ran around to the side and up an alley, looking for

another door. I didn't find one, but in one of the basement-level rooms which I could look down into, a man was conducting a class of some kind for a handful of adults; I crouched and rapped on the window. Startled, the man looked up and understood what I meant when I pointed to the front of the building. He came up and let me in.

When I found the door with the sign SAMUEL GLAZIER ASSOCIATES on it, I burst into an empty waiting room, walked quickly down a short hallway, looked into a room on the left and saw a tall, thin man sitting there smoking a cigarette. "Mr. Glazier?" I asked.

"Sam," he answered. "I couldn't imagine where you were."

"Oh, God, the train was late."

He motioned to me to take a seat opposite his. Both the chair he motioned toward and the one he was sitting in were salt-and-pepper-colored easy chairs, frayed on the cushions, with a look of great wear and tear and tiredness about them. As I was sitting down, I thought to myself, How much sadness and misery have sat in this chair! What happened to those people before me? What was going to happen to us?

My shirt clung closely to my body, wet and smelly from exertion and tension. My heart was pounding, and I needed a moment to catch my breath and compose myself. Sam seemed to understand this and did not press me to begin. He was thin, with a nervous, restless air that seemed to preclude fat clinging to him. At times he tucked an elbow behind his head, as if holding himself back from hurtling into motion. He had heavy glasses, a large, curved nose, black hair parted in the middle that fell down untidily. His eyes were a prominent part of his sharp face, leaping out in their brightness. They looked to me as if they could be ferocious in their intensity, but now they were soft and patient and waiting. He had lit up another cigarette and was looking at me expectantly.

I blurted out what had happened two days before, but what now already seemed an eternity ago to me. I was surprised at the attention he paid to detail, breaking in from time to time to ask me for more precise information: "What were her *exact* words?" . . . "Tell me again how she put it." . . . "You said what?"

I broke down repeatedly as I talked—deep, painful sobs so that I could not continue for many minutes. When I did cry, he would say, "That's okay, I understand," or, "Go on, don't worry about it." He asked me if there had been any other man in Jean's life and I immediately answered no. Then I remembered she'd told me about a friendship with the education minister at her church and I told him about that. He nodded thoughtfully and ground out his cigarette in the ashtray. I told him I couldn't live without Jean, without my children, that life would have no meaning. And I kept coming back to how much I needed his professional help, how everything depended on him, how he was our only hope.

At one point Sam stopped me and said, "I want you to remember that I'm not a miracle worker. I can do my best, but I can't produce miracles. So keep that in mind." I heard what he said, but in my mind I was saying, Our situation doesn't require a miracle. This isn't some marriage which has been on the rocks for years and now they're bringing the cadaver to you and expecting you to pump some life back into it. This is an alive and vital and positive relationship; something has gone wrong—we don't know what, but you must be able to find out, and then you can help us fix it up again.

He went on to say something else: "We don't really 'save' marriages down here, we try to help individuals."

Sam seemed to sense that I couldn't understand this just now or that it might alarm me unduly because he quickly went on to say, as if to minimize his earlier words, "But you'll see better what I mean later, so don't worry about it."

I hadn't the slightest idea how a marriage counselor worked or what would happen or even how much it would cost. He said that Jean and I would talk to him and to a woman therapist for one hour a week. We would start that way and see what progress could be made. If this didn't go well, we would try some other approach: group sessions with several couples, or individual counseling with each of us for limited periods, or even marathons lasting a whole weekend. I got the reassuring feeling that there were a number of sophisticated treatments available to meet any of the needs we had. The sessions would cost twenty-four dollars an hour.

Then Sam said, "There's one awfully important thing. Will your wife come for counseling? Without her, I don't really see how we can do anything."

I said I couldn't imagine her not coming, but I couldn't safely speak for Jean these days. I admitted that she hadn't made any commitment to come and told Sam that probably the best we could do was to go ahead and start on the assumption she would join us after she got back from Texas.

Sam moved on to explain how painful the period of counseling and therapy would be, how we would both learn things about ourselves that hurt, that there always were two people to blame in these situations, but that if we were really willing to work at it, there was no other way to do it except this rough, torturous, risky method. He also said that he couldn't guarantee the outcome.

That bothered me. I thought, A doctor always says, "Now take this medicine and everything will be all right." Why didn't it apply here? But I was so relieved at being a part of a scientific approach and to be talking to an expert who could do something about this problem that his words of caution didn't put a damper on my spirits. Sam seemed so sharp, so competent, so perceptive, that I couldn't imagine all those talents not being able to unravel our mystery and solve it happily.

Sam made no effort to cut me off in my spilling out of my fears and hurts. But now it seemed I had said everything that was troubling me up to that moment. Instead of saying, "It's time to quit," he looked at me with an "is that all?" expression and let me suggest myself that we stop for the night. I looked at my watch. It was near eleven. We had talked nonstop for an hour and a quarter.

On the way home I was tingling with relief and rising spirits. I felt like laughing. Iron weights seem to have been lifted out of my body. I talked to Jean as I drove. "Jeanie, darling, I love you so much. You mean everything to me; you always have; you always will. This has been a horrible experience for both of us. I don't know what I've done to cause it. But I am dreadfully sorry. Everything's going to be all right. I know it will. We have the kind of help that can get us there. And we'll have something better, something beautiful, and something lasting for you and me and the boys."

When I got home, I tried to restrain myself. I was afraid that if Jean wanted a divorce so badly, and I came back exuberant from counseling, she would be convinced it was a place where I would get my goal—reconciliation—and she wouldn't stand a chance of achieving hers. I didn't want her to think I was leading her into a trap or a situation loaded against her. I thought she felt this way already, because of her reluctance in agreeing to go. So I wanted to convey enough of the goodness I felt to make her curious, but not to frighten her away.

She was in the kitchen, cleaning dishes and pots out of

the drainer. I told her a little bit about what Sam and I had covered and how good the session made me feel. She listened, kept at what she was doing, and asked no questions.

Earlier that night she had called her parents in Texas and surprised them with the news that she and Mark were coming down for a visit. Jean had said she was tired, it had been a long, wearying winter, and she simply needed a rest. She would be down on Wednesday, two days from then.

On Wednesday I stayed home to drive Jean and Mark to the airport. On the way down I was still so exuberant about the counseling that I tried to get her to agree to go. I mentioned how much we had at stake, how much we owed each other and the children and our families. Would she just give me a promise that she would *begin* the sessions? "No, I'm not going to, not now," she said firmly. "I'm just going to get away from it all and think."

Mark, excited at going to see his Nanna and Pappap, kept popping over the front seat from the back. When he and Jean got ready to board the flight, I crouched down and gave Mark a big hug and kiss. Then I went to hug Jean, but she turned away. That hurt, but trying to make light of the rejection, I said, "How about taking one for your mother from me?" She grimaced but nodded okay, and we exchanged a quick, dry kiss.

On the way home in the car, up the Van Wyck Expressway, over the Whitestone Bridge, onto the Connecticut Turnpike, I alternately raged and wept. I shouted angrily at myself, "Goddamn it, this has got to stop, this is ridiculous, this is crazy" . . . then wept in helplessness and misery, screaming, "Oh, Jean, how could you? How could this be happening? What can I do?"

With Jean gone for a while, there was a novel spirit about our house, a challenge for the boys—for four of us—to make do. Jim knew how to work the dryer because he had used it often when his clothes got wet. It was difficult for me to get close to Jim, the oldest, who was a sophomore in high school and beginning to assert his independence, but this common plight gave us a happier groundwork. I figured out how to use the washing machine by reading the directions on the inside lid. Dan, who was thirteen and in the eighth grade, liked cooking skillet lasagne and other ready-packaged foods, so he became the chief cook. Dan was more like me in personality, and I found it easier to talk to him. Charley, who was nine, fed the cats and the dog, and set the table.

None of the boys knew the real reason why their mother and Mark had gone to Texas, so they had only their normal, usual feelings about our family and our home. From my own feelings and from the children's presence, I drew a happiness and comfort that I had been desperately lacking for the past few days. The boys enjoyed the luxury of a Dad's shopping: I bought things we liked to eat, not just what we needed. Other couples from within the Modern Liturgy brought us complete dinners from time to time; many called to pick up kids to take for a visit with them. It was a pleasant and different experience for all of us.

At night, though, or in moments alone, I felt the dread, fear and anxiety come over me. In this house that was running so smoothly and joyfully, only I knew the real danger we were in. But I was mostly in a state of suspended animation, buoyed up because the immediate problem was gone for the time being, and hoping that the euphoria that was built up at my end would carry over when Jean came home.

III

BEFORE JEAN RETURNED, a letter came from her father. Pap wrote that he and Nanna were totally stunned and saddened when they learned the real reason for Jean's visit. They hadn't the slightest idea that something like this was even a remote possibility. They saw us as a perfectly happy couple, deeply in love, without a problem between us. Their reaction, in Pap's words, was: "It's like a nightmare, a bad dream. . . . We hope we'll wake up and find that it's not real. . . . We have a numbness, a disbelief that it's really happening." Pap told how he'd been awakened early that morning by a noise close to him. When he sat up and looked, Nanna was sobbing into her pillow. His letter meant a great deal to me. I felt I had two very important and very influential people in our lives working toward the same goal I was: keeping the family intact. An indication of how they could influence Jean where I couldn't was contained in this sentence: "Jean has expressed a willingness to undergo counseling." That was the best news I could have gotten at that point.

While waiting for Jean's return, I made a few more visits to Sam. The sessions became the backbone and purpose of my existence. From the start, I accepted the blame for whatever had happened between us. Just what I had done or what caused this disaster was the agonizing mystery.

To get at that, I went over with Sam in our meetings what I was doing as a husband, how I was looking at my actions, and why I thought they were contributing to a happy marriage and not to a divorce. I told him about how Jean and I had shared the responsibilities for where we found ourselves at various stages of our life, for how we as a pair related to the daily realities that made up our existence. How, going back to the birth of our first baby, I had always shared the responsibility for raising the children. And how, when Jean was faced with the necessity of keeping a home running, first a small one and then a big one, I'd had no reluctance to pitch in with the housework when she needed help—washing floors, waxing furniture, cleaning windows, vacuuming. (I'd done all these things as a teenager during World War II when my mother worked in a defense factory, so why not do them in my own home for my wife?)

I told him how money had never been a problem between us since we had never had a surplus of it and we didn't think it was of primary importance anyway; whatever we had to spend for all our needs and desires was placed in cash envelopes and in a joint checking account, to use as we both saw fit. How sex had been consistently enjoyable, and although I had been the more eager and aggressive partner, Jean certainly never seemed reluctant or dissatisfied with it.

Whatever I could think of that went into our relationship, or whatever I thought a counselor should know about us, I poured out. I remembered, too, something that I'd really enjoyed doing all my married life: buying clothes for Jean. We talked about that a great deal. I explained that finding a dress or a blouse or some jewelry for Jean was a challenge because she had such excellent taste. I did it because I loved her and wanted to please her. I also did it because I was so proud of how beautiful she looked in these clothes. Jean would often say, "I'd never spend money on myself like that. I'm glad you did it"—and I was glad I did, too.

By telling him all this, I wanted Sam to understand what kind of husband I was trying to be, but instead of reacting one way or another, he accepted what I told him noncommittally. Finally, Sam did say one thing that made me think a lot: "Maybe you were serving yourself by all those things more than Jean." What did he mean by that? But there was too much coming at me too fast; I didn't have time or the ability to sort it out and ask questions. All I could try to do was listen.

And then Sam criticized me sharply for that: what he called my "not listening." He said I didn't hear what he was saying. But I thought I did. I listened as if my life depended upon it, yet he frequently scolded me: "Open your ears, Al! Didn't you hear? What did I just say?" The maddening thing was that he wasn't asking me just to listen, but to know what he meant. I could hear the words, but they didn't seem to get the reaction he wanted.

One thing I learned at those sessions was that Sam was not there to prop me up or offer me any encouragement. After a few minutes of a session, I was emotionally prostrate, shattered by shock and anxiety, and Sam's method seemed to be to kick me even harder. Sam would say repeatedly, "You've got to get up off the floor!" But how?

That's what I was there for. But what he did and what he said booted me even further down.

Sam analyzed what I thought was the good life Jean and I were leading and said it sounded to him like there was a great deal of satisfaction in it for me. But did that mean no one else was happy or satisfied? I asked. He couldn't say. He returned to the way I had described my conduct in the home and suggested I could have been making Jean feel inadequate as a mother when I took over the children at night, that I could have been telling her she couldn't do the housework by herself when I helped out, that I was foreclosing her own choices when I selected dresses for her. I was confused, shaken, in doubt about what I had been doing, whether there was any validity to the kind of life I was leading after all. My own vulnerability magnified and compounded the effects of his words.

It was a rough, cauterizing process, but I knew I had no choice. Counseling was turning out to be something far different from what I'd expected, but I had to undergo it, succeed with it, and through it, save Jean's and my marriage and family. So I clung to the sessions, counted the hours between them, entrusted my whole future to their outcome. If that process meant being torn apart, that was okay as long as it achieved the outcome I wanted. I had complete trust in Sam. I didn't understand why he did what he did; I couldn't see where we were going; frequently I didn't agree with the observations he made, but I gave myself over to each new session as completely as I knew how. I also realized that maybe even more would be required of me, for we were just beginning.

After Jean came back, she disagreed at first with her father's report that she had agreed to go to counseling. She said she had only indicated she "might." For several days she would not give a positive response; then she finally agreed in these words: "I'm *not* going in order to save the relationship but to satisfy myself about my reasons for wanting a divorce." I was appalled by this attitude, but I was tremendously relieved that Jean was consenting to start counseling, whatever the reason. So three weeks after Jean dropped the bombshell that exploded our lives, we went to our first session together.

February 26, 1972

Jean and I drove to the session in vastly differing moods. I was holding back excitement, anticipating the beginning of a process I'd been looking forward to for weeks. Jean was quiet, withdrawn, distracted.

In the waiting room, I had a strange, uncomfortable thought. What if we met someone we knew there? They would be embarrassed and so would we. Just our presence there said so much. It seemed wrong, inappropriate for Al and Jean Martin to be there. Of all the places to be on a Saturday afternoon, how did we wind up there?

Time went by, right past our appointed two o'clock hour. It was almost twenty minutes before a couple—older than us, and both serious-faced—came out. I looked away quickly; I didn't want it to seem as though I was prying or staring at them. I wouldn't know what to say or how to act. Nothing seemed right except not to be there.

Sam peeked around a corner, motioned to us and went back into the room he and I had been using. When I showed Jean into it, there was a woman standing there with Sam. I introduced Jean to Sam and he introduced both of us to Gloria.

54

Gloria was about our age, in her mid-forties, with dark black hair swept up on top. She was solidly built but with, I thought, a pleasing femininity and softness about her. I liked the gentle, friendly warmth I felt from her.

The four of us sat down, smiled and looked at one another. Jean was chewing gum, which, she explained, was her "cigarette." She had never smoked in her life. I normally smoked a pipe, but I was determined not to rely on it in these sessions. The pipe tended to make me relaxed and comfortable, and I wanted to be as alert and attentive as possible.

Sam began casually by asking Jean how her trip had been. She said it was fine, that she always enjoyed visiting her parents. There was more small talk about how it felt to go back home when you're an adult and how parents seem to us at various stages of our life. Then there was a pause.

Sam broke the silence by saying to Jean, "Why don't you tell us why you are here."

Jean chewed on her gum a little harder for a few moments, cleared her throat and began. "Well, I'm unhappy. I don't love Al any more. I've asked him for a divorce."

That struck me as a curious phrase: "asked him for a divorce." Did that mean I had a choice? If so, and if I said no, would we all get up, thank each other, say how nice it had been, and walk out the door?

Jean's voice had come out slightly higher than usual, with an edginess to it, a slight breaking, so I knew she was nervous. Not as nervous as I was, I supposed, but showing some tension anyway. Beyond that, I saw obvious control and determination in her. The biggest impression I got from this woman I loved and had known for so much of my life was that she had emptied her emotions. As she began speaking, there was no uncorking of pent-up anger, no opening of floodgates of frustration, no scathing denunciation of what I had done, or of why she was forced to be there. In fact, what she was saying now didn't seem to involve me directly at all.

"I want a fresh start, new beginnings, a simpler life. I need to find myself, be myself, have my own identity, get out from under a smothering relationship," Jean was saying. "I want a relationship that is spontaneous, that is alive."

Up until then I'd been nervous because I'd wanted everything to go right, but now I became completely absorbed in what Jean was saying.

Gloria interrupted Jean to ask if she could describe more precisely what she wanted.

"Something more useful and with more of a purpose," Jean said. "Like the Vista Corps. That isn't it, but something along those lines." She went on: "What we have now, our suburban way of life, doesn't make sense to me. It's phony, artificial. Our home is too big, it's impossible."

I thought, My God, *she* picked the house!

Gloria was now asking Jean how long she had felt this way.

Jean hesitated in her answer. "I'm not sure," she said. "Six months, maybe a year. I know something hit me hard last fall when my minister's wife died. That made me realize how much my own church and my own religion meant to me. That day of the funeral, standing in the parking lot at church, I had a talk with Leon Smothers, our assistant minister. He understood me, he understood what I was talking about."

"What did that have to do with your marriage?" Gloria asked.

"Only that it started me thinking about myself, who I

am, what I wanted to be. And I wasn't being any of those things at all."

"Did you come to this realization alone?"

"Mostly. Leon helped. He enabled me to see for the first time that I mattered as a person, I was important. I've been looking at things differently since then. We've had a number of discussions over the past months."

I listened closely. I knew Jean spent a lot of time at church, but I didn't know this series of conversations had been going on.

Sam asked, "Did you try to talk things over with Al?"

"Yes, I did. We had a number of talks late at night," Jean answered. "I felt something was wrong, that things were not right somehow, but I didn't know what. I just knew I was restless and dissatisfied and unhappy."

"But, Jeanie," I broke in, "you never said anything was wrong with us. You never mentioned divorce or separation or things you wanted changed."

"I shouldn't have had to!" she snapped. "Something was wrong, you should have sensed that much!" For the first time in the hour she showed emotion: anger at me.

I went on to say that the talks Jean and I had had didn't make sense to me, that Jean had been complaining about *something* but she couldn't say what. The conversations usually wound up with her crying, me saying, "Everything will be all right," and feeling puzzled, and me assuring her I loved her deeply because I thought one of her problems was a concern that I was going into some male middle-life spree. I certainly never felt threatened by the talks or even felt a hint that they warned of disaster for our marriage.

Sam said to both of us, throwing it out to whoever wanted to answer, that he'd like to hear about how we lived, what kind of life we had together. Jean was silent. I looked at her and waited. She still said nothing. I wanted to talk about it, I was eager and anxious to tell about something I was proud of, so I began. Some of what I described Sam had already heard, but I repeated it for Gloria's benefit and so Jean would know how I felt about our marriage.

At first infrequently, but then more and more, Jean would break in to differ with what I was saying. She would not contest what I was saying as being untrue, but rather how she felt about it. "Wait a minute, Al, that may be how you reacted to parties we gave," she would say, "but I didn't ever like entertaining a dozen people at once. I also didn't like the way you 'produced' those get-togethers. I would have preferred much more intimate gatherings."

At first I was startled by her interruptions. Then I began to get angry. "Why didn't you say that back then?" I demanded. Or, "Jean, you never told me that at the time!" When we would be at loggerheads, Sam or Gloria would say, "Okay, okay, go on," to both of us. The clashes were minor but frequent. I was struck that not a syllable or comment had been uttered by the counselors about Jean's wanting out of the marriage and into a completely new life style. Neither had questioned the consequences of such a major decision—how it would affect the boys and me, or what any of its long-range effects would be. It seemed strange to me that they accepted such a staggering decision in the same vein as they did our talk about which couples we might entertain on a Saturday night.

But now, with the hour coming to a close, I was pleased that we had gotten through without Jean's threatening to quit or any indication that we wouldn't be returning for more sessions. The first hour had turned up some differences in outlook unknown to both of us before, and I had learned a little about how Jean was thinking now.

Most important, we were underway. If we kept at it, I

was certain it would only be a matter of time before everything would be laid out for us to see what was wrong; then we could put it back together the way it should be. Any couple would want to do that rather than split up, especially if they had the background Jean and I did; that was simply sensible. And there was a nice, easy informality now about the relationship among the four of us as we stood up and chatted casually about things light-years removed from Jean's and my personal problem.

Whatever comfort and security I took from the fact that the counseling had at last started leaked out soon afterward, like air from a punctured tire. Within hours I felt the same terrible fear and the same ball of hurt inside me that had begun three weeks before. These feelings were now with me almost constantly.

I knew very well what the basis for my fear was: that I would be left alone; that everything I had would be lost, taken away from me; that all I had to show for the best years of my life would be myself, stripped of all the people who were precious to me, and forced to start all over again. I felt as if a sledge hammer had been taken to the whole foundation of what I was and what I had, and Jean was swinging it. No situation before, no sensations, no feelings, no bad dreams or imagined catastrophes had ever been like this. The worst physical and mental agony of Army basic training, the months spent overseas away from loved ones, the worst moments of college when I thought I would surely flunk out, the uncertainty about beginning a career, all the ups and downs of life—none of this was in any way comparable to what was happening to me or could in any way prepare me for it. There was no way to prepare for the bottom dropping out of my life.

That night after the first session, I did something which

was natural and comforting for me. I wrote down what I was feeling, what I was going through. I found that setting down on paper my fears, hopes and reactions put together in one place something tangible of myself, something that I could see. It gave me a reference point for the tumbling, chaotic existence which was my life. I could go back every now and then and check whether I had imagined something or whether it really happened.

I couldn't understand how a relationship between a husband and wife could go on seemingly unchanged on the surface, but could become so radically different underneath. A turn of Jean's head away from me could cause pain and instability lasting for hours. Every nerve ending was raw with hurt. Being with Jean used to be an automatic joy; now it was a source of agony. And it had only been a month since all this began.

By contrast, Jean, as I perceived her, was calm, collected and absolutely sure of what she was doing. Reasonably, I knew this couldn't be true—she had to be in great turmoil herself—but from everything I could see and hear, she was firm and determined. Jean was brushing me—and everyone else who expressed disapproval of what she wanted—aside and was steaming along straight on her course to divorce. Even in agreeing to go to counseling, she had held steady: she was going to clarify why she wanted out, not to find out how to stay in the marriage.

I'd heard of friends' wives who were radically changing their lives; I also knew the forces for change, such as women's lib and consciousness-raising and encounter groups, were a growing part of our culture. But Jean had never participated in any group of this kind, had never gone to a meeting or even spoken in a way to indicate that these forces were influencing her. I knew she was generally sympathetic to the cause of women's rights, but in a nonspecific way, not tied by anything she'd ever said to changing roles in marriage, or least of all to her own situation.

The biggest force for change she had mentioned in the past month had been a book, *To a Dancing God*, by Sam Keen, but I couldn't imagine a book, any book, could be the cause of such a profound change in a person. Keen combined a background in theology and psychology; he had studied, among other places, at the Esalen Institute in California. He wrote in his book that he had begun to live after he asked himself the question: "Who am I?" Jean was tremendously impressed by the book and quoted from it all the time. She quoted especially Keen's ideas about the "vibrant present" and his emphasis on "spontaneity" in relationships. She read to me with great emphasis: "My identity is secured by my awareness of the resident sacredness of the present moment in time." Jean was also moved by Keen's passages commenting on religion. She seemed to understand what he was saying—although I had to admit I was left in the dark—when he wrote: "Justification by faith leaves me in exile from the historical time of my incarnate existence if it makes belief in the unique atoning work of Christ a condition of salvation."

In the past we had shared books we liked with each other, reading aloud or recommending parts for the other to read. Now this book, and others Jean was reading, seemed to be a wedge she was driving between us. I tried to read Keen because I wanted to be able to understand how Jean was feeling and reacting, but I could not get much out of him.

There was one other change in Jean's habits; this had to do with reading, too. Books on human behavior and psychology began to appear in great numbers on our coffee table. They were part of the wave of popular psychology, books that urged people to find themselves, to get in touch with themselves, to look within. I read them, too, and I saw a lot of good in them, but they also showed me what a changed world we were living in. Two decades before, Jean and I had been married in a time of "togetherness." This was a concept everyone in our generation took for granted as the basis for a happy relationship. Think of your partner first and you'll never have trouble; be considerate of others—these had been the foundation for our conduct towards one another all these years. What I was seeing now was a different world from that.

In the counseling, too, I thought I detected an echo of this new idea: the individual is what counts; look within, identify your needs, satisfy them. *That* was the way to happiness. I seemed to be out of step, or the step had changed and I hadn't. Now I had to live each tumultuous day, trying to meet the realities such as earning a living, handling the kids, understanding Jean; and at the same time I had to try to understand change and change myself. I knew I had to do it—there was no choice—but I didn't know how.

March 7, 1972

The surface normality of our lives and the conflicts going on beneath clashed painfully this evening. Jean was to come into New York where we were to go to a reception and have dinner together. As the afternoon slipped by, my anticipation grew greater. It was just like old times. As I walked down to Grand Central Station to meet her, I thought of the familiar events that had occurred at home: Jean rounding up the boys and feeding them, picking up my parents to babysit, trying to find a parking space at the railroad station, and then having to wait for the train, it being late as usual. This was an involved, complicated procedure, and we only went through it when there was a good reason to meet in the city.

Tonight provided such a good reason: a reception at the French ambassador's apartment to honor a friend and old network colleague, who was being inducted into the French Legion of Honor for his contributions toward keeping the American public informed about the French people and nation while a correspondent there for many years.

For a change the train came in not far past its scheduled arrival time; with mounting excitement, I watched the people walking up from the track. Whenever I was waiting for Jean's arrival like this—in Washington or in Los Angeles or in many other places—I was always thrilled at the effect her appearance had on me. The small, dainty figure, so distinctive, filled me with delight. Tonight was no different. Jean was wearing what she called her "genuine fake-fur coat," black, curly material. Underneath she had on a black dress with silver buttons off the center; the entire look accentuated her trimness and petiteness. She was wearing long, shiny black boots. I felt the surge of pride and affection for her I always did, and with that feeling, started to greet her with a hug and a kiss. She brushed aside both gestures, said hi evenly, and kept moving toward a cab.

In the taxi Jean told me how everything had gone that day, what the boys had done, and how the train ride had been. I thought she spoke with more animation than usual and far less disinterest, and I was encouraged. "It's good to be in the city," she concluded. I couldn't have agreed more. Her presence brought back memories of our courtship, of the lure of New York for us both that had brought us back from Texas, of countless evenings in the city for plays, ballet, network functions, visiting friends. I thought of the weekend alone we took each spring, midway between our birthdays in April: a crowded time of seeing plays, eating in restaurants we liked, and enjoying the city and each other, away from the children and home. Perhaps it was the memories of those times, or just being in the city, or the fact that we were going to see an old friend, but Jean and I seemed to be hitting a good stride together again.

From the moment Jean skipped inside the door, and gave our friend a big kiss on the lips, my hopes began to climb even higher. There were the first introductions, the need to get a feeling for the place and for the people. Then as we drifted over to old friends and began absorbing the mood that was already in the room, the occasion took hold completely.

A change I had noticed within me during the past month also began evidencing itself. Being completely devastated as I was, I'd become open and receptive to people beyond anything I'd ever been able to achieve. I absorbed their feelings and reactions like a sponge, sensing dimensions and aspects of people I'd never been aware of before, even people I thought I knew well or had known for many years. Off in one corner I found myself engaged in an intense, tremendously satisfying conversation with a woman from the network whom in the past I'd always found prickly, defensive, and almost impossible for me to relate to.

From time to time, just as we always used to, Jean and I would drift back to one another, chatting for a while, commenting on people and conversations, joining other groups, putting in finishing or supportive remarks for one another as we did almost automatically. For a few moments we even held hands until Jean realized what was happening and pulled hers away. Champagne, poured freely and unobtrusively by deft waiters, was producing a warm, mellow glow over the gathering.

At last, the time came for the guest of honor to receive his medallion from the ambassador, and he capped the evening by responding in French—very good French, I thought—to the accompaniment of cheers and bravos. Then the delightful affair was over, and Jean and I were back outside, trying to think of a place to have dinner. The mutual choice was Au Steak Pommes Frites, a place in the West Fifties we had enjoyed for many years. When we got there, we sat down at a corner table, quiet and relatively private.

I thought what a lovely night it had been. All the old spark and spirit were there. I felt the same love for Jean, the absolute confidence that she would bring charm and warmth to the affair, the anticipation of sharing our impressions of the evening afterwards.

We began chatting over a bottle of wine, talking about friends we had seen, news we had heard, observations about people at the reception. We also talked about the nice feeling of familiarity the restaurant gave us, and about previous occasions we had been there; then we reminisced about other nights in New York.

During moments like this in times gone by, we might even have leaned across the table and exchanged a light kiss or held hands while we talked. Tonight I longed to do both. There didn't seem to be any reason why I shouldn't. The wine was making me deeply affectionate and nostalgic. Flushed with the luxurious feelings I was having, I reached out for Jean's hand, took it in mine, and with tears swimming in my eyes, said, "Jean, I love you so much." All the pain and yearning and desire I had been holding back for the past month poured out in that one gesture. Jean seemed taken aback, flustered. Then she firmly took her hand out of mine, looked me squarely in the eye, and said, "Al, I don't feel that way any more. I wish I could say that, but I can't."

For several minutes neither of us said anything; we both looked down. Everything about what I had been feeling was excruciatingly real: my sense of closeness to her; my feeling that we were relating well; my desire, my need to reach out. But it had all run into a firm rejection. How could that be? What could I do about it? I was confused. But I was determined not to lose the mood that had existed.

With an effort I pulled myself back to concentrating on what we would have for dinner. We both looked at the menu and exchanged comments about what we might order, filling in the awkwardness that had settled over us for a few moments. Soon the flow of conversation between us had been restored and we began to relate again, talking about what tomorrow held in store, what needed to be done this week.

On the train going home, Jean was reading. After a while she got sleepy and turned her head and body so that she did not rest on me. But in dropping off to sleep, she had shifted position and rested her head on my shoulder, just as she used to do. Looking at her, a peaceful, tranquil face with childlike features, I felt tremendously protective and loving, pleased that Jean, even unintentionally, was resting against me.

By the time we got home, it was near midnight. As I waited for Jean to finish her shower, I thought of the mood that would set in on nights like this over the years. After an evening in the city, even though we were tired, we usually finished off the night by tenderness and love-making. Tonight I wanted desperately for that to happen. Why couldn't it? We were still husband and wife; no doors had been slammed finally; we were still trying to work out some very difficult problems between us, but maybe this would help. My heart began pounding at the thought. It had been such a pleasant night, except for those brief moments in the restaurant, that maybe the mood would carry over and Jean would feel as I did, that we could try again.

When she came out of the shower, I was thrilled and excited by her nakedness. I took her hand gently, and with all of the feeling that was surging within me, said, "Jeanie, can't we . . . can't we make an effort to let love help us around these rough corners?" As I began to speak, she had put her towel up quickly in front of her. Her answer was quick: "Al, I don't feel it. Nothing has changed. There would be no point."

Sadness, frustration, hurt all flooded into me. I didn't feel anger; I guess I was too numb, too overcome by this tragic turnabout which was engulfing me. Filled with disappointment, I climbed into bed beside her—next to Jean, whose warm, breathing, appealing body was settling down to sleep —and tried to find rest myself. After a long time, I too fell asleep.

Next morning Jean and I had an appointment with a guidance counselor to talk about Jim's lack of interest in school. Since we had gotten to bed late the night before, I told Jean I would get up and make the boys' breakfasts and get them off to school and she could stay in bed.

After the boys had left, I slipped back in bed. It was a dark, rainy morning, the kind Jean and I would have gratefully taken advantage of before. She was still asleep, on her side, facing away from me; I nestled gently against her and felt the warmth of her body. I wanted so badly to make love to her. I moved a hand softly and gently to her breast. She did not move, did not push it away. I caressed her delicately. Still she didn't move. My desire and emotion made me tremble.

Jean let me fondle her for a few moments without stopping me, then said over her shoulder, "I haven't changed since last night." It wasn't a command to stop, just a statement of fact. I said, "I know, Jeanie, but let's at least try. Let's see if making love can't bring us closer together again. Please, let's try." There was silence, no answer. Then, almost with a sigh of resignation, she relaxed and I knew I could go ahead.

Having felt so miserably a sense of loss for weeks, I now felt the resurrected joy of regaining. To a degree unknown before, every touch, every sensation, every contact which meant we were one brought a reaction within me. Without Jean even showing any response, without her giving back any love, I was for that moment full of love for her and happiness. I wanted to show her how important this relationship was to me, so I tried to convey this in every touch, every word I said. Still Jean remained uninvolved, passive, simply enduring. It was terrible love-making; but for me it was somehow encouraging just because it was happening. I told her this, my words gushing out in relief and joy. Jean said coldly, "There has to be love on both sides, not just a physical act, not just a service." I knew that, but the reality was that for me that love existed. For her it didn't, but we were at least trying, making an opportunity for change to take place. After a month of hell and emptiness, this was a small beginning, and I clung to it frantically.

I thought to myself, As long as Jean and I are together in the same house, as long as contacts are still happening, we can succeed; we can save our marriage. Part of our world still existed and we could rebuild the rest into a fantastic new whole. For the first time since my nightmare began, I felt hope growing out of something that happened between us.

WITH FLICKERING SIGNS of what I saw as improvement in
our daily relationship, I pressed even harder for the counseling sessions to give us help. But wanting help and getting
it in the way I imagined were not the same thing. I had
thought I could depend completely on the counseling process to teach Jean and me to lead a better married life; that
was why, I surmised, we were there. But so far there seemed
only to be a picking apart, a grinding away of what I saw
as a solid, healthy relationship between the two of us.

At one of the sessions we talked about Jean's personality,
the way she related to people. I couldn't have felt more
comfortable and secure talking about anything else. Everyone liked her; it was impossible not to. In the ballet company, she was one of the few people not the target of envy
or backbiting or tearing-down criticism. Jean was the kind
of person others rooted for: they hoped she would get good
parts; they were happy when she did. Many people found
in her a quality they could trust: she was the one they went
to when they had a problem; she was the one they chose

to represent them in the dancers' union. Over the years she had been the same kind of open, accessible person wherever we lived or whatever kinds of people we met.

When Sam asked Jean to describe how she viewed herself, Jean began by saying she thought she was a friendly, outgoing person who liked people and was accommodating to the views of others. I thought this description was modest, and I chimed in with my own feelings and with what I had observed others to feel about Jean. "She is just the most wonderful person I've ever met," I said.

Sam asked her, "How did you generally look at people?"

"Mostly, up," Jean said. "I always used to look up to certain people. I'd been taught to do that. You know, like teachers, ministers, parents, older people, all adults when I was a kid."

"How about people your own age?"

"Not so much that way, but I generally felt they were a little better than I was. I don't know why. I guess that's something I picked up in childhood. But lots of times I did what I thought people wanted me to do because I thought they knew better."

"Any other reason?"

"I wanted to be liked. I had been brought up to be nice to people and they would be nice to you."

"Did you treat certain people as idols?"

"Yes, I think I did. My ballet teacher in Dallas. Daddy. People like that."

"Al?"

A pause. "Yes, I guess so."

"So you looked up to some people, put them on a pedestal. What about now? Are you still doing it?"

"No, I don't think I'm doing it now, if I can help it. I'm being more critical. Even of my father and mother."

"And Al?"

"Yes, I believe so."

Gloria asked, "Before, how did you go about relating to these people?"

Jean thought for a few moments. Then she said, "I was acquiescent. I was a very passive person. I did what I thought was right because others wanted it, not because I thought it. I was very accommodating and self-effacing."

"How do you think you're relating now?" Gloria asked.

"I'm not being passive and acquiescent. I'm thinking for myself. That's the big change."

Sam asked, "How do you look at Al in all this change?"

"I guess I did a lot of things he wanted that I resented but I didn't say anything about. I know I felt he ran our lives, that what I wanted didn't matter."

"Why didn't you say something?"

"Because I'd been taught that nice girls didn't do that, they just did what was expected of them. I thought I'd be weird if I did. That's just the way I was."

There were a few moments of silence, of thought about what had been said. Then Sam turned to me and asked how I had been getting along since last week.

I described for them a long walk I had taken during lunch hour the day before. All that morning I had been tortured by thoughts of our family breaking up and of losing Jean forever. As I writhed in the grip of that dread, my arms and legs stiffened with tension, the back of my neck became taut, my lips burned, my stomach tightened like a drum, and I ached all over. I wanted to get up and scream, to bang my fists against the walls, to smash through them, to let off the relentless, unbearable strain pressing on me.

During lunch hour I began walking up Madison Avenue, not knowing where I was headed or how long I would be gone. It felt good to step out; my cramped, hurting body began to unwind, to let go. It was a mild day for March, so I didn't wear a topcoat, yet I was still sweating as I walked. I felt just as alone striding along through the crowds on Madison Avenue as I did when I walked along a remote country road from my house to my favorite spot by a waterfall a mile away.

As I walked, I wondered if Jean was experiencing this same feeling of aloneness now, going her own way, pushing me aside, having to go against what her parents wanted her to do. What had I done to drive her to this? There was no question in my mind but that I had done it. Yet what could account for such a negative and, from my viewpoint, disastrous reaction? Had I brought this about by what Sam was pointing out: that I didn't listen? Was I really doing things for my own satisfaction and not for hers? Those were certainly possibilities, and I wasn't trying to duck responsibility for any of them. I felt the sooner I found out the better, because then I could begin correcting my faults and we could work to save our marriage. I didn't know yet exactly what I was doing that was so destructive, but I was determined to find out, to work as hard as it took to get that answer. When I had walked more than twenty blocks, I started back, feeling better after having gotten away to concentrate on the problem and face it honestly.

Gloria was the first to react to what I said. "It's fantastic," she began. "The power balance is incredible. Jean has all the power and Al is on the floor."

What did she mean by that? I thought what I'd told them indicated that I was making progress, I was facing the problem unflinchingly and working at it.

Gloria was now talking to Jean. "We have to find out what really are the faults in the marriage and what are the problems within you that you are bringing to it. But to do this, Al has to at least sit up, so all the power burden isn't with you." Power burden? That didn't make any sense to me. If she meant that Jean had all the advantages, that she could choose to make or break the marriage, that she had the legal weight riding with her, then I could agree to that. But how could that much power be a burden? If it was, I'd gladly have her hand over some of it to me.

Gloria went on: "When we start counseling a couple, we have to examine all possibilities. We have to consider, for instance, that your own personal emotional crisis—maybe an identity crisis not directly related to the marriage—is at fault. Al may not be contributing to the feelings you have in the way that you think. You may be using him to handle situations you can't face any other way. You may be seizing upon faults present in most marriages to work out your own needs, your own problems."

I was absolutely riveted by what Gloria was saying. For the first time, she seemed to be bringing the world "out there" and the world "in here" together. I glanced at Jean, and she was chewing on her gum harder, nodding to show that she had heard.

"Al said earlier that he felt you 'stacked the deck' against him, Jean," Gloria continued, "and that's a good description of what could be happening. You may be looking at everything he does, everything he says, from a certain specialized perspective, one that suits your needs now."

Jean paused, looking at her fingers locked into one another, then began to speak about the way she had been brought up. "I always had to do things a certain way, just so. My mother was especially fussy about that. As a housewife and a mother myself, I knew exactly what was expected of me. I never thought to challenge any of this, to decide for myself whether it was right or not."

Sam had been listening with hawklike concentration to

what Jean and Gloria had been saying. His left arm, the elbow a sharp triangle, had been hooked behind his head. His right hand clutched a cigarette which he guided unerringly to his lips without once taking his eyes off Jean. I sensed more than I saw him shift forward in his chair; now he was leaning on his forearms propped on his knees, his eyes blazing even more brightly. He had caught Jean's attention and she was staring at him curiously; Gloria was beginning to, too. All at once, with his left forefinger stabbing the air for emphasis, Sam leaned forward and pronounced, "This is a weak woman!"

At first I didn't think I heard what I heard. Jean's eyes blinked and her jaws worked. I couldn't believe yet what I had heard. My mind was running through the events of the past five weeks: Jean's coldly telling me she wanted a divorce, shoving aside my pleas and objections, ignoring her parents' opinions, determining to throw away eighteen years of married life and start something new. And now, Sam was calling her a "weak woman." Impossible! I was flabbergasted.

I found words, finally, to say what was pounding in my mind: "Sam, she thinks you are full of shit!"

Sam whirled at me furiously, stabbing the air now in my direction. "That's what you've been doing for years. Why didn't you let her answer for herself? Why can't you let her say what she wants?"

I fumbled and flustered helplessly. I had only wanted to help Jean. I thought Sam was insulting her and what he said was so preposterous it had to be answered. Sam lashed out at me again. "You don't give her a chance to use her own mind. You don't give her credit for having one. You should be happy at what I said, but instead you mess it up by jumping in with your own two cents."

I didn't know what to say. Something was happening here I didn't understand at all. I only wanted to help my wife and the try had exploded in my face.

"Sam," I pleaded, "I don't know what you're talking about."

"Don't ask me for guidelines," he said curtly.

"I'm not. But what should I do?"

"Unplug your ears. Listen for a change."

"How can I possibly understand when I don't know what to listen for or what to do with it if I hear it?"

"Dig!" he growled.

And then the session was over, no casual small talk, no pleasantries, just an abrupt end.

That evening I was more desolate than ever. Nothing was going the way I had hoped, or even in a way I could comprehend, in the counseling. Rather than heading in a direction which would improve our relationship, we were more strained, confused and uncertain. It was a battering, merciless operation. I didn't know how to cooperate with Sam, and he didn't seem inclined to want to show me. I was filled with despair. Still, everything depended on what took place in those sessions; I couldn't give up, not for a minute. I had to do better, to make progress. But right now there was no solace, no comfort, no lessening of the pain from what was happening there. Living each day was just as painful, just as frustrating as it had been. The nightmare was deepening, and I was only making it worse by my actions, not better.

Jean wouldn't talk to me. When we were alone after supper, I tried to ask her if she could help me understand, make more sense out of what was happening. I tried to clarify what she thought Sam meant by his statement that afternoon, but our conversation lasted only a few sentences.

Jean said tersely that she felt Sam had meant that "all these years I've never spoken up, just gone along with things, so that I was weak. But I don't think he's right now. What I'm doing takes strength, not weakness."

I certainly agreed with her. By way of conjecture, I said to her, "Maybe he meant also that a strong woman would find a solution in some way other than divorce."

Jean snapped back, "Stop spending your time analyzing me. Look inside yourself." And that ended the conversation.

But how could I look inside myself? That's what I wanted to do, but nobody would show me how. I didn't even know where you started the process, what it felt like, how you knew you were doing it. I did know that all around me a horrible reality was unfolding and I was powerless to influence it or stop it in any way.

Still, I had to go on living, go on carrying out the responsibilities of my job. So the next day, a Sunday, I went off on my first business trip since the breakup had started. Jean drove me across town so that I could pick up a limousine to the airport. My organization was holding a directors' meeting in Raleigh, North Carolina. As I got out of the car, I said to Jean, "Maybe I'll find that after all these years we really haven't had a substantial relationship after all." Those were brave words on my part because I was so loaded with desire to regain her love, so desperately in need of loving her, that I was barely able to face making the trip and being away from her.

In Raleigh, I walked around in a dream. All the people who used to excite me—the illustrious people who were on our board—were there, but I was so aching and tortured with tension that I was in my own self-contained capsule, unable to reach out or to be reached from the outside. I wanted so badly to tell someone about the pain I was carrying around with me, but that seemed like a totally inappropriate thing to do. I was also afraid of opening floodgates of emotions I might not be able to handle. I even thought about calling Sam and having a talk with him, but I realized immediately that he might only hammer me down even more. So I went through the motions of being a human being—smiling, chatting, making believe I was whole.

Dinner was a disaster. I ate with a member of our board of directors, an elderly, aquiline-nosed gentleman who embodied all the qualities I had fancifully attached to New England, and with a woman who was also on our staff. Besides being removed from any kind of real and effective communication with them, I found my steak tasted like liver; their stroganoff and fish both smelled bad. Every dish was sent back, but the replacements were no improvement. So calling it all a complete loss, we said good night and went back to our separate rooms.

It was then about nine-fifteen, and I began to pace. The room was spacious and practically soundproof. I was able to scream, yell or talk to myself. All day long I had been fighting despair and now I let it all come out.

Walking, talking to myself, I could feel myself struggling past discouragement and pain into something still deeper inside me. I hadn't reached that place yet, but I seemed to be heading in the right direction, through levels I'd never been to before. I focused my thinking on why I hadn't listened to Jean in the past and why I hadn't heard right even as late as yesterday's session. Why wouldn't my ears unplug?

As I paced, I got a stronger and stronger feeling of purpose and determination. Even if I didn't know how to listen yet, I was at least trying to look inside myself, sticking with it, pushing myself, scolding myself, demanding: "Think, you dumb son of a bitch, try, dig. Why do you act the way you do?" Doggedly reminding myself of how I felt during five-mile endurance hikes in the Army, I kept grinding away at it. I kept forcing myself to stay on the subject. Goddammit, this was going to be a start.

What *was* I doing when Jean was talking to me? Why didn't I hear her as I should? What was she saying that I never heard? When I put myself into the situation of Jean talking and me listening, I realized what I was doing immediately: listening as a reporter. I was noting her words, but really only scanning them, picking out what would set up the next question or comment for me. I wasn't reacting in depth to what she said, or exploring any dimensions beyond the words. My God, had I been carrying over my professional approach into personal conversations? And how long had I been doing this?

Then I asked myself, Why did I do this? That was harder to answer. Simple answers came easy. That this way of listening and reacting had been trained into me from about twenty years of being a reporter. Something else that occurred to me was that I'd never had an example in my home of parents communicating in any depth; they were just never capable of this. But there were still harder answers than these, there had to be. Was I afraid of a deeper, two-way relationship with Jean? Did I intentionally keep the conversation at a certain level to avoid it? I didn't think I was afraid of a deeper relationship with Jean, because I knew I loved her. Still, that was a possibility which had to be explored. I didn't know that I could do this on my own; Sam and Gloria might have to help me beyond the point of my raising the questions.

For almost three hours, I kept at it. It was now after midnight, and I felt exhausted, but good. I had made some progress—not a tremendous amount, but I had moved a few feet toward where I had to go. I had unraveled one small knot and was on the way to discovering where others might lie. And at least I knew something about myself and how I acted that I hadn't known before the night began.

When I got in bed, ready for sleep, I thought for the first time that night about Jean and the boys. Normally that thought would have made me homesick and lonely. Tonight, though, I felt different about myself, much more self-sufficient. I would like to have had them with me, but I wasn't uncomfortable being apart from them. I fell asleep even before I expected I would.

Next morning there was a new feeling inside me: the absence of pain. It had been so long since I had not felt that gnawing, draining sensation that at first I couldn't adjust to its absence. I felt light, free, floating. The speech I wrote for our corporate chairman to deliver at the meeting went over very well, and that also made me feel good. Then I got up on my feet before the directors and delivered my own report, which came off calmly and confidently. The day before, I had feared that I wouldn't be able to do it, that I would go blank or falter or even collapse. By the end of that afternoon I felt even stronger, more satisfied and content with myself than I had felt in weeks.

The next morning—five weeks to the day Jean had picked me up at the railroad station and told me she didn't love me—she picked me up there again. As she drove up, I searched her face anxiously for any hint of change, any indication of relenting from her decision to get a divorce. Within moments I knew that nothing had changed. She was cool and diffident in her greeting, businesslike in wheeling us on our way. She asked no questions about the meeting, offered no information about what had happened while I was gone. I had to ask her specifically what I wanted to know about her and the boys while I was gone. When I ventured a description of what had happened in Raleigh, she nodded without taking her eyes from the road.

As Jean concentrated wholly on driving, I studied her face. I thought how much she had changed. Her whole look now seemed dry and arid. There was no softness, no radiance. There had been about her a joyfulness and a gentleness. These were gone now. Instead, there was a hardness in her eyes and in the way she set her mouth. She looked older to me. I knew that her trust and love had disappeared for me but I wondered if they could still exist for someone else.

As always, I was happy to be back home. I had brought each of the boys a small gift and some candy for Jean. Snow had begun falling earlier in the day, and now it was causing excitement because enough had stuck to cover the ground. Through the big picture window in the living room we could see the yard disappearing under a huge blanket of white, the arms of trees beginning to stick out dark against the whiteness.

Charley and Dan brought some firewood in from the garage and we soon had a fire crackling away. I was home. The company of these people, the snugness of our home— these things were the core of my world. Everything might be normal again now: games with the boys in the living room, ping-pong downstairs, stories read to the little kids before bed.

As I thought about this scene taking place around me, many things about the counseling didn't fit into a perspective I could accept. Sam and Gloria were critically picking apart the relationship between Jean and me. It seemed as if very little we were doing was right. And yet something had to explain this family, this mood, the reality which was unfolding at that moment. This was actually happening, not being faked for anyone's benefit. The boys didn't know anything was wrong between Jean and me; they were just acting naturally. There was no way I could look at this scene and say that it wasn't good. And it included Jean and me, too. Didn't this count in a meaningful relationship? If we had faults in communications or listening or relating, wasn't this also part of being husband and wife? We were that, and we were also parents: there was nothing theoretical or abstract about these roles. I was puzzled by the negative way in which my buying clothes for Jean and helping her around the house had been interpreted by the counselors. But surely there were no two ways about this evening scene. If there was anything more basic to what life was all about, I didn't know it.

As I thought about this, I remembered I still wanted to tell Jean about my digging in Raleigh. She had gone to the bathroom to roll up her hair for the next day, so I followed her in and talked to her as she combed her hair. With all the depths of the feeling I'd felt pacing my hotel room, I told her what I had discovered, what I had found that I'd never realized before. From time to time she would nod or say yes to indicate that she heard. But there was no strong reaction to anything I said, no approval or disapproval or encouragement; she simply didn't seem to care. And, I realized, my reactions were tied so closely to hers that as she rejected me, I began once more to deflate, to feel crestfallen, confused, lost. I began to wonder if I might not have done the digging to gain Jean's approval, rather than to learn something for myself, but wasn't that somehow what we had been taught when we were married: that life was sharing, togetherness?

When we settled in bed, I put my hand between Jean's thighs, a practice that years before she'd said she liked because it gave her a "comforted" feeling. Tonight she took my hand and pushed it away. "I've never liked that and I don't now," she said irritatedly. I was bewildered. What was true any longer? How many reversals and turnabouts were there coming? I didn't know, but I felt as though I had to hang on and ride out Jean's changes because that was the only way I could save our relationship.

Jean went away today for four days to a church meeting in Pennsylvania. I was struck by her eagerness to leave. Her enthusiastic departure brought out a major difference in how we were reacting: she couldn't seem to wait to get away from the house, and I couldn't bring myself to be away from her and the boys. It was plain to me that Jean was doing absolutely what she wanted and I didn't matter at all. She never asked me about the trip, never discussed any of the complications, simply announced she was going. For two decades, anything we did, we did together or worked out between us beforehand. A group of six was going from her church, including the Reverend Leon Smothers, the education minister. As I thought about that, I was troubled, uncertain about the relationship between them. In a way I felt silly: going to a church meeting with six people was hardly a setting for a romance. But I also hadn't known about their discussions over a period of several months. I was shaky and insecure all day.

But when I got home at night and plunged into getting our supper, my mood lightened and I felt comfortable again. The boys, too, seemed to be expressing a sense of working together, the "making a go of it" spirit they had shown when Jean was in Texas. Charley came in from doing his homework to set the kitchen table. Mark fed the cats and dog. Jim built a fire in the living room. Dan hadn't gotten home yet; he was ice-skating with some kids from school.

I began to feel my own personal needs, and they were showing through clearly that night. If I lost this way of life, the things I was doing just at that point, then I lost myself. It was that simple. I had never realized what all this meant to me, but I did now. The anxiety clinging to me during the day was giving way to a sense of contentment. The warmth from the stove, the aromas, the kids passing in and out, cats and dogs comfortably fed and nodding drowsily—all these things made the kitchen a pleasant, cozy and important place to be. I thought of how much living we'd done in that room. I thought with an ache that the bedroom was terribly important, too, for two people, but that aspect was nonexistent now for Jean and me.

The dinner I was preparing was almost ready, but my thoughts about where Jean and I stood just then needed to be explored a little further, so I slowed down the heat under the pots and thought some more. It seemed to me that Jean had really found a new family in her church. Her vital involvement and commitment were there. She was using her creative talents to plan worship services and programs; she was using a minimum of her talents to keep our house running. Home was a stage wait for Jean in between rushing out to church activities. There was substantial physical evidence to show that she was not home very much: the boys' rooms upstairs were a mess, beds hadn't been changed or made in days, clean clothes were in short supply, meals were uninspired and repetitious. At church she found no significant differences of opinion, no complex, continuing problems that involved other lives intimately, or money, or demands on her. The Vista Corps she wished for was a worthy cause, but something she could throw herself into without complicating full-time commitments. And somewhere amidst all that, there was a relationship with the Reverend Smothers. Just what kind, I didn't know, but I was worried. He was eight years younger, married, and the father of a child, so romance didn't seem practical. But in some way he fit into the scene, and I didn't.

There was one last grim irony I thought of before the insistent cries of "Supper ready?" from the other room brought me back to practicality. That was that Jean and I were supposed to be in marital trouble to one extent because we didn't communicate with each other well. But ever since we had learned that, or since Jean had told me she wanted a divorce, even less communication had taken place. Jean simply would not talk to me.

Serving the spaghetti became the most important matter before me, and Jim, Charley and Mark came in to eat it. Each seemed in a talkative, outgoing mood. Jim proudly announced he'd passed a French test the other day; we all cheered. Charley said he had done well on his science project—a volcano he built. Mark, who was in kindergarten, didn't want to be left out of things, so he made up a "test" he'd had that week, while Jim, Charley and I exchanged knowing smiles. Dan came home from skating as we were finishing up, so he ate alone while I cleaned up the dishes.

The four days from Thursday to Sunday went smoothly and were for me a break from the stress Jean and I were experiencing. On Saturday night, our last night before she came home, Mark slyly trapped me. As he was getting ready for bed, he said, "Dad, you're going to miss Mom and I'm going to miss Charley [who was sleeping over at a friend's house], so why don't I sleep in your big bed?" The thought was so charming and the reality behind it so true that I agreed, and we made a big production out of bringing his stuffed animals, blanket and pillow into my room. When he was settled in bed, the tiny red-haired figure seemed lost in the covers and pillows. We read a story, said good night to all the animals and then turned out the lights. As I looked at him later, sleeping peacefully there, the thought of what could happen to him and to our family hurt me even more. Why did people have to do this to one another? Why did children have to suffer for what supposedly grownup people couldn't work out? Weren't there other answers, better answers? For the moment I was thankful nothing like that had actually happened as yet. I prayed that it wouldn't.

Holy Thursday, March 30, 1972

Jean had come back a few days before, and as a family we picked up our normal routine. That included a religious service the Modern Liturgy was holding on Holy Thursday. Our group had moved out of the parish in which we began and was now an official experimental parish meeting in the local Catholic high school. Most of the families that had started it came along with the experimental community and many newcomers had been attracted.

The service was a Seder. Several families had studied the Jewish ritual with a rabbi at a nearby temple and had adapted it to our Christian worship. Tables in the school cafeteria had been pushed together and about forty families were to take part in the meal and service. Each had brought along the prescribed food and wine. This element of novelty added to the customary bedlam of a family affair: adults mingled together, talking over the noise; little kids by the score visited with one another; teenagers gathered in their own knots. When it came time to begin, families drifted back together and sat, two or three families at each long table.

I was delighted by what we were doing, especially having Jean with us. The kids were obviously enjoying themselves with their friends. As the ritual unfolded, it was also joyfully apparent that the regular sipping of wine added another dimension to the event. Soon there was a pleasant, humming mellowness to the congregation. Jim and Dan were smiling happily and saying that their Jewish friends had a pretty good deal after all. Charley and Mark had never been allowed so many sips of wine. All around us, there was a warmth of companionship, of people who were glad to be together. At our table was another family, the Quinns; Tim and Marie Quinn had been having marital difficulties for the past year, but tonight they too seemed swept along by the spirit of the Seder. Jack Connors was conducting the service.

A great peace and happiness settled over me. This was what I thought a family should be doing: taking part in a religious service involving all the members, enjoying it, experiencing something new, being with people who meant something to them. The cafeteria was a sea of good feelings, happy sounds, people relating warmly and easily. This was such a far cry from the troubles and crises of the past six weeks. As I looked at Jean, who was gesturing intently in what seemed to be a light-hearted conversation with Tim Quinn, she seemed like the Jeanie of old.

Then, Jean happened to turn in my direction. Our eyes met. My happiness and joy reached out to her; my spirits were soaring with elation. She held my gaze. Noise crashed all around us; joy and togetherness hung like smoke in the air; life surged vitally in every direction. My eyes told her how much this moment meant, how happy we could be together, how much I loved her and needed her. She seemed hypnotized by my gaze. Her eyes seemed at first to wonder, to question, even, I thought, to understand. Then suddenly her eyes communicated a full answer: no!

Suddenly, I had to get out. I broke off eye contact with Jean, got up from my seat, and almost ran to a door and the darkness beyond. Tears blurred my eyes. A cold, chilling rush of night air hit me as I hurried on, not knowing where I was going. I was sobbing now. I started to walk across a field, away from the lights behind me. Different lights picked out the path ahead of me, and I followed them without knowing what they were. When I got closer, stumbling several times in my confusion due to the tears in my eyes, I realized I was at the Lutheran church across the field. I looked up: a white spire was silhouetted against a clear, star-filled sky.

Lurching up the stairs, I tried the front door, and it opened. Rows and rows of shining, varnished pews stretched ahead of me, terraces of mahogany against whiteness all around. Stained glass broke against the sea of white. The church was empty. Hesitantly I walked up the center aisle, turning to see if anyone was in the choir loft. No one.

I slumped into a pew about a third of the way toward the front and buried my head in my arms. I cried, "Oh, God, why did this have to happen?" My whole being felt as if it were spilling out in the tears streaming through my fingers. Everything inside me was groaning in pain. How much of this could I take? Where was it all going?

I felt I knew where it was going: divorce. The situation

was utterly, completely hopeless. I wanted to be away from it, away, away, anywhere. I thought of San Francisco and how I'd always wanted to work there. Yes, that was it. I'd take off and get a newspaper job in San Francisco. I couldn't win. There was no point in fighting any more. Jean would get the boys anyway, the home, everything. Why was I struggling? Why was I tearing myself apart? Why didn't I just accept it?

When I thought of being apart from Jean and the children, I was plunged into total misery and loneliness. But what else could I do? I couldn't make her love me again, make her want to keep the family together.

Then, I began to come back together. I was stiff, chilled with sweat. I remembered the Seder. Could it still be going on? I got up. My legs were unsteady, so I gripped a pew for support. How long had I been gone? I had no idea. Painfully, hobbling, I made my way back up the aisle, out the door, into the night. Lights were still on in the school, but there seemed to be much less noise now.

When I walked into the room, the affair was breaking up. Jean briefly glanced up from her conversation with Tim; her brow furrowed with curiosity when she saw my face. But then she looked back at him and went right on. The boys looked at me with interest, and Dan shouted, "Hey, Dad, where have you been?"

"Just outside, getting some air. I didn't feel well."

I drove home at a wild clip. Inside me, anger, frustration and sadness were all churning. At times the boys became anxious about my speeding: "Hey, Dad, watch what you're doing." I remained silent and sped on. At home I jammed on the brakes, slammed the car door behind me and let Jean take care of putting the kids to bed.

Jean went right straight to bed after them, without

saying a word to me. I sat in the living room, thinking, smoking my pipe, trying to compose myself. There was a reality I couldn't escape: I was trapped. There was no way out of this horror I was in. Jean was unreachable. Whatever she decided to do, I had to accept. She could strip my life of all meaning and purpose and I would have to go along with it. I could think of going to San Francisco, but that would be a form of suicide for me.

The stark reality tortured me. Most of the night was now gone. Just before dawn I fell asleep, but a few hours later I woke up. And once more I began searching for answers, the same answers I hadn't been able to find in six weeks of searching.

The Saturday before Easter was a beautiful day, and unaccountably I felt happy. The trees, the grass, the flowers —all were springing to life for another season; maybe our life could renew itself, too, and there would be sanity flowing out of all this madness.

As we settled down for the Saturday afternoon counseling session, Sam said immediately, "You both look happy." I looked at Jean and she was smiling with a softness I hadn't seen in two months. I said, "Yes, that's true, but I don't know why. Nothing's changed particularly. The events of the past week don't add up to that feeling. And I don't feel Jean has been any less hostile to me than since we saw you last."

I realized that my use of the word "hostile" didn't touch off a negative reaction, but was accepted by Jean as well as the counselors as a description of reality.

"Why don't we talk about your feelings of hostility, Jean?" Gloria began.

"I do wonder about them from time to time," Jean said.

"I think they are tied up with what you told us about how you looked up to idols most of your life. Your feelings about teachers, grownups, Al. It looks to me as if you assigned yourself a certain status in relation to them which was 'inferior.' You seemed to think they were better than you. For most of your life this was uncomfortable but acceptable. You went along with it because you thought this assessment was right and made sense for you. This pattern developed way back even before your marriage and of course continued after it."

Jean listened quietly, nodding that she understood. I strained to hear every syllable.

"Now, though," Gloria went on, "with a desire on your part to be a person, not just to play a role, this sense of inferiority may have caused an overload. You've kept it to yourself, but now you can't carry that load any longer and you may be dumping some of it off on Al. You may be finding situations in your relationship to him and your marriage which allow you to direct your resentment and hostility against them, rather than against yourself."

Jean still said nothing. Throughout most of the counseling, I'd had a terrible time understanding the implications of what was being said. And no one seemed inclined to want to spell them out to me. But I could comprehend Gloria's analysis, and it offered an explanation of the most baffling and hostile aspects of Jean's recent behavior.

Gloria asked Jean if she could give an example of what she resented in me.

Jean thought a minute. "I resent Al hovering over me," she said. "I don't trust his solicitations and his attention. I think he's doing them for his own purposes, to trap me, and I'm not going to let him do it. That makes me angry and resentful. I don't think he's any different now than he was before."

90

"Again, you're interpreting everything your own special way," Gloria countered, "a way that could be suiting your own personal needs. This is really a form of narcissism. Some of it is needed in the way we look at people and events. But I don't like the extent I'm seeing it in your situation now."

I felt a deep sense of gratitude toward Gloria. Partly because she seemed to be taking a more critical attitude toward Jean than Sam did; partly because she was asking the questions that were usually in my mind; partly because I felt Gloria's probing made the whole of our relationship more accessible, while Sam usually concentrated on my faults alone.

Then Sam gave me the "what's been happening to you?" look, so I told them the entire story of the Seder. When I got through, Sam sat blinking, crushing out his cigarette, looking intently at me. Gloria's eyes glistened; she seemed stunned, totally absorbed. Even Jean had propped her chin in her hand and was staring at me, not with hostility, but with deep interest.

"My God, you never talked that way in here before!" Sam finally said. "I was absorbed in every word you said."

Gloria nodded her head vigorously in agreement. "It was beautiful, Al."

Even Jean responded: "In eighteen years, I've seldom heard you speak with so much emotion."

I was taken aback, but delighted. I didn't think I had done anything extraordinary.

Sam went on: "You expressed yourself so clearly, with so much power. You've had no force behind anything you've said here before. There was commitment in what you said; you're getting yourself up off the floor. You should be pleased with yourself."

I was, but I wondered what this so-called new commitment in me meant? Why had I reacted with "so much power"? As we ended the session, there were lots of smiles and positive feelings exchanged.

Afterwards, I felt like whooping with joy, jumping in the air, hugging Jean. I had done something to show progress! It was ironic, I thought to myself, that the whole incident as I viewed it before was a show of my weakness, my desire to run away. That was the crazy thing about counseling: things didn't come out the same when brought in there. But the feeling I was doing *something* right overrode everything else. It even made me think some of my observations and conclusions about us and our way of life might even be correct, might even have some validity to them. Up to then, I hadn't felt so at all.

When we got home, I purposely kept away from Jean, trying not to put a triumphant touch to the afternoon's mood. Down in the cellar, I put the football equipment, hockey gear and parts of bikes where they belonged. I busied myself past the time Jean and I would usually have had a drink before supper. Then I finally went upstairs.

Jean immediately began a conversation. It was the first time in two months she had initiated anything other than routine exchanges of necessary information. She was excited, and enthusiastic about what she wanted to do in the months ahead.

"There's a course at Yale I'd like to take this summer," she said. "Theology, but not something over my head, something I could handle. Somehow I'd like to use my dance background, too, with worship services or in something like dance therapy. Did I tell you there's a chance I may teach a course in dance movement at a summer camp the church is running? It would try to use movement, simple stuff, involving the whole congregation."

One statement tumbled out on top of another. Her eyes

sparkled as she spoke and her whole attitude was animated, alive. I was delighted at what I was seeing—a coming to life on Jean's part—but I didn't want to dissolve in emotion, rendering myself of no use to her, so instead I listened to what Jean was saying and gave her occasional helpful reactions to it. I said it sounded wonderful, that her biggest problem seemed to be deciding which direction to choose. Any way was okay with me as long as she was happy.

But strangely, right in the midst of her bubbling enthusiasm, Jean would stop and suddenly begin crying. She had never let that emotion out in front of me since our ordeal began. She would sob and say, "Someone's going to get hurt. I don't want to hurt anyone."

When she cried, I wanted so badly to hold her, to kiss her tears away, to say that we could handle anything together, to cry with her, to laugh with her, but I didn't want to snuff out what she was saying, to smother her feelings as they said I'd done in the past. So I just listened and told her I was terribly excited for her. At one point Jean said, "I feel less hostile toward you than I have felt in weeks." And life began to flow back into me.

With that glow still upon me, the evening meal went off nicely. Charley and Mark wanted to get started coloring Easter eggs right away, so there was no fooling around on their part at the table. As soon as the table was cleared, they began dipping eggs into cups containing different colors, putting designs on some eggs with transparencies, marking their names or initials on others with a clear wax crayon so the writing would stand out when the egg was lowered into the coloring. They had to work quickly because Easter-morning sunrise services dictated an early bedtime.

When the little boys were sound asleep, two "Easter

bunnies" took over. Jean got out the baskets we'd used every year since the big boys were tiny. I collected all the stuff we were going to put in them and portioned out the nuts, fruit, candies, games and gifts (such as hairbrushes or jackknives) that the "bunny" had assembled. Then Jean and I carried the filled baskets into the living room and tried to figure out someplace to hide them that we hadn't used in recent years. When this was done, we hid jellybeans on window sills, in ashtrays, anywhere off the floor where the cats and dog couldn't get at them. In the morning the boys would hunt for their baskets first, then try and see who would collect the most jellybeans.

As far as I could determine, this was a normal, happy activity for two parents to be doing for their children. There was nothing about the ritual or how we went about it that differed from any other year. Jean was talking to me as if nothing was wrong; we were relating without any tension or pain or conflict. I wondered why we couldn't build on moments such as this to close the gap between us and save all of us from the terrible consequences which lay ahead.

When Jean and I settled into bed, I wanted more than anything else to hold her and to give her the affection I felt so deeply. Wasn't this, I asked myself, the spirit of this Christian holiday: reconciliation, resurrection, rebirth? What was so difficult or irreconcilable that we could not do this? Instead, Jean merely squeezed my hand as we lay side by side and said, "Good night, Al," more gently than she had in weeks. Just that tenderness lifted my hopes. I thought about Easter and about us and about our children and prayed to that God we both believed in that this night might be a turning point. It was very late when I fell asleep, and we had to get up at four forty-five for services.

In the chill dawn light in the outdoor courtyard of the Catholic high school, families gathered, whispered greetings, exchanged hugs, hopped around to get warm. Tall, thin tapers were passed around and each person lit one. When they were all flaming, the flickering line of tiny white lights circled the courtyard in a procession, all of us singing hymns. Slowly we wound into the band room, where the Mass was to begin. Jack Connors and the co-planners had selected short, simple scriptural readings: the theme was "God created the world." Jean sat next to me, with Mark and Charley next to her, hypnotized by their candles. Most Modern Liturgy services reflected an ambitious creativity; this one was quiet and plain. In the candlelight reflecting off the faces around us, I saw the people Jean and I had known and grown close to. I felt part of them, part of a larger family. And Jean was part of it with me.

After the service the entire community had breakfast together. There was a subdued, thoughtful feeling about the group. Drinking the hot coffee, which woke up my sleepy senses, I told Jean how wonderful it was to have her there. I said I'd be delighted to go down to her church with her later that morning.

"No, Al," she answered. "Thank you, but I'm not ready for that yet." But she said it gently.

After Jean had gone to her church, she joined the rest of us at Grandma and Grandpa's for Easter dinner. My father had a shirt and tie on, one of his "special-day" outfits. He looked younger than his seventy-six years in his colorful outfit. My mother was fair-skinned and needed to wear bright colors to give her a lively look; she had on a blue dress and it gave her the sparkle she sometimes lacked. My brother Ralph and his wife Carla had come down from Vermont for the holiday. They had brought some sparkling burgundy along with them.

Out of the kitchen came the parade of food which Grandma had fondly labored over: ham, mashed potatoes, string beans, broccoli, baked eggplant, mince pie, apple pie. Grandma and Grandpa had Easter baskets for the children, too, and a dollar each to spend. Before the meal Grandpa—his gruff, unpolished voice struggling to find the special words for the day—said grace. Without knowing the terrifying problems Jeanie and I were having, he prayed that "God will let us all be together again next year to enjoy the Easter meal."

I looked around at the happy faces—my parents', my children's, Ralph's, Carla's, even Jean's—and tears filled my eyes. I prayed inwardly that this would indeed come true. I was always moved by occasions like this; I liked the sense of family, of continuity. I thought of Jean's father saying grace when we lived down there, and of his father, Granddad Singleton, praying with his sturdy, rough-hewn profile bent forward, eyes closed. I felt all of this was something important, a vital part of me and of my family.

Afterwards, as Ralph and I were doing dishes in the kitchen, I spoke to him in guarded whispers about Jean and me. He and his wife had known about our situation from the start because I called them the first weekend it happened. Over the following weeks I had called them periodically to let them know what was happening. My first phone calls had been so filled with my crying that they could barely understand what I was saying. But today I was telling Ralph how much better I felt about things, how much hope I got out of yesterday's counseling session, and how normally Jean had acted last night and that morning. I said, my voice breaking at the words, "I think we've turned a corner."

By late afternoon we'd loaded the kids into the car, carried the containers of ham and leftovers Grandma had divided up among us, and headed for home. I felt it was one of the most beautiful days we had experienced in months. At home the boys bounded out of the car to find their friends and see who had gotten what for Easter.

Jean and I were alone in the house. I came into the bathroom where she was combing her hair. I put my arms around her slender waist, as I had done for so many years, and looked at her in the mirror. She looked back steadily at me, still combing her hair.

"Al, I feel less hostility toward you, but I don't feel any affection."

"Jeanie," I said, "what they were saying yesterday gives us a chance to look at this whole thing differently. Maybe you've been looking at what I do a certain way and—"

"Okay, cut that out!" she said sharply. "You're using the session against me, out of context." She turned and pushed my arms away from her waist.

"I don't buy a lot of the things Gloria said," Jean said firmly. "The whole process is superficial. How much can they know about us from one hour a week? They aren't God. They can't know everything. They can't know how I feel. I'll listen, but I'll decide myself what I'll do."

Cold shock hit me. In a moment everything changed back to where it was. Had I imagined a softening between us? What had happened to the lovely mood of last night and this morning? Hadn't it really happened? And what was she saying about counseling? It was our big hope, the one place where we—or I—had placed all our reliance, where some positive steps could be taken on the road back together.

"But, Jeanie," I said, "what you're saying sounds scary. It sounds to me like you'll go through the formality of the sessions, but you won't necessarily believe what's in them."

"No, that's not so. There are just some private areas of me I'll never reveal to anyone. Only I can know them."

"But if you hold something important back from the process, it can't work."

"That's the way I feel, Al, and you'll have to accept it." With that, she brushed by me and headed into another part of the house.

I waited a moment, not knowing whether to pursue her or to go away myself. Then I walked out into the sinking sunshine. I asked myself: What does Jean want? What was it she was demanding? And I had no answer.

SPRING CAME TO CONNECTICUT early in April. With it came a new cycle of activities around our house.

Baseballs flew around the ball field, fishing tackle came out of winter storage, storm windows came' off and screens went up, and soil was turned over and vegetables planted for our garden. The hockey games on the coffee table, ping-pong in the basement, fires in the fireplace—all these became part of a season past, put aside now to be picked up again in the regularity of their turn next year.

The normality of our patterns was one of the things I counted on as a factor working in favor of what I wanted most. Spring meant time spent in the yard working on flower beds; it meant long chats sitting on a stone wall in the lazy sunshine; it meant for the kids an almost completely outdoor existence and for Jean and me the option of enjoying the outdoors or the new quiet and privacy of the house. Each spring activity threw us into contact with a similar event that had happened a year or two ago or somewhere in the past: they were all part of the history of what we were as a family. My recurring hope was that the reminder, the fresh association with what had been before would somehow shake Jean from her implacable course.

April brought two events that were important in the pattern of our family life: birthdays, Jean's and mine. Hers came early in the month, mine later. We were both going to be forty-three. And as I look back now, the way we responded to these two events reflected accurately our separate reactions to the tremendous changes in our life.

I was determined to make Jean's birthday exactly as we had always celebrated it in the past. Birthdays were a special thing in our house. For that day the person whose birthday it was held the center of attention. If it were one of the kids, it meant no feeding the cats or dog, no taking out the garbage, no setting the table. This was *his* day. He could name his menu for the birthday dinner, have his bunch of friends over for an afternoon party, choose the kind of cake he wanted, draw up a list of gifts he'd like to get.

In the case of Jean, the boys and I had always made the meal, set the table, served her, let her sit back and enjoy the day. I would get suggestions from her for the things the boys might give as gifts. As for my own gift for Jean, I would look forward to the prospect of buying her a dress or a blouse or a skirt.

But this year was different. When I asked Jean what she would like us to fix for her birthday dinner, she said, "I'll do it," including the baking of her own cake. And since the counseling had shown that many times in the past Jean had received my gifts of clothes negatively, it wasn't appropriate to go through my anticipated shopping ritual. Still, when I asked Jean what she would like from me for her birthday, she startled me with the answer: "Clothes." However, I made sure that she gave me a specific description of what she wanted. In an abbreviated shopping expedition, I bought her an orange and white summer outfit I felt she would like.

When the day of Jean's birthday arrived, I couldn't wait to get home from work. I left my office a little early and on the train looked forward to the happiness and pleasant emotions that always surrounded a birthday celebration.

I hurried up the front steps by twos and gave Jean a hug and a kiss amidst the boys' greetings; even her dry, perfunctory kiss and the feel of her body holding back could not diminish my enthusiasm.

"By golly, I always found older women attractive," I said, picking up a theme Jean had to contend with every year.

"Yeah, Mom, how does it feel to be forty-three?" one of the boys chimed in.

"How about being the oldest one in the house?" someone else asked. Jean usually took the kidding in good grace, but tonight she was restrained about it.

In a few minutes the boys were pouring themselves sodas and Jean surprised me by saying she would take a cocktail, instead of the beer she had pretty much restricted herself to since February. This simple gesture sent my spirits lifting higher. While the children drifted in and out, Jean and I sipped our drinks and chatted. When dinner was ready, there was a flow of enjoyment which made me feel good. The spirit of the special occasion was shining in the feeling of having fun that everyone was showing around the table. As I looked at Jean from the other end of the table, amid the feeling of love I had for her, and the happy feelings the boys were showing, I wanted to reach out to her and say, "Jean, we could have all this if you will only let it happen."

Jean reacted to the mood around her with firm control.

She had relented in having a cocktail, and I knew she was enjoying in a general way what was happening—these were, after all, her children and her home—but she was also withholding herself as she never would have before. When Charley and Mark carried in the birthday cake with its candles blazing away on top, she seemed pleased, even mellow; she beamed as we bellowed our ragged chorus of "Happy Birthday." The little gifts the boys gave her appeared to please her. But when she opened my gift, she did so with deliberate care, taking a long time to look it over carefully before saying simply, "It's nice. Thanks, Al." In other years she would have gotten up and come over to give me a kiss, now she was making no sign of moving. The joy, the relief, the hope I was feeling were too much to hold back and I got up and went to her chair. Jean looked up, startled and confused, and yielded a quick kiss.

When my birthday came, a few weeks later, Jean was not home. She had gone away the night before to a weekend church meeting. That Friday night, after she had gone, I mentioned to Jim, with some of the hurt I was feeling showing through, that Mom had gone away without thinking of my birthday. Jim said, as if I should know, "We're going to celebrate it Sunday night, when Mom gets back. She told us that."

With Jean gone for most of the weekend, the boys and I fell into the routine that had by now become familiar. On Saturday morning there were chores to be done. Getting the boys to work when they didn't want to was not easy, but with much grumbling and protesting they fell to. Jim and Dan raked the dead grass, sticks and stones from the ball field. Charley did the banks leading down to the field. Mark and I mended stone walls.

Saturday afternoon meant the counseling hour, and even when Jean was away I went to it myself. When the sessions were with me alone, Sam and Gloria concentrated on my personal reactions and attitudes that they had observed. Today, after we had been chatting a few moments about what had been happening during the week, Sam went back to something he had wanted to point out before.

"One thing I've noticed," he said, "is that you tend to fight some of the things we tell you. For instance, the other day I said that divorces are terrible and messy, and they are even worse when two people can't agree and fight over kids or money. Everyone gets hurt. Do you remember what you said then?"

"Oh, something about 'What do you want me to do, just give up without a fight?' Or, maybe it was 'Shouldn't I fight for my children and my home?' I guess that was it. Is there something wrong in saying that?"

"No, it's not a question of that being wrong, but it shows how you received the information. I didn't say you *shouldn't* fight. But you took it as that and went a step further. How do you generally feel when someone gives you advice or information?"

"I guess it depends. If it threatens something as important as my marriage and family, I take it as challenging my view, as opposing my position. And I react defensively, as I did to you. What other way should I react?"

"As if you are receiving input, as if someone else is giving you information, sharing what they think for your consideration."

He was right. It was wrong for me to react the way I did. I didn't know I was doing it, and I would have kept on unawares if Sam hadn't pointed it out. I thought that practical observations like that were helpful, and I wanted more of them instead of the frequent feeling I had that I didn't understand what Sam and Gloria wanted me to understand.

"Look," I said, "I've been coming here for months now and feeling a lot of the time that you two and Jean are carrying on on a wave length I can't tune into. I've wanted as badly as I know how to make progress, to dig into myself, to work with you, but I've felt all along I'm just not doing it. The three of you seem to be able to understand and speak the same language so much better than I can. It makes me feel depressed and discouraged. Jean is so damned good at getting in touch with herself, is so far ahead of me in this business, that it's almost unfair, it's so one-sided."

Sam had been sitting alongside Gloria, both facing me and both looking intently at me. When I described Jean as being good at getting in touch with herself, they both burst out spontaneously, "Oh, no!" It was loud and emphatic. I was startled by the volume of their response and by its nature. Hesitantly I said, "Come on, you're just saying that. I know Jean is very good at this process and I'm not."

"Did Gloria or I exchange a look?" Sam asked.

"No, I didn't see any. You didn't have time. You both just blurted out together."

"We didn't rehearse anything or know you were going to say that. It's just a fact that we believe Jean isn't very good at what you say she is. She's working at it in her own way, and so are you. But you've got it sized up wrong."

I was astonished. The session, which had concentrated on me, suddenly and accidentally had shed a tremendously intriguing bit of information about my wife. I had been convinced that Jean was sure and precise and absolutely right about all her feelings. I knew I wasn't, because my emotions were confused. But what the counselors were saying was that my observations were at least as good as hers, that we both could benefit from listening more intently.

That evening, I took some steaks out of the freezer, put some potatoes in the oven to bake, unfroze some peas, and opened a can of beer for myself. One by one the boys came drifting back at suppertime. Jim had been fishing in the lake across the street, but it was still too early in the season to catch anything. Dan had ridden his bike down to a friend's. Charley was building a tree hut in the fields near the lake with his gang. Mark had run through our woods and played with the kids whose house we could see only in the winter, when the leaves were all off the trees. The boys bunched around in the kitchen, talking to one another, to me. The whole excruciating mess of Jean, Sam and Gloria faded into the background.

Why didn't Jean just let me stay like this? If she wanted to find herself, to fulfill herself, to be liberated, to find her own identity, why couldn't she leave the rest of us alone? I didn't want our way of life disturbed; I was pretty sure the boys didn't. This was what we all wanted to be doing.

When supper was ready, Jim, Dan, Charley and Mark sat down hungrily. Steak and baked potatoes was an easy meal; it was hard not to make that appetizing. Nobody mentioned Jean's being away or my birthday. Instead, we talked about fish that weren't biting, bikes that needed brakes tightened, tree huts that were coming along fine and the joy of new swings at the house through the woods behind us. After supper Jim and Dan walked down the pitch-black country road to the Congregational church and the Saturday-night teenage coffeehouse there. Charley, Mark and I played a new hockey game I'd bought on the living-room floor until it was time for them to go to bed.

When they fell asleep, I was at last alone in the big,

quiet house. In other years I would have been terribly lonely and hurt to be left by myself on an occasion like a birthday. But tonight I felt strangely peaceful and content. This was not a life situation I wanted; I would have given anything to be out of it. But that evening the feeling of being responsible for the boys, of being amid my family, made me feel that these were priceless moments I wouldn't trade for any amount of self-fulfillment. From where I stood, in the roles and responsibilities I had assumed, this was fulfillment and identification. I couldn't imagine what else could be.

Sitting there alone, I got the urge to express myself, to produce something that would say that I was a creative, expressive human being, able to do something other than suffer and endure. I got out my portable typewriter and perched it on my lap. I began to think of my childhood, my early days in a Polish parochial school. Sister Anastasia came back to me, her face rimmed in white cardboard, the huge mass of brown robes with a thick white cord belt knotted at her waist, the heavy metal crucifix bouncing off the muffled bulk of her body when she moved, her pale-blue unfeeling eyes peering out from behind round metal-rimmed frames. I thought of us kids cowering in her class—children of working-class families in the South End, girls who got up and did the wash or ironed before they came to school, boys who lugged coal or ice with their fathers after school. Mine was not that life situation—my father was a mailman—but spiritually we were from the same mold.

I remembered Cecelia, an awkward, gawky girl whose head was too large for her body; she was the maverick and the independent one in the class, a fearless girl who suffered wicked beatings from Sister Anastasia in order to cling stubbornly to her independence and her freedom. I imagined a little incident between Cecilia and Sister, an amalgam of many that actually happened, and began to re-create in words the tension and terror we all had felt. For three hours I wrote steadily, only stymied from time to time, driving myself to keep going, reminding myself I was writing only for me, not for anyone else's criticisms or comparisons. When I had finished, I had a short story—not a bad one, I thought as I read it over—the first I had written since college. I felt a strong sense of accomplishment, of having stuck to something and finished it. I looked at my watch; it was past midnight. I was now a day beyond my forty-third birthday. I was still in a horrible crisis, my wife still wanted a divorce, but I felt good nevertheless.

The older boys had come home from the coffeehouse while I was writing, said good night and gone upstairs to bed. I made my rounds, checking on them and the little fellows, all sound asleep. I prayed and hoped that this night was somehow the beginning of new strength for me.

Jean came home just before suppertime on Sunday, and we held my birthday party. When she came in, I looked at her anxiously for any signs of change, any softness in the way she looked at me, any return to the gentle, friendly person she had been, but she was just as hard and aloof and distant as when she left. I felt uncomfortable and uneasy. Birthdays were always times of celebration and happiness; I didn't know how to act any other way, but I also didn't feel any of those emotions. Still, the physical ritual we went through, the spirit that couldn't be stifled, nudged me into better feelings. Jean had dutifully bought me a raincoat. But the tone of where we were was more accurately reflected when I said grace before the dinner. I thanked God for the birthday and the family and all of us there and prayed that "the wife I love" and I might have the ability to grow and develop together. When I said the words "wife I love," I glanced up hopefully at Jean and she was glaring at me with irritation.

As the weeks went by and my feelings of love and affection for Jean did not lessen at all, my frustrations at not receiving her physical love or any emotional response grew stronger and stronger. She was still physically Jean: the trim, delicate body, the lovely little breasts, the long attractive legs. The effect of her movements, her closeness to me were the same as they always were, but now even greater with each passing day as the pressure of desire built up in me.

As soon as our counseling session began one Saturday in April, I let loose the anger I had been carrying around for some time—anger which I had already partially expressed to Jean, but which would have shaken our home and turned our daily lives into a battlefield had I released it completely.

"My God, how can she do this to me?" I demanded. "We are both human beings. We both have feelings. I know I do. We have been making love for eighteen years and now suddenly she stops. I want her. I love her. I want to make love to her desperately. How can she torture me this way? What have I done to deserve it?"

Sam and Gloria merely listened. No one interrupted me or offered a response. That angered me further, so I went on.

"What the hell discomfort is she suffering? She doesn't have any feelings, she's not interested in sex, she hasn't any worries about losing her children and her home—the courts always give them to the mother. If she insists on a divorce, she can always get one somehow; there's no way to stop her. But why do we all have to go through hell for one person? Why do we have to have our lives shattered and everything that means anything to us? If I'm so unfit to live with, why doesn't she leave?"

Jean broke in, started to make a point, then let it drop. My emotions were so aroused that I scarcely noticed the interruption.

I finally ran out of angry words and sat tensely in my chair, glaring at the three of them. Instead of responding to me, Sam turned immediately to Jean.

"Do you realize what you just did?" he asked. Jean looked at him in surprise and shook her head. "You started to make a point, then stopped, let it drop and never said anything more. But I'll bet you didn't stop thinking about what you were going to say or feeling what was bothering you. You just didn't push it far enough. You never expressed what you were feeling."

Jean nodded, indicating that she understood.

"You give up too easily. I think this has been going on for years. It's part of the communications problem you and Al have. You don't have either the strength or the confidence to break in and say what you want, and he goes right on. After a while, you begin to feel as if what you want to say isn't important. What does it matter? Why make the effort? And that makes you feel inferior, unimportant. Out of those feelings, I think, have come a lot of the anger, resentment and hostility you have towards Al."

Jean thought about it for a few moments. "Yes," she said. "I think you're right."

This was a valuable point for Sam to make. I certainly never could have seen that Jean was reacting to me in the way he pointed out. Yet this process must have been going on, and it must have done its damage.

Gloria then said she thought Jean was approaching our

marital problems the same way. "Rather than taking the situations one at a time as they come up, breaking in and saying, 'Wait a minute, I don't like that,' and working them out, you seem to be seizing on a complete solution to the whole thing at once, a radical solution, a divorce. That way is sure and definite. However, it may not be the right direction for your children, for Al or even for you, but it is easier that way."

Sam continued, "There are definite patterns between you and Al that we can see. Some of them aren't good, and we can point these out. What you do with them is up to you." He paused, then went on, still addressing Jean.

"From what I'm hearing, you allowed your marriage to develop this way because it was what you wanted. You must have been sensitive to Al's need to be protected against anxiety. He's terribly anxious now, and that's why he's suffering—he's not used to it. You used to reassure him against that anxiety. Al continued to think he was the strong, dependable male, which was what he needed to think, but he also was getting the reassurance from you. And you in turn received a strong sense of security and protection from him, which is what you needed."

Something struck me about what he was saying, and I asked, "Sam, isn't that what married people do all the time? Isn't that what the idea of partnership, of helping one another, involves? What's so unusual or destructive about that?"

"It's a question of degree," he said. "You obviously were very emotionally dependent upon Jean. Now she is withdrawing that support, for reasons of her own, and the reality is you are flat on your back and you can't face the thought of life without her."

That certainly was true. After nearly nineteen years of

married life, could it have been any other way? I couldn't imagine it. How could two people commit themselves so completely to a joint life, bring four lives into this world, face thousands of decisions of mutual concern, and not have some kind of emotional dependence tied up in each other?

Sitting hunched in his chair, Sam had been twisting his bony fingers together and waiting for someone to continue the discussion. He did not push or hurry a response; this was one of those times for reflection and sinking in. Several minutes passed. Then, with a gesture as if he were closing the cover on one subject and turning to a new one, he said, "Look, Al is gripped by fear and anxiety right now. He can't think of anything except what might happen. And so he can't work at this as he should." He stopped, looked from Jean to me to check that we were listening, then went on. "Jean, you seem set in your own decision that what you want to do is best. Neither of you can examine alternatives if you stay frozen in these positions." Another pause, an upraised eyebrow as if to ask, "Any questions?" None.

"I propose, for the good of everyone, that we drop all talk of divorce for the next three months." Pause. "Al can have the freedom to let go of his dread for a while and work on means, not ends. And you, Jean, can think about whether there is another choice or if you want to continue in the direction you are now going."

I didn't need any time to make up my mind, so I said, "That's fine by me, Sam."

Jean frowned, looked hard at Sam, studied her hands locked together in her lap, and then finally said, "Okay."

"Fine. I think that will help," Sam said. "Oh, yes. Al began this hour complaining about his lack of sex and any affection from you, Jean. He's obviously hurting because he can't touch you, can't give you any of the love he genuinely feels, can't have sex as he is used to it. How do you feel about this?"

"I'm sorry," Jean said, "but I don't feel that way about him."

"How *do* you feel when he touches you now?"

"I cringe!"

God! The word stabbed me with pain. "Cringe." What joy the touch of each other had brought us over the years. We used to hold hands whenever we walked down a street. We even had a special signal worked out when we were with other people at a party, or sitting next to one another at a dinner gathering: we would hold hands briefly and squeeze three times; the signal meant "I love you." Touch was one of our constant forms of communication. And now Jean said she "cringed" when we came in contact.

"It seems to me," said Sam, "that this is part of what we talked about earlier, your feeling put-down and unimportant. You felt then that Al was rejecting you, so a lot of hostility and resentment built up within you. Now you're rejecting him and he's the one who's hurting."

When we came out into the brilliant mid-April sunshine, I could feel the sun's rays warming my skin and was soothed by the heat. But there was another part of me that was equally real, that was as substantial as the me whose skin the sun was burning, a stranger who in some fragmentary, incomprehensible way was being dragged into my awareness. The sessions were only starting to reveal his dim outline.

In the weeks since our ordeal began, I had had very little contact with my parents, except for the Easter dinner. Their home was within five miles of ours, but with my life and emotions in turmoil I had no desire to complicate matters further by letting them know what was happening.

My mother was very emotional and could get upset and cry over matters far less serious than our situation; I felt I could not bear the burden of their anguish as well as mine. Besides, I was hopeful that our problem could be solved without them ever knowing what we had been through.

Since February, when Jean announced the change in her feelings towards me, she had also begun pulling away from my parents. Now the only time Jean saw them was when she dropped the children off to be babysat. From the beginning of our courtship, Jean had been very close to Mom and Dad. Both children of Polish immigrant families, they had been entranced by the Texas Methodist ballet dancer. As our marriage and family progressed, my parents had come to love Jean deeply, and she was wonderfully loving in return. Then suddenly all that had come to a halt. My mother would ask me pathetically, "Al, why don't you and the family come over more often?" We were all they had, the center of their love and the joy of their old age. My brother and sister-in-law lived in Vermont, did not visit that often, and had no children; so our children gave them the deep happiness that came from being grandparents.

Until Easter I had continued to keep the truth from Mom and Dad. Because I had expressed so much hope and optimism to my brother that day, he felt he should end the confusion and hurt they were suffering and told them the situation Jean and I were in. At first Mom had broken down and wept uncontrollably. Ralph had firmly but gently told her she couldn't behave that way; that we had enough problems without adding her tears to the burden; and that she had to pull herself together in order to help matters. Both Mom and Dad were deeply shocked. Like everyone else, they thought we were a perfectly happy couple.

So one day in April, when I had finished work early, I

drove by their house on my way home to pay a visit. As I parked my car in front of the little brown shingle home where I had grown up, I was torn two ways. I felt guilt and concern that I had not seen very much of my mother and father recently. On the other hand, I still had no desire to spend long periods talking about my situation, going over the same ground—and most visits to them turned out that way.

When I opened the front door, my mother got up to greet me with a surprised look and happy hug.

"Al, how good to see you! Come on in. Sit down!"

Mom was small, about five-two, gray-haired, a little bit stout. She looked, as the older boys put it, "just like a grandma is supposed to look." The house had seemed plenty big when I was a kid, but now my family and I filled the living room when we came there. My mother and I sat down opposite one another and for a few seconds an unsureness settled over us. Neither of us knew what to say. She was struggling not to ask the questions which she ached to ply me with but which had left me irritated and hurt after our recent conversations.

"Mom," I said, "I know how worried you are and how anxious you and Dad are to know what's going on." She looked at me gratefully. "There really isn't too much to tell. Jean and I are going to the counseling regularly. It is tough, real rough going, and I have to say, sadly, that Jean hasn't changed any so far. I don't know if she ever will. You know how badly I want her to, and that I'll do anything if it will bring us back together again. But there's no way of telling what will happen, so that's all I can say."

She had listened to each word anxiously. When I said that Jean hadn't changed, I could see the lines on her face deepen and the hurt and bewilderment creep into her eyes.

She wrung her hands helplessly, shook her head, and then finally, after I had finished, burst into tears.

She held her hands over her eyes and wept bitterly. I went over and put my arm around her and tried to console her, but I felt my own tears beginning to flow. "Al, how could she do this? What's happened to our Jean? What's wrong? How could she?"

"Mom, I don't know. I don't understand her either. There are faults, there's blame for both of us. But why she wants this, why she wants a divorce, I just can't understand."

The sound of a car door slamming outside made us both look up. "That must be Dad."

I looked out the window; Dad was taking his tools out of the back of the car. He used to come frequently to our house and fix things: stuck doors, leaky pipes, broken windows. Dad could fix anything; he could do plumbing, carpentry, wiring, painting. He was known as "Mr. Fixit" to the children; any broken toy was immediately taken to Grandpa and pretty soon was restored to working order. This was his whole life now, since he'd retired from the post office. He wanted to be useful, to help; and when he was doing it, he was a happy man. But it had been weeks since he'd come to our house to work.

Seeing him coming up the front walk, smiling as I hadn't seen him smile in weeks, I was struck at the additional hurt we were doing to this man. Not being able to see his grandchildren frequently and knowing that his son and the daughter-in-law he loved were having grievous problems was bad enough, but to take away his purpose, his usefulness and his joy in life, by just letting him stagnate here, was even worse. How had I let this happen?

I knew I could not handle the feelings I felt, the words I wanted to say but couldn't. I went over to my mother, hugged her and said, "I'm sorry, Mom, about the way things have been. We'll see more of you and Dad, don't worry. Somehow we'll work it out. I'll call you."

Then I got up, stopped for just a moment to squeeze my father's hand as we passed on the porch, and ran to my car. "I'll call you," I shouted back as he looked at me, stunned and disappointed.

May was upon us—three months had gone by since Jean's announcement. She still would not soften her harsh attitude toward me. There was no chance to share directly what we were going through or get at each other's insights or explore where we stood at that moment because Jean didn't want to talk. She brushed aside my attempts and insisted we had to work on ourselves.

I began to try as hard as I could to convince myself that a divorce and life apart from her was really for the best: for me, for the boys, for her. But the effort was not meeting with much success deep down within me. When I saw how little of this conviction had reached into my guts, I realized the gigantic change that would have to occur within me to let that happen. There would have to be a basic upheaval of who I was and what I believed in.

I tried my feelings out on others every now and then and got a reaction as to how they sounded. One day when I thought I had convinced myself I could bear to be apart from Jean, I telephoned Stu Robertson and said, "Stu, I don't want to be divorced, I don't want to lose Jean, but if I have to, I can do it." Stu was merely listening, so I went on. "If Jean can't accept anything else, I can face the reality that exists. I'm ready." There was another pause. Finally, Stu said, "Say that again for me, Al." I went through it once more—even more firmly, I thought. After I was finished, Stu said, "You haven't convinced me." He was right. I hadn't convinced myself either.

Divorce meant the death of a relationship, and for some, a new life afterwards; but not for me. Three months after the initial shock, I was still praying: "Please, don't let it happen." And the prospect of what I had to go through if a divorce happened meant to me living a slow daily death.

One night Jean and I were supposed to go to the Robertsons' house for a party, but on the way we had a fight. In almost nineteen years of married life and twenty-two years of knowing each other, it was the first fight we'd ever had. It began when we were almost on the doorstep of the party.

I was driving and the low-key conversation had been about how we should be relating to each other during this period. Suddenly Jean burst out, "I wish I were away from you! I don't love you. I hate to be near you." Her outburst had happened so quickly that as I was about to turn the wheel into Stu's driveway I hesitated, pulled the car straight ahead and slowed down a moment to think. I couldn't face going into a party seconds after my wife had said that; besides, I wanted to know what caused her to say it.

So we kept riding and I said, "Let's go somewhere near here and talk for a while." I felt no strong reactions to what she said, other than my normal disappointment. There was a dead-end street coming up, so I turned into it, slowed down under a streetlight so we could see each other, and turned off the motor.

I leaned back on my side, looked at Jean and said, "Now, could you tell me what prompted you to say that?"

"Because I feel it," Jean said angrily. "I'm tired of you and I'm tired of this hassle." She was half turned toward me, but not talking directly to me, more toward the wind-shield and the front of the car. "I got a letter from Mother this week . . ." Her voice had mounted in anger but she paused, not seeming to know which direction she wanted to take. Then she said quickly, "There's one thing she has to realize, and you do too. That's how seriously I take the *other* relationship."

"Other? Which other? . . . You mean, Smothers?" My temper was now rising, and I could feel my heart pounding faster. "The son of a bitch! I thought he was your education minister!"

"He is, but he's more than that."

"What do you mean by that?"

"I mean that our relationship is serious."

"Serious enough for you to go to bed with him?"

"No, it's not that kind."

"But you would break up a marriage of eighteen years and hurt four children for whatever it is?" Then I remembered something. "The night before I went away to Phila-delphia, you woke me up and had me make love to you. How could you do that if the other relationship was so serious? How could you do it if you didn't love me?"

"I'll tell you, but you may not like it. I did it that night to keep you in a good mood so you wouldn't mind if I went down to the church again the next night to see him."

The cold-blooded admission struck me like a sledge ham-mer. "Goddamn you . . . goddamn him. How *could* you!"

"Don't you know? Can't you see? I don't love you and I can't be happy with you. I've got to get out so I can breathe again."

"Get out, go. What the hell's stopping you? Go with the son of a bitch if that's what you want. Find yourself a new existence, a new life. But don't destroy mine and the boys' in the process. You don't know what it means to think about them or anyone else but yourself."

Now we were both talking rapidly and loudly, railing at each other with voices shaking with emotion.

"I've gone over this nine hundred and ninety-nine times with you about what this means to the boys," she shouted. "*I'm* the one who has been victimized by this marriage, not them. *I'm* the one who has been hurt. I don't think I can ever forgive you or trust you again because of it. Do you realize what energy it would take for me to try to work out this whole damnable mess with you? And I don't want to! I want out . . . away from you!" She was crying, pleading, spitting words out angrily, all at once.

"You'd rather walk away from it, wouldn't you, without even giving it a try," I shouted back. "You had your mind made up even before we began. What can be more important than this? What else is there to life except what we have in us and in our children? We know some of the things that have been wrong. Why can't we work now to do something about them and go on from there?"

"You say that as if it was so easy. You don't know what this whole thing has taken out of me. I'm burned out. That's what Sam says happens to love over the years. It gets ground out or burned out or beaten out."

"Beaten out? For Christ's sake, first you were talking about self-fulfillment, finding yourself, meeting your needs. That's the reason you said you wanted your goddamn divorce, to seek your identity. Then it was the *other* relationship. Now it's because I treated you so badly, tromped on you, put you down, beat the love out of you. How come you didn't know it when it was happening? Did someone have to tell you? Did Sam have to—otherwise you wouldn't have known? How come no one else knew it was happening . . . your parents, mine, anyone who knew us? When did it happen? Where? How? Tell me!"

Jean was beginning now to sob and moan, to sputter beginnings of sentences, then choking them back in tears, shaking her head, struggling with rage and agony.

"Oh, God," she cried. "You're saying, 'Be happy with me under any circumstances.' I can't! I can't! You talk about the boys. You *always* talk about the boys. You always use them. If I can't be happy with you, the way you want, then you use the boys against me." She stopped, then she said with a sneer, "God, how solicitous you've gotten of them lately. Anything they want, you give them."

"Bullshit!" I shouted. "If *I* don't give them any attention, they won't get any. You're never home. You never give it to them. They can't get it if you're at church conventions or at meetings. Don't tell me I'm doing anything new. I've been bringing home Friday candy treats, playing hockey with them—and baseball and football and tennis—and going on walks and playing games in front of the fireplace for as long as we've had them. There's no change in any of that."

I was getting angrier and angrier, screaming loudly. "Now everything's a plot, my plan against you. Before, it was our way of life, the way we did things, willingly, happily. Every choice, we made. Now I spoiled the kids. Grandma and Granpa have. You've made no contributions except to be martyred. I'm 95 percent to blame for what's wrong and you're maybe 5 percent."

"No, 75 percent yours and 25 percent mine!" she screamed back. "You don't understand the hurt I feel. You say, 'You shouldn't have it.' Well, goddamn it, I have it. I have it! Do you hear? I have it!" She was shouting at the top of her lungs, her face contorted by rage and tears, the

light from the streetlight illuminating the redness and wet-
ness of her face. "I'm not going to get trapped again.
You're so full of concern for me. You say you love me.
Shit, shit, shit! I'm not going to fall for that again."

I was exhausted, sick over the emotions which had carried us this far. In a tired voice, drained of all the anger I
had felt, I said, "I don't think you are so all-powerful or
wise or have all the answers. You are just as weak and just
as faulty and just as much to blame as I am."

Suddenly Jean yelled, "Jeee-susss!" and swung at my face.
I could see the blow coming and snapped my head back
to avoid being hit, but her hand glanced off the side of my
head and my glasses went flying to the floor of the car.
Before I could move, she smashed me again, flush across
the face. I was quivering, trembling with shock and rage.
She had never done that to me before, ever. We had never
felt the naked hatred we were feeling at that moment toward one another. My voice was shaking as I said, "Now
I'm looking right at you. Hit me again if you want." She
glared at me, swore, crossed her arms and sank down into
the seat.

There was silence—a crushed, heavy, defeated silence.
We were both breathing heavily. I felt physically ill, as if
I might throw up. My hands were shaking, my insides con-
vulsing.

In a few moments I started the car. I drove slowly, feeling as if I were in a dream. We passed the Robertsons'
house; now there were cars parked all around it and lights
spilling out of every window. People we knew and loved
and had spent two intimate and unprecedented years with
were there, laughing, drinking, talking, feeling the deep
bond which we had felt. Tonight we were in another world.
Three months ago no one would ever have thought—I cer-

tainly never would have—that Jean and Al Martin would have been through what had just happened to us. We drove by the patch of brightness; then there was darkness and the road ahead. It was impossible. It couldn't be happening. But it was.

The shattered mood stayed with us the rest of the week. There was a spent quality about our relationship. Hurt and rough times were part of what I thought people had to go through at times in their lives; I felt no matter how much we had wounded each other Saturday night, we had to persist and come back together. I knew we had the ability to overcome any of these problems if we only had the will. And for the sake of the children, for our own sake, we at least had to try our hardest, so we could either succeed or know that we had made the utmost effort. But there was not even a hint from Jean that she would ever feel that way. The week went by with us making little real contact. Teenagers kept pouring into our basement room for after-school jam sessions punctuated by dips in the lake; flowers blossomed; trees thickened with foliage so that once again we could not see the houses around us any more; vegetables poked through the ground in our garden, bringing Dan in with reports like, "Hey, the lettuce is up," or, "You can see the row of radishes." But Jean and I were untouched by these daily occurrences.

Work was a dreadful, wearying experience each day. I could not sleep for long periods at night, after wanting to do so all day. My levels of tension and anxiety had dropped since Sam suggested the moratorium on divorce talk, but the real situation was still buried not far beneath my consciousness. When Jean and I used to make love, the event would provide a feeling of security and affection, so I slept soundly afterwards. Now there was no beginning and no ending to the constant tenseness; the time spent in bed was only an excruciating reminder of what used to be and what could be. Sometimes I would wake up during the middle of the night, find Jean deep asleep, and snuggle close to her just to feel the warmth and strength from her that I had known for so long. Nothing could replace Jean during the waking hours of my life, and nothing seemed to be able to do it at night. In a painful procession of similar days, we moved on to another Saturday-afternoon session.

The argument of the previous weekend had overshadowed everything and obviously had to be put before Sam and Gloria. Jean had no desire to do it and so I began. As I talked, she interrupted occasionally to clarify what she meant by a certain remark, but she didn't dispute my account of what happened.

When I had finished, both Sam and Gloria were thoughtful. Sam poked a cigarette out in the ashtray. Gloria fiddled with a ring on her finger and looked as if she was concentrating hard. Finally Sam looked up, turned to Jean and said, "It sounds to me as if you'd like to get rid of Al."

There was a silence for a few moments; then Jean said, "Yes, I think so."

Another silence. All eyes were turned on her, waiting, watching; a heavy mood was settling over the four of us. Then Jean went on: "But I haven't thought it all through yet."

Sam asked her if she wanted me to leave the house, and she hesitated a moment, then said, "I'm not sure."

Did she seem uncertain, or was I imagining it, hoping for it?

Gloria turned to me and asked, "How do you feel when you hear Jean say that after all you've done these past three months, all the changes that you've made, all the effort, it doesn't matter?"

"I guess I feel I'm not surprised by what Jean is saying, so I can't say I'm disappointed. I didn't really expect otherwise, although I hoped for it. I'm discouraged. I've suspected Jean might have had her mind made up all along and it didn't matter *what* I did. But I had to do it, and I'll keep doing it. There's no other way for me."

Turning to Jean, Gloria said, "I've heard about what Al has done, or tried to do, how he has changed or tried to change, but I haven't heard much about you changing, Jean. Do you think you've changed any in these past three months?"

Jean started to answer several times, but stopped each time. She was flustered and uncertain. "I . . . I . . . haven't changed my *initial* feelings. But I . . . I've arrived at them differently. I think about this all the time; the process goes on constantly."

Sam had been listening quietly, but now he asked her, "Well, where does all this leave you?"

Then Jean said very evenly, without a pause and very calmly, "In love with the wrong man."

Her words hung in the silence with shattering simplicity —no dramatics, no major pronouncement, just a straightforward comment. Everyone was quiet, eyes riveted on Jean. I was stunned. After eighteen years of married life, my wife had just casually said that she was in love with another man, a man I presumed to be Smothers, who was supposedly dedicated to the high principles of the ministry, married, eight years younger than she, and with a son of his own.

In the extended silence Jean began now to look agitated. Her hand found her mouth and she rubbed the area around her chin. She was looking down and the color began rising slowly over her face. She seemed to be breathing now in short, hard breaths.

"I presume you're talking about your minister friend," Sam said. Jean nodded. Then she said, "I'd like to have a private meeting with you and Gloria to talk this over, because there are some things I don't want to discuss in front of Al."

Sam looked over at me questioningly. "That's fine," I said to him, "but I want both you and Gloria there."

"Why?" Jean asked.

"Because the tough, critical questions to you in here are always asked by Gloria, and I want to be sure she's there to ask them."

"For who, you or Jean?" Sam said.

"For me. I want to protect my own interests."

I left boiling with anger. My wife had said she was carrying on with her minister, wanted to walk out on me and smash up our family. I was furious with Jean but also with the counselors. No one had raised a voice to her to say, "Hey, wait a minute. Do you realize what you're doing?" No one had even suggested that there might be something wrong in this. She could have said she was going shopping for groceries afterwards and they would have reacted with as much concern. What in God's name was going on in there? Did anything go? Could you say you had just murdered six people or raped your mother and still get a benign acceptance? Weren't there any values or rules left? What kind of insanity was this?

And what about that son of a bitch Smothers? What kind of a "man of God" was he? As Jean and I walked to the car, I raged about him, about the "deceitful goddamn bastard God-playing hypocritical minister, trying to steal my wife away. I could kill the son of a bitch with my bare hands!"

Jean had regained her calm and poise now, and she asked matter-of-factly, "What would that accomplish?"

"A helluva lot for me," I shouted back.

When we got home, I slammed the car door, stalked up to our bedroom and picked up the phone.

"Smothers? This is Albert Martin." I spat out the words. "Meet me in your office in fifteen minutes. And you'd better be there, or I'll come to your house. And I'll break the goddamn door down if you don't open it." There was a short silence at the other end, then a muffled "Okay."

I was at the Methodist church ahead of him. Nobody was there. It was late on a Saturday afternoon. The door was unlocked, so I presumed a staff person must have been working somewhere in the building. I paced back and forth outside Smothers' office, shaping and controlling my fury, molding it into the club I wanted to swing.

In a few minutes Smothers arrived. He climbed out of his car and walked toward the door. He was wearing a dark suit and tie. He was tall, taller than I, but had sloping shoulders and an awkward bearing. His black hair was combed straight back, revealing his slightly receding hairline. He had round silver glasses and blue eyes that seemed to be concentrating all the time. He smiled automatically at me, then wiped the smile off his face when he saw the look on mine.

He led the way into his office; I slammed the door shut behind us and said, "Sit down, you son of a bitch!" He looked around and sat on the front of a straight wooden chair. I paced in front of him. "My wife has just told me that she's in love with you. What do you have to say about that? What do you intend to do?"

126

Smothers frowned even more deeply, looked at me unblinkingly and said, "I don't know." His voice was gauzy, fuzzy—not from fear or nervousness, but because, it seemed to me, to reflect a deep, basic uncertainty about himself. He was slumped forward, accentuating the slope of his shoulders. I thought, What a miserable wretched son of a bitch! And *this* is what Jean chooses over me. The thought intensified my anger, and I snarled, "I could smash your head through that wall. I could kill you, you bastard!" Smothers simply looked at me, unflinching, accepting. "I'll tell you that you had better begin to think about some of the goddamn consequences of what you are up to. Jean may be out on her ass and you'll have your balls cut off by the Methodist church if I have anything to do with it. Nobody wants a cuckolding bastard minister around, and I'm going to expose you for that."

Smothers still said nothing but listened to what I was shouting, nodding to show he understood. When he began to speak, his mouth was dry; he had to swallow hard and continually lick his lips. "I think a great deal of Jean. I don't know if I love her. I don't know if I'm going to marry her. I just don't know."

Amidst my anger, I suddenly felt pity for him. The poor bastard. Maybe he was as bad off as I was. Maybe Jean was the pursuer and he the pursued. He certainly didn't look like any romantic hero ready to storm the ramparts for his loved one. Instead, he looked like a wretched, miserable, tortured, uncertain guy.

"Look, Smothers," I said in a softer tone, "I don't know how much you've contributed to this. I'm telling you that you had better do some deep thinking. You may find yourself involved in an alienation-of-affection suit and the subject of a big scandal in this church. I'm not going to take this lying down. I love Jean. I want her. I'm going to fight to keep her and to keep my family intact. I'm just warning you that you'd better know what you're getting into. Any questions?"

Smothers sat there, looking at me, studying me, something working in his mind. Then he shook his head and got up.

"Fine," I said. "Goodbye, you bastard!" And I slammed the door as hard as I could.

That evening, sitting out on the porch overlooking the patio, the ball field and the wall of green woods beyond it, I thought that this whole, bizarre, unbelievable experience had reached the height of its incredibility. The utter insanity was at its peak. Within the past few hours my wife had revealed she was in love with another man; I'd confronted that man and said I wanted to kill him; Jean had come home and made a delicious supper that we all enjoyed and ate together amiably; and now I was contemplating a beautiful, gentle twilight. Surrounded by blissful suburban quiet, I was looking out over a scene of children playing and dogs and cats romping. The scene could have qualified for a *Family Life* cover.

I tilted back comfortably in a porch chair and thought to myself, The whole world has gone crazy. Things like this don't happen to forty-three-year-old normal people. As I sat there, the aches, the tension and the anxiety I had felt so long were momentarily dissipated in the feeling of freedom and wide-open space which filled me as I gazed at the massive cluster of trees, branches waving majestically in a slight breeze, and past them into infinity, into a cloudless sky.

Jean came to church with the boys and me because it was Mother's Day. The sermon was fine: not heavy with clichés about motherhood, but a mature reflection about accepting people sometimes without understanding them completely. It may not have been a conventional Mother's Day sermon, but I thought the theme was good for Jean and me.

After a light lunch Charley and I took off for his Little League game. A fine rain had been falling most of the morning and we weren't sure the game was on, but we had to show up anyway. At game time, the rain slowed to a very light sprinkle, so the boys began to play. As there were no stands in the school ball field, all of us had brought folding chairs; I settled myself into my porch folding chair, put up an umbrella over my head, snuggled into my raincoat and felt like a dry island looking out on a sea of wetness.

The game was the usual high-scoring, freewheeling kind, nobody holding a lead for more than one at bat, but fun for the boys. Charley played catcher and did all right, making some good stops. Like Jim, he was a much better fielder than batter, but he got a piece of the ball a couple of times and looked like a batter. His team won, 11–10, which made the parents on our side happy. During the game I had been carrying on the running commentary that was always going on in my mind; talking to Jean, thinking about us, asking questions, supplying answers; the reality of us never left me. As I was folding up my chair and gathering up the other gear, a new set of parents began arriving for the next game.

I looked up, and suddenly the sloping, ungainly figure of Smothers was in front of me. The short, chunky figure of his wife was beside him, and their son, holding a baseball glove, was running across the diamond. Smothers had seen me already and was nodding recognition—not a greeting, just an acknowledgment that we were both trapped. I nodded back automatically, not sure of which emotion to follow: anger, indifference or civility. The two of them were so close together as they passed that I thought I saw them holding hands. Then Charley said something to me, and as I answered him, the Smotherses passed out of my view.

All the way home my mind raced over what I had seen. I thought of how I might have handled it, changing my mood each time. Then the utter irony of the domestic scene struck me, and I wanted to laugh. Smothers and his wife, hand in hand, going to a ball game. Jean should have been there to see that. Anger grew in me.

When we got home and Charley had gone upstairs to change, I played my little scene.

"Saw someone you know at the game today," I said.

Jean was hesitant. "Really, who?" she asked brightly.

"Smothers and his wife." I let the words sink in. "They were holding hands. It was a lovely, touching sight."

She looked at me stunned, visibly shaken. Before she could respond, I spat out angrily, "Wouldn't that be ironic as hell! Smothers and his wife make up and live happily ever after, and you get your ass kicked out of that twosome and out of here, too. Wouldn't that be too bad!"

A few days before, Jean might have fired back a tart answer or even swung at me in anger. Now she just stood there helpless, looking like a child about to cry. I wanted to grab her, tell her I was sorry for hurting her, kiss her. I wanted to say, "I didn't mean it. For God's sake, this is all crazy. Let's forget about the whole mess and go on from here." But I had been hurt too many times, distrusted what she would do too deeply. Instead I looked coldly at her floundering in her indecision, and went to the sink for a drink of water. I had played my game, but there was no joy in it. Jean had moved to the pantry, out of sight. In a moment she brushed by on her way to the other part of the house.

I kept myself busy, peeking in the oven, looking into pots, resisting the temptation to go to her. Finally I couldn't stand it any longer and hurried to where she had gone. The bathroom door was closed, so as an excuse to talk to her I said, "Jean, do you want me to start the charcoals outside yet?" There was no answer. Then she opened the bathroom door and just stood there, tears streaming down her face. We looked at one another for a moment; then we both took a short step forward. Suddenly we were in each other's arms. I held her as tightly as I could, and I could feel her arms clinging to me and her body pressed against mine. I kissed her eyes, her forehead, her lips. "Oh, Jean, Jean, I love you. I didn't mean to hurt you."

"Leon won't be with us at our conference next weekend," she blurted out. "I don't know who will be . . . but he won't be going."

"Thank you. Thank you for telling me that. I was worried, but I wasn't going to ask. I'm glad." We were still holding each other tightly, and I was kissing her softly. "Jean, we're just two people hurting, going through terrible pain right now, reaching out to one another. I accept this as just that." We stepped back to look at one another, then hugged each other again. She turned her face up and we kissed as we used to, deeply and warmly. "Darling, darling," I said, "we need one another. There's no right or wrong, just two people trying to do our best." I could have screamed for joy; this was the moment I had been dreaming of, praying for. I knew it had to happen. Everything else was a nightmare; this was really Jean and me as we should be. It was just a moment—I knew our troubles weren't over—but it was a beginning, a touching in the way we used to. It felt so unbelievably, deliriously good to hold her in my arms.

After a time we began to feel awkward, uncertain, embarrassed. Jean stepped back first, straightened out her dress, smoothed back her hair and smiled faintly, then went into the kitchen.

In the following moments we were both disoriented. We didn't know how to relate to one another, what to do. We both talked quickly, almost desperately, and about the most trivial things we could. Charley came in and we both gratefully seized him as the focus for our attention. I felt a tentative, cautious joy, as if to seize it completely might make it go away or crush it.

When we sat down to dinner, I was still delicately trying to fan the sparks of contact between us. I said grace before dinner and carefully steered away from anything presumptuous. Instead, I simply offered thanks for Mom on Mother's Day.

As the evening went by, Jean gradually pulled away from me, and I sensed that her mood was changing again. Very subtly she seemed to harden; the signs were in the way she carried her head and her shoulders, the look in her eyes, the slight edge to her voice. After all the children were in bed, I tried as gently as I could to find out where Jean and I stood at that moment. I didn't want to draw my own conclusions from what happened or to assume too much. I asked her if we could talk for a few moments about what had happened that afternoon. "Only if you make it short," Jean said wearily. "I'm tired."

"Well, I'd really like to have some understanding between us about where we stand," I said. "I know how I feel. Those moments this afternoon were wonderful; I'm deeply grateful for them. But it was only a moment, and I don't want to take anything more from it other than the hope that there may be others like it."

"It sounds to me like you're trying to impose on me what I should think about it," she said tersely.

"I don't mean to do that. I just wanted to know how you reacted to it, that's all."

"Look, Al, we take different conclusions away from the same event. We do it in counseling, so it's no surprise we do it here. I think I was only feeling low and needed someone to comfort me and you were there. Nothing more. That's it. Period."

These words crushed the hope and promise of the afternoon. I had sensed the direction she was moving in; now her words confirmed that for me.

Inside I was struggling with disappointment, discouragement, rejection. The moment had apparently not been even the smallest thing I was hoping for: a tentative beginning. Jean was not offering the slightest chance that it could grow and develop. For her, it was over, forgotten.

That I had to accept. But at the same time I had glimpsed a small crack, a tiny breakthrough. After months of no hope, even this slight glimmer was gratification enough to try even harder.

VI

Whenever I expected *anything* out of the counseling sessions, something entirely different happened. That occurred again the next Saturday when I went by myself; Jean was away at a church meeting in upstate Connecticut.

I was expecting encouragement about what I considered to be a breakthrough. I also hoped for some comment about the progress we were making in communicating with one another more realistically, even if it involved angry words and fights.

Instead, Sam lashed out at me angrily. "You're still spending 80 percent of your time trying to figure out how Jean is reacting and 20 percent of the time looking into your own reactions and feelings," he thundered. "What's the matter with you? Why are you afraid to look inside yourself? You're depriving yourself of the luxury of self-examination."

Startled by his unexpected anger, I stammered, "Well . . . I guess it's mostly because I don't know how to. When something as emotional and explosive as this happens between Jean and me, I want to know what caused it and where we are at."

"That's crap," he snapped. "What do you mean, you don't know where you're at? That's bullshit. You know damn good and well."

"I know a lot better than I did three months ago, but one minute I think there's hope and the next I'm crushed by despair."

"Okay, tell me what you know," he snapped tersely.

"I know a lot of things going on between Jean and me were not what I thought they were. My buying clothes for her, my getting up with the kids at night, my doing dishes and helping with the housework. I thought these were good, positive things, but it turns out they were bad and negative, at least as Jean was seeing them. I thought all along I was strong and decisive and giving Jean the support she wanted, and you say things were just the opposite, I was dependent on her. And—"

Gloria broke in: "Okay, Al, what do you know now that was *positive?*"

I was thrown off stride completely by her question. Nobody up to now had ever asked either of us what was *right* with our marriage.

"Hell yes, I can think of lots of positive things. For instance, I'm proud of what we were. We weren't some kind of cardboard cutouts or cartoon characters, with the words coming out in balloons floating over our heads. We were real, distinctive, interesting people, with values and priorities, making worthwhile, concrete contributions to society. We weren't robots moved around the country every two years by some giant corporation, pulling up roots fifteen times so that we could climb up some goddamn corporate ladder. What we did in the community and who we were and what we did with our lives was something to be proud of!"

"Al," Gloria said quietly, "first you mentioned the negative things you've learned. And you associated yourself first person with these faults. But when you started talking about the positive things, you switched over to 'we' and you suddenly sounded as if it was some impersonal listing about someone else."

I didn't realize I'd done that.

"You should think some more about that," Gloria continued. "You didn't have to accept all the burden of blame when you and Jean first came here. Nor, at the same time, did you have to reject it. You could have kept an open mind instead, saying, 'Let's see who really did what.' But you accepted all the blame, and you lay on the floor for so long because of it."

I looked at Gloria for a few moments, trying to absorb all that she was saying. Then, without thinking, these words came out: "God, I haven't even begun to list the ways Jean may have hurt *me* in our relationship."

Sam shot out of his chair. He walked around it and looked back at me, eyes blazing. "You have *never even mentioned* that aspect in the entire three months you've been coming here. Do you know that?"

Gloria chimed in: "It's true, Al, you haven't." There was excitement ringing in her voice.

It hadn't occurred to me. "Well, I'd like to go in that direction for a while and see where it leads."

"I want you to," Sam said. "I want you to think about that lots more. Spend some time thinking about it between now and our next meeting."

As I started to get up, Gloria smiled warmly. "You're doing okay. You're making progress."

When I came outside, I was exhilarated. For the first time the session had taken a positive turn, from my point of view. There was more of a balance, a larger scope to what was happening, and I felt better because of it.

Because I felt better, relations with Jean were better that evening. I wanted to do *something* with her that night, just to enjoy the new sensations I was feeling. A funny movie seemed just the ticket. Jean, however, did not feel like going out, so I went alone to see Barbra Streisand in *What's Up, Doc?* The choice was perfect for my mood; I hadn't laughed so heartily in months. Afterwards, I treated myself to a hot-fudge sundae and began to drive around slowly in my car, eating it and thinking.

One thing I could see clearly now was the completely different positions Jean and I had started from on February 5. From the moment she exploded her bombshell I had to start from scratch on a whole new life. For months Jean had been mulling, preparing, working toward that moment, and that explained her toughness and the readiness with which she moved past it. Now we were wrestling with two processes: the staggering changes within our lives, and at the same time the day-by-day concerns of living which could not be ignored—job, children, friends, and so forth.

Driving around slowly, aimlessly, letting cars pass which were in a hurry, I enjoyed the nice, unpressured feeling of being alone, thinking, getting in touch with myself. This was a process I'd never thought to do in all my years of knowing Jean; we always did things together and I thought that was the only way married people behaved. There was a calm luxury about being alone and letting my thoughts and feelings roam where they would.

I thought of Jean's stock phrase to end all discussions, the phrase for which I had no answer up to now, "Al, I don't love you any more." I began to wonder about love. Obviously Jean and I differed hugely right now about what the word meant. One day she had said, "I look out the window at you coming up the driveway and I don't feel about you the way I used to." I guess she meant on that basis she didn't love me any more. But was that the basis for love for two people as far along in life and in a relationship as we were? At age forty-three was love still a gushy, gooey visual contact? Or wasn't it embedded in grubby things like waxing a floor so she wouldn't have to do it, or getting up with a sick kid because she was tired? As I saw it, love was helping Jean; it was concern, care, tenderness and regard. It didn't focus on personal identity, self-fulfillment, growth and all the psychological factors Jean was now so exclusively concerned with. What we had been doing in our own natural, perhaps "unenlightened," way was for me love. Now Jean's whole understanding of love had changed, along with almost everything else about Jean. We had to resolve these changes within the central relationship of our lives, our marriage, or else we would be putting an end to the relationship. How could people like us follow our feelings and hang the consequences, whatever felt right for the individual was the right thing to do? How could you run families or stable societies that way?

As I scraped the last bit of hot fudge from the plastic cup, I felt with satisfaction that it had been a good, a worthwhile period of reflection alone.

The next day, May 23, was Dan's fourteenth birthday, and just seeing Dan provided plenty of gratification in itself. The scar on his upper lip was barely noticeable; he had no speech impediments; all the complications of nose, ears and throat we had been warned about in cleft-palate babies had not materialized. He was now a fine, handsome normal boy in all respects, and his own ordeal—four operations, the years of speech therapy and orthodontics—had made him a strong, self-reliant individual.

I thought about all the work and sacrifice on the part of Jean and me to help make Dan what he was today. I wondered how it would have been achieved in a period of self-fulfillment and self-importance. In order to pay the thousands of dollars in medical bills we'd owed on Dan, I had taken a spot on the network's overnight staff, working from 1:00 A.M. until 8:00 A.M. That meant getting up at midnight to go to work and living an inverted life, sleeping mostly in the daytime. What if I had gotten in touch with my feelings and followed them: "Screw getting up in the middle of the night. This routine stinks. I don't like to do it and I won't. My need is for a regular daytime job, and Dan will have to make out as best he can." Jean had to drive Dan to countless sessions of speech therapy and medical and dental appointments; she could have said, "I've got a life of my own. I'd rather be dancing or painting or taking a sewing course. Dan's needs come after I fulfill my own." Didn't we have to take into consideration other people's needs, sometimes sacrifice our wants for those of others, in order to make a family work? Wasn't that what grownup, mature people bargained for and clearly accepted when they became parents?

But where was any hint of that bargain in the kind of counseling we were getting? Shouldn't Sam say one day, "Wait a minute. Let's talk about where you are in life. Jean, it's true that you are not getting maximum fulfillment out of your marital relationship, but this is an imperfect world and the challenge is to make something viable out of what you have, not to chuck that away and expect to start from scratch with all new beginnings."

Dan's birthday celebration had everything we could give him to make him happy: his choice of lobster tails for his birthday dinner, the icebox cake he loved for dessert, and a ten-speed bike from Jean and me as his gift. But the greatest gift I thought we could give him, the assurance of a stable, unified family, seemed farther away from realization than ever. And that, amid my pride in his progress towards manhood, made me troubled and sick at heart.

As the weeks went by, Jean continued to be away from the home a great deal of the time. She went out to meetings two or three nights a week and spent most of the weekends away. When she was home, she talked on the phone almost incessantly. I wanted her to have her own interests and activities, but their extent was affecting the children and our life together as a family; the house was getting more and more run-down. If I tried to put my foot down angrily and say, "Stop it, cut it out. You've got to be home more," I was being demanding and domineering. One night as she was going out, I tried to discuss what I felt was happening.

"Jean, I hear the boys complaining about a lot of things, and from what I can see, I think they are right. They say, 'Mom is never home. She's always on the phone.' The house is filthy; you can tell that if you just look around. Our meals have been pretty lousy and usually late. You never used to be like that."

"Al, you mind your business and I'll mind mine."

"Yes, but our business is these children and our home. I think you're neglecting them, and you won't even listen to them or to me."

She stiffened. "Don't you start telling me—" Then she looked at the clock: "It's late. I don't want to get into this now!"

"Wait a minute. I want you to listen to one thing more."

She grimaced impatiently, shifted her position and stood waiting.

"There are two ways of looking at where we are now. One is that I'm the whole cause of your disenchantment with our marriage and that's why you don't love me. That could be, and I am dreadfully sorry for what I may have contributed to your feelings. I'd rather have you, this family, and our home, intact, than anything else. No one wants a divorce less than I do."

She began to shift her weight again and frowned irritatedly; looking impatient, she told me to get to the point.

"The second possibility is that you are going through some immense personal upheaval yourself. Sam and Gloria said it was a possibility, your own 'personal identity crisis.' You aren't the person you used to be; you never did things like this before. Couldn't we at least begin to talk together about that possibility? We've never even discussed it among ourselves."

Jean had started to listen very carefully when I began talking about the possibility of her personal change, and anger began to show in her eyes and in the line of her lips. Now she said hostilely, "You'd like that, wouldn't you? It would get you off the hook. Everything would be my fault then, wouldn't it, and you wouldn't have a thing to do with it. That would be nice for you, wouldn't it?"

"No, good God, no! That's the last thing I'd want to happen. I *want* you. I love you. I want all of us here, together, in this home. That's all. Believe me, Jean, that's why I think we've got to at least consider that possibility."

She had picked up her purse, her car keys and some papers she was carrying. "Al, I don't have time to talk about that now. I don't trust you anyway, so I can't believe you. That's how I feel and you'll have to accept it." And she brushed by on her way out.

The next Saturday afternoon at our counseling session, the same theme came up again. Sam remarked that Jean had missed several appointments because of her church commitments; he said he felt we couldn't make progress if she kept that up.

"That's one of my problems at home," I said. "We can't make contact if she's not there, and even the boys are complaining about Mom not being home."

Turning to Jean, Sam said, "I don't see how being out to meetings so much can make a contribution to the family."

"It does. It helps me cope better with the boys and things around the house."

"Well, Jean, what do you think?" Gloria said. "Do you feel as if you are going through a personal crisis?"

Jean began to say something about her religion now—how important it was to her, how she wasn't acting any differently.

Gloria broke in: "But you haven't answered my question."

Jean began again, but this time she talked about her realization that she didn't love me, how she felt about life, how her outlook had changed.

As I listened closely, straining to hear this important answer, I thought, Either she doesn't understand what Gloria is asking her or she can't get the answer out. Because what she was trying to say wasn't coming across to me. Sam and Gloria were listening closely, too; I don't know what they heard, but they did not question her.

Instead, Sam turned us sharply and decisively in another direction. Without any preliminaries he asked Jean, "Do you still want a divorce?" Just as quickly, she answered, "Yes."

Jean was not reacting emotionally; she was very simply and coolly answering his question. The only sign of any inner excitement was that she began to chew her gum a little more rapidly.

Sam asked, "Why do you want to end your marriage?"

"Because," Jean answered, "I don't want this kind of complex, mechanical relationship. I want a spontaneous one, where somebody knows me automatically and understands me."

Then Jean launched into a list of complaints about our marriage and how we'd been living. "I'm tired of Al and everything about him. I don't feel any love. I'm tired of Catholicism and how it's turned off the boys. I'm tired of our big house, of the entertaining we did. I just don't want any part of it any more!"

Sam listened carefully, and when Jean paused for a moment, he said, "You've listed all the reasons why you want to be divorced *from* a situation. How about telling us what it is you want to go *to?*"

Jean shifted in her chair, rubbed her chin with her hand and replied, "I really haven't made up my mind on that yet."

There was silence. My depressed spirits picked up a bit. If she was uncertain about what she wanted next, there was still a chance.

Gloria had been studying my face and she asked, "Al, how do you feel about what Jean said today?"

"Terrible. I don't want a divorce. That's not the answer for me. I know we're not perfect, we've got faults. But despite them we've had an awfully good life together. I know *I've* had. I'm not looking for ideal solutions. I want to go on from here to make a better life for Jean and me and our kids. Nothing else has made sense to me and nothing still does."

Jean broke in: "You've always been more concerned with the family than with our marriage."

Maybe she was right, but before I could answer, Sam said, "Gloria and I have been listening to you both for about four months now, and we know enough about you and about the problem. We will all have to make up our minds what to do about it. I think we have to get down to the nitty-gritty. We'll start with that next time."

That night, a few hours after Jean had reiterated her desire for a divorce, we sat side by side and entertained six people for dinner in our home. We carried on lively conversations, talked to and about one another, acted as if it were any other Saturday-night social event during the past five years.

When everyone had finally gone home, after midnight, I began the cleanup process which was part of our routine. Jean got ready for bed while I washed the dishes, put away the leftovers and got the kitchen in shape for the morning. But while I was doing that, my mind was wrestling with this question: how could we pull off an evening like this, get along so well, bridge our differences so successfully, yet not be able to turn the same process to bear on our personal problem?

Summer was rapidly approaching. The boys were already checking off the remaining days of school on the calendar. Now they were asking, "What are we going to do for our vacation this year? Are we going to go camping again like last summer?"

This summer we were to go to Maine, where we had

rented a cottage on the coast for a few weeks, and the boys wanted to know when we would be going. I couldn't give them an answer because I didn't know this far ahead what Jean intended to do. The moratorium Sam had worked out about talk of divorce would be up by that time. I could only give the boys evasive answers and live on hope.

Events of a simple and enjoyable nature could turn for me into occasions of great pain. One of these was Charley's final recital with the school orchestra for the school year.

Getting ready that evening, Charley was so excited he could barely eat. I helped him into the white shirt bought especially for the recital, and even managed, after several tries, to tie his tie for him. He brushed his long golden hair carefully and wet it down a bit so that it would stay in place. While Jean and I got ready, he opened his violin case, propped the music up on the piano, and practiced one of the pieces for the dozenth time. Mixed in with a nine-year-old's pride at performing in front of an audience that included parents was the nervousness that he wouldn't do well. In the car going to school, we tried to assure him that we knew he would do very well; Charley could manage only an uncertain smile in response.

When the orchestra filed out onto the stage, I felt a thrill of pride in the well-scrubbed, handsome boy trying to find us by sneaking a look out of the corner of his eye. At one point while he was waiting for the cue to begin, he did locate us, and there was an almost imperceptible nod of assurance. Then they began, and my nervousness, which must have been at least the equal of Charley's, began to disappear. They were good! That was our boy up there playing as if he were part of a professional orchestra. I looked at Jean and she was beaming proudly, too; we glanced at one another and exchanged a look of pride and relief. All around us, couples were being pleasantly surprised and settling down to enjoy the evening.

As I sat immersed in the good feelings and glow of the moment, the sudden thought hit me that I might soon lose evenings like this forever—the joy and pride of going through these events with my children, the sharing of the moment with Jean. I began to sweat and to feel hot and flushed and smothered. I struggled with the dread and anxiety of being cut off from evenings like this, reacting as severely as I had during the first days after Jean's announcement six months before.

The rest of the evening I smiled mechanically, applauded vigorously, joined other parents in exchanging words of pride and in giving congratulations, but inside me I was unable to loosen the grip of fear that held me.

Afterwards Charley was bubbling with relief and happiness, and we both told him how fine he had done. By way of celebration, Jean and I took him to the ice cream parlor for a soda, crowded now with other parents and kids from the recital. We beamed happily with him and were part of the excited crowd, but my mind was fixed on other nights which might be different from this one.

From an outsider's point of view, Jean and I carried on as we always had around the house. For me, that was easy: I hadn't changed in my feelings toward Jean, and it was a natural and comfortable outlet for me to show what I really felt inside. For Jean, behaving as if everything were normal had to be difficult; but there was no sense in telling the children anything because there was nothing definite to tell them just yet. There was not even any hypocrisy in-

146

volved in our daily routine because I did what I felt comfortable doing and Jean did likewise; the children couldn't have known that the morning and evening kisses I gave her, as I always did, were largely one-sided, or that the hug I would impulsively give her made her tighten to my touch. We talked normally most of the time because there were no flaming feelings of hatred or anger; Jean's deadness to me did not exclude civil and sometimes even lively conversation.

Sex was a continuous and serious problem for me. My mentioning it at the counseling session had brought about no change in the situation. Jean adamantly refused to allow us to make love. I would not even consider an outside sexual relationship, just as I never had during all the years of our marriage, because Jean was the one I loved and sex without love does not appeal to me. But this was also something the boys couldn't be aware of, so it seemed to them as if nothing were wrong.

Our social life had been busy before, and momentum kept it that way. We went out together, entertained when we had to (far less than before), and seemed to most of the outside world the same as ever. By now, however, many people knew that we were going to marriage counseling and that Jean wanted a divorce. I had talked about my reactions in the most realistic and detailed terms I knew how—with Jack Connors, Stu Robertson, and others.

Among our closest friends, some difficulties and complications were beginning to show. Feelings of antagonism toward me or toward Jean would flash from friends who unconsciously sympathized with one or the other of us. I felt sharp and hostile reactions from a few women; the men gave me sympathy and support. Evenings with our close-knit group from the Modern Liturgy would suddenly become tense when some comment touching on Jean or me laid bare deep emotions.

June 28, 1972

The necessity of a business trip and Charley's tenth birthday combined to take me back to Texas. Since I had to go to Dallas for a meeting and school had just let out for the summer, we decided to let Charley fly down with me to spend his birthday with his grandparents and perhaps stay a week or two after I returned.

This was the first time Nanna, Pap and I would be seeing each other since our comfortable relationship going back two decades had been radically altered, although we had corresponded frequently, Pap and I exchanging long and frank letters.

From the moment we stepped inside the Dallas terminal and the trim, wiry Texan stepped up to give us both a firm handshake and hearty hug, I felt I was back in a world I could understand and which was a welcome relief. All the warmth, the friendly kidding, the open acceptance—qualities which had disappeared completely from my relationship with Jean—were here.

On the ride down to the retirement home which Nanna and Pap had built south of Dallas I could feel tenseness and anxiety leave me. My frame seemed to grow taller and freer; there was such joy in talking to someone I loved who loved me back. I reveled in the familiar companionship.

Charley, too, was basking in the affection of his grandparents, excitedly telling them all the things he'd stored up: about the last days of school and the good report card he had gotten, about the Little League baseball team, about our garden, about the kids in the neighborhood. The hour-and-a-half drive seemed short; soon we were at their house, which was built on the side of a lake. Charley was full of pent-up energy from both the flight down and the car ride, so he, Pap and I threw a ball around while Nanna made supper.

Dinner was the one Charley had been hoping for: fried chicken, and afterwards a birthday cake Nanna had baked. Adding to my pleasure was the presence of Aunt Myra, Nanna's sister, who had come to live with them now that she had retired from schoolteaching. Myra had enough of the seriousness of the teacher about her to impress Charley and keep him on his best behavior, but he knew that beneath the reserve there was a gentle, playful personality. After supper we played dominoes and talked and enjoyed being with one another. When Charley's bedtime arrived, Aunt Myra excused herself, took him upstairs and also went to bed. Nanna and Pap and I were alone.

Throughout the evening there had been no reference to the difficulties Jean and I were having, not even when Pap and I did the dishes together, smoking our pipes like old times, talking about religion, politics, relatives and friends we knew. Even now I didn't want to disturb the lovely, relaxing atmosphere by discussing our problems, but I also didn't want to avoid talking about them. I tried to put how I felt as frankly and gently as I could: "It is wonderful just being with you again. I didn't come down to bring our problems into your home. I'll leave it up to you. If there is anything about Jean and me that you'd like to know about, anything that's bothering you, I'd be glad to talk about it. If not, if you'd rather just put it aside for now, that's okay by me, too."

Pap shifted in his chair and puffed thoughtfully on his pipe. "We appreciate that, son," he said, "and of course we're terribly concerned about what's happening. We just don't know much because Jean doesn't write about it. We found out she resented our probing too much and some statements we made, so we generally stay away from that now in our letters. We're pretty much in the dark about things."

The way he said it seemed to me an invitation to at least catch them up on a few basic points: where the counseling stood now, what it had turned up, what the situation was in regard to Smothers (I knew Jean had written to them about him). I took several minutes to tell them about how Sam and Gloria operated, what I had learned about my dependence on Jean and then about my confronting Smothers.

Pap drew a few puffs on his pipe, narrowed his eyes thoughtfully and then looked at me again. "Of course, Momma and I could see problems for you two a long time ago, but that's not the kind of thing young people listen to, or can be expected to listen to. We could see your religious backgrounds might cause trouble because they were so different. And when the children came along, the way you handled them. We don't want to be critical— please understand that—but we always felt you indulged the boys, spoiled them, Al. I know you didn't mean to or want to, but that seems to be what happened."

"Pap, I know what you're saying. I understand. But I don't think those things explain a divorce. Religion wasn't a problem for Jean and me for eighteen years, and it's not now, at least in the way you see it. The same thing is true with the boys. I'm not locked or fixed or saying, 'It's got to be my way and no other way.' I'm willing to try, to do my best on any new approaches. God, I've found I had faults I never knew existed, but I don't mean to keep them. We've got to try to work together, however, and that doesn't appeal to Jean just now. Why, I just don't know."

Pap tapped the ash in his pipe bowl down gingerly with one finger, puffed some new life into it and asked, "Do you think—and Momma and I have talked about this a great deal—that Jean could be going through a change of life of some kind?"

"I do, but it's not physical at this time. I mean, she's going through a tremendous emotional change, it seems, but it's not physical menopause. At least she says it's not; she doesn't have any of the physical symptoms."

In the quiet room we sat thoughtfully, talking only when someone had a question to raise, deep in our own reflections. I thought to myself: what incredible people. They are undoubtedly wrenched by the deepest anxiety about their only child; how easy it would be for them to hurl accusations at me, defend her, be antagonistic simply because someone had to be blamed and it could easily be me. Instead they spoke with such openness and listened so acceptingly; they were the model of what had struck me about Jean when we first met and what I'd always cherished about her. I looked up at the picture of Jean balanced on toe from her ballet days, at her in her wedding dress, holding her bouquet. Her presence was there with us. She was a part of these people; she was basically, soundly what they were, and what I was feeling so at home and comfortable with. I had a surging conviction that somewhere, at some level, Jean was still this, and we would rediscover it and live it again as we once did. It was impossible that we couldn't do this.

The clock chimed twelve; we were beginning to yawn. Nanna was bleary-eyed with sleepiness. She got up, stretched, and excused herself. Pap and I were alone, quiet, smoking, thinking. At last he stirred, took off his glasses, rubbed his eyes and said maybe it was time we went to sleep. We stood up, and I felt a deep, profound love and admiration for this man. I reached for his hand and shook and held it. "Thanks, Pap." He looked at me with a soft, tender smile and said, "Thank you for being our son."

Myra drove me into Dallas next morning so I could go to my business meeting. On the way up we had carefully skirted talking about Jean. Myra had not married, and Jean was like a daughter to her. As we got near the city, though, she began talking about Jean's surprise visit four months ago.

"Jean frightened me," Myra said. "She looked to me as close to a nervous breakdown as a person could be."

"Good Lord, Myra," I said, "no one has suggested that before. What do you mean?"

"She was confused. She didn't know what she wanted to do. She just didn't seem like she was handling things at all. I had never seen her act like that."

We rode along in silence. I felt a deep pity for Jean, thinking of how Myra had just described her. Could there be any truth in it? Why hadn't Sam or Gloria detected this or said anything? I didn't know what to make of Myra's suggestion. Finally I said, "You know, don't you, that if Jean will let me, I'll do anything to make things work out between us and to help her."

"Yes, we do, Al," she nodded, "and we appreciate that. We love Jean very deeply, we love all of you." Her voice broke; her eyes were swimming with tears.

We were now into a new month: July. Sam had said we were now going to get down to the nitty-gritty in our counseling sessions. One item to come up early in the first of these sessions was the Reverend Leon Smothers. Sam brought him up. "Jean, there's one factor that we've said several times we can't deal with here. That's simply because the person isn't here. Your other relationship, Smothers. He's still in the picture, and because of that we can't deal properly with your and Al's problem. That relationship contaminates what we're trying to do here. It's not fair to all of us."

Jean shifted uneasily in her chair. I could tell she did not like what she was hearing.

"There are a lot of things I don't understand about that," Gloria said. "You say your relationship isn't genital. You haven't had sex relations. Yet you say you love him, that you love him enough, in fact, to want to end your marriage. Do I understand correctly? Do you intend to marry Smothers?"

"I don't know, I just don't know yet," Jean replied. Her tone had an edge to it, an annoyed defensiveness.

Gloria said, "It just sounds unreal to me. You please each other with words, but you can't carry on a fuller relationship in the confines of a church building, and that is the only thing you seem to be doing so far."

"Yes, so far that's what it's been," Jean acknowledged.

"Jean, you're going to have to purge that relationship— even if only temporarily—for your own good," Sam said firmly.

"What do you mean by 'purge'?" she asked.

"I mean give him up, at least personal relations. Don't have those long conversations. Don't continue the relationship as it is now," he answered.

"Why?" Jean asked sharply. "What's that going to accomplish?"

"You owe it to yourself to try to work with Al, for whatever comes of it," Sam said. "You've got to try to become involved in real relations with him. You aren't now. In fact, I'd go so far as to say you are terrified of him."

We both looked shocked.

"I think this fear goes back many years, but you're handling it differently now," he continued.

"Jean," Gloria said, "did you love Al when you married him?"

"I thought I did, but now I realize that perhaps I didn't," Jean said. "I'm not sure."

"Do you remember loving him?"

"Oh yes, I did."

"Okay, then you did," Gloria said. "Al has talked a lot about the things he liked about you and about the marriage, the positive things. Can you give us a list of positive things?"

"Uh"—Jean hesitated—"the children, of course. And the causes Al worked for. And what he did at the network."

"What about that? How do you feel about his work?" Sam asked.

"Well, I don't think Al is a creative type. He's more an administrator, someone who sees things get carried out," she said.

"Hmm," Sam said, raising his eyebrows, "I don't see that. From what I understand about what he does, he's a writer; he puts things down for other people to say on TV. I think that's being creative."

"Well, okay," Jean acknowledged, "but he's not like some people who carry an idea out from start to finish."

"I'd still say he is a creative person," Sam insisted. Jean finally agreed.

"Is that your positive list?" Gloria asked. "Is that all you want to talk about now?" Jean said yes.

"Well, let's get back to relationships," Gloria said. "You've discovered a defense mechanism you never knew about before: the withdrawal of your love. Sam said a few minutes ago you're handling the situation differently now. I think that's one of the main ways you're doing it. And it's worked beautifully. Al is floored. You've cut off the relationship. He can't do a thing about it. But you can't use this all the time; you've got to use it sparingly. You've started the effort to find yourself alone, and you don't seem to hold out the possibility that you can do it with somebody else, at least not Al. But you've got to try with him—for your own sake, if for no one else's."

"But I don't want to do anything dishonest or misleading . . . for Al's sake," Jean protested.

"What does honesty or dishonesty have to do with it?" Gloria asked firmly. "What's at stake here is the question of your involvement, your willingness to participate in a real relationship, not honesty or dishonesty."

"Yes, but you can't expect me to change the intellectual knowledge of what I have to do into real feelings very easily," Jean asserted.

"Who says it's easy?" Gloria asked. "I don't mean to say it's easy. It's not. It's hard; it's work. But you've got to try!" she insisted.

I'd been listening intently to the exchange between the two women. Then I asked, "Sam, did your 'weak woman' statement have anything to do with what they're talking about here?"

"Yes, that's part of it," he replied.

There was a pause; everyone seemed to have said what they wanted to for the moment. "Okay," Sam said. "I want you, Jean, to consider both a halt to personal relations with Smothers for a while and the need of trying to work on a *real* relationship with Al, wherever it might lead."

I felt wonderful. I thought the session was tremendously constructive, much more along the lines of what I thought we needed than any one before. The "nitty-gritty," if that's what it amounted to, was okay by me. Jean was angry and upset. When on the way out I ventured a few comments on how helpful I thought the session had been, she jumped on them curtly. I decided to let the case stand on its own merits, without my comments.

July 15, 1972

Most of the time the social life Jean and I continued to lead unfolded on a level apart from the troubles between us. Tonight, however, our difficulties were the center of an evening of deep emotions and conflict. Not surprisingly, this happened among the people we were closest to in the Modern Liturgy and with whom we had learned to be as frank and open as any adults we'd ever met.

The occasion was a dinner party on the large screen porch at the Noltings', one of the four couples who founded the group with us. Besides Sara and Gene Nolting, Stu and Marilyn Robertson, Elaine and Bob Johnson, and Jack Connors were there. It was always good to be with these people, for there was no need to pretend or maintain artificial poses; I could simply relax and enjoy being in their presence. Tall summer drinks served by Gene soothed us, and the conversation flowed along easy, interesting channels. Jean took part in it with enthusiasm. The buffet dinner, which we ate sitting on porch chairs or sprawling on the floor, fit right into the friendly, informal mood.

After dinner, however, the mood gradually changed. It became harder to make casual talk. Everyone seemed to be

156

waiting to say or hear something more important, but no one knew exactly what to say or how to say it.

Marilyn Robertson edged the conversation toward more serious and controversial areas by saying she had seen *A Clockwork Orange* a few nights before and hated it. "I thought it was horrible to spend a whole movie just looking at that side of life," she said. "Maybe it exists, and maybe that's something to look out for in the future, but it was just one unrelieved look at sordidness."

Jean and I had seen *Clockwork* recently, too, and I recalled our reactions. I had thought it was fantastic, a superb success on a number of levels. Jean didn't like it. She had objected strenuously to the portrayal of a minister in the film; she thought he was made to seem like a fool.

Jack Connors said, "Good criticism of society doesn't have to be positive; it may even be more effective by being so negative."

Bob Johnson suddenly brought the discussion closer to home by referring to Sam and Marie Schwartz, a local couple recently separated. "Take the case of Marie Schwartz as an example of a force run amuck. Here's a woman with six kids who says she is expressing her creative personality by running off with boyfriends and leaving Sam to take care of the kids. Now, for Christ's sake, what kind of behavior is that?" Bob was a crew-cut former Marine officer, very decisive in his opinions.

Now I felt I had something to say. "I think that's a pretty sick situation. She's asking for a divorce now and wants to turn her back on her husband and the six kids."

There was a noticeable tensing around the room. Bob sat waiting for someone to pick him up; clearly he expected much more to be said.

"I just don't know enough about the situation to have an opinion either way," Sara Nolting said.

Bob's wife Elaine said to him, "How can you have such a decisive opinion when you don't know all the details?"

"What more do you need to know?" Bob said firmly. "You know she's a married woman; she has a husband and together they've had six children. You also know she's been into every liberal cause and worked on every project, and now she's calling what she's doing 'artistic expression.' For Christ's sake, do you think she deserves a medal?"

My turn again. "It seems to me that Marie has become a symbol for a lot of women in this town who have problems of their own with their life styles. They're getting a lot of vicarious kicks out of what Marie's doing. Maybe they want to do it themselves. She's a heroine to many of them, a sort of Joan of Arc. I think that that's evident here."

Elaine said, "I don't know about that, but I do know she's a human being."

"What do you mean by that?" Gene Nolting asked. "As I understand them, human beings are supposed to be responsible."

"I guess what Gene's just said is what made me able to connect *Clockwork* with Marie Schwartz," I said. "The film says to me that excesses in anything—violence, government mind-fixing, doing away with any values in society—can lead us into an insane jungle. We have to do something that ties us to our humanity and to being responsible. Balancing the excesses is one of them. There are structures breaking down all around us, and the Marie Schwartz case is one that's close to home. We all have wives, husbands or kids, and presumably want to act responsibly toward them."

Jean said little during the exchanges. She joined the other women in saying she "really didn't know enough" to make a judgment of Marie. Otherwise she was on the sidelines in the conversation, watching and listening.

158

Over the years Bob had expressed himself strongly and emotionally. Sometimes he monopolized conversations by his passion. Now he had been getting visibly more excited and was chafing to say something. When he had his chance, he jumped in again.

"Goddamn it, this is ridiculous. We sit here, all of us grownup and intelligent people, and we say we can't even say whether it's good or bad for a woman to commit adultery and leave her husband and six children. I think this is absolutely crazy. I haven't heard anyone mention Sam or those kids or even care what happens to them. My God! You sit here saying you can't make judgments. By Christ, I can! I say this Marie Schwartz is a disgrace. She is sick!"

He was getting into the full swing of his anger and indignation. "Any woman who has a reasonably successful marriage and kids has responsibility. She can't hide it or duck it or call it anything else. She has to make that marriage work no matter what it takes because at her stage in life it's too destructive to do otherwise, and she owes it to all of them to do that. She should have her ass kicked if she doesn't, not everyone trying to understand or forgive her."

I looked at Jean's face. She was crimson. The lines of her mouth were drawn in a bitter, tight grimace. Fierce anger hardened the whole cast of her look. She seemed on the verge of bursting with emotion, but she still said nothing.

Elaine Johnson moved quickly into the gap. "Well, I realize in my relationship I have to move myself more, if Bob has moved himself, to try and get in the same places. Maybe a woman has to see that and recognize that."

Her comment deflected the confrontation that Bob's words had thrown before everyone. Sara added quickly, "But it takes two people. That's what I've been saying: we don't know what part Sam has played in all this."

"Those are pretty heavy remarks you made, Bob," Stu said. "I don't agree with many of them. But I'd like to know what an outsider to the married state thinks. Jack, you know all of us intimately and the problems we face. What do you think about what Bob has said?"

Jack picked at the fuzz on the carpeting thoughtfully for a few moments, then shifted himself on his elbow and began to speak. "Well, I'm appalled by a lot I see going on around us. As I said, I think *Clockwork* was beneficial and says something. I agree with Bob that you can make some comments about the Marie Schwartz situation even if you don't know the intimate details. I mean, it is bad from a number of standpoints. For one thing it is tremendously destructive for the children. Can you imagine what effect all of this is having on them? You have to believe something pathological is involved here to account for Marie's behavior.

"What bothers me is that bits and pieces of what she and other people like her are doing have added up to an epidemic loose on our society today. There's a tremendous danger of self-gratification creeping into what we do, and it's awfully hard for a person to avoid if society says it's okay. There is plenty of validity to change. The old won't do; nobody wants that. We can and should get in touch with our needs and see what they are. I guess Marie has done this; I'm not sure, because it could be she's just confused. But to act on needs in disregard of consequences— that's no good. That isn't growth, it isn't creative, it's just irresponsible. And I can't see that she's looking out for her kids' needs or anyone else's.

"When it comes to marriage, which is what Stu asked me about, I see a special relevance. The fact is there are commitments, there are responsibilities, there are accommoda-

160

tions people have to make. And I don't think people are paying too much attention to them. It's too easy not to. What ever happened to suffering? If things get rough or hurtful, don't we drop them now and run away? That's what I'm worried about. I'm afraid too many people are doing that. I think women, like Marie and like others, are too prone to do this in our atmosphere today, in the fever which is gripping our society. If a marriage was corrosive from the start, if it was destructive and there is no way to change it, then I can see ending it. But after a certain number of years and with several children involved, marriage is a whole different ball game. The reasons have to be very great, and expressing 'creative feelings' or wanting to begin something new just aren't enough for me."

Everyone had been listening intently to what Jack was saying. Over the years each person in this group had felt free to say what was deepest in his heart. Intimacies of the most personal kind had been bared, emotions let go unashamedly, sharply differing views expressed. We had laughed and cried and shared eloquent silence together. We had reached depths of communication we never achieved anywhere else.

But now there was a strained, tense joylessness. Real people's lives—not those of Marie and Sam, whom we barely knew, but Jean's and mine—had been exposed and commented upon unmistakably plainly. I had a feeling that if one more comment was made, the gathering would blow up from the power of the tension crackling among us.

Stu was pulling on his cigarette and looking thoughtfully at Jack. Each person was isolated, looking down into his drink or his hands. Jean said nothing, but consternation and churning emotions came through to me. There was wariness and restraint among us now. The evening had tapered off into grim, unspoken feelings. In a short while people made their move to say good night, and soon the evening was over.

Jean and I said very little in the car going home. I was glad that many things had been said that night. I wanted to know how Jean felt, but it would have been too provocative, I felt, to come right out and ask her. Her only comment was a general one: she hated weekends.

The anger Jean had felt at the dinner party spilled out at me over the next few days.

"You should have stopped Bob," she said to me the next night. "You knew he was hurting me."

"Why are you angry at me?" I asked. "You ought to have directed it at Bob."

"You *agreed* with him, I know that!"

"Yes, of course I did, but why didn't you answer Bob on the spot? You rave and rant at *me* now, but he's the one you should have taken on. I'm not a ventriloquist. He said what he wanted to."

Early Monday morning I awakened before dawn as I had for many months. My thoughts went back again to Saturday night and all that had been said. I tried to lie still and not bother Jean, but I was now fully awake and it took an effort not to move. I thought of Jean's angry statement of yesterday that I should have stopped Bob Johnson because he was hurting her. And then a scene came to mind of what would have happened if I *had*. Jean: "You cut Bob Johnson off last night and wouldn't let him say what he wanted to. You assumed you had to protect me, that I'm a child without a mind of my own. You have to speak for me. That's what you've been doing all these years, and you haven't changed in the least. You don't even give me credit for being able to think or speak for myself!"

I thought of another incident—a real one—that had happened earlier on Saturday night. Jean, Jack and I happened to arrive in the driveway at the same time and were walking into the Noltings' together. I was struck with how lovely Jean was dressed and how beautiful she looked and I said impulsively to Jack, "Doesn't Jean look trim and youthful tonight?" In her anger Sunday night, she had thrown that remark up to me testily: "There you were, showing me off proudly for your own pleasure and glory. Why don't you just let people make up their own minds and not tell them what to think?"

Then it occurred to me that I couldn't win. Lying there in the dark, I began to see how completely boxed in I was. Jean wasn't going to let the relationship have a chance to work if she could help it. The counseling was concentrating on us as individuals and not paying much attention to saving the marriage. I wasn't making any progress that I could see toward preserving the marriage along those routes, at least for now. There was one direction, one I hadn't thought seriously about before, that might give me support in what I was trying to do. As I thought about it, I realized more and more clearly that I had to see a lawyer.

VII

As he listened, Harold Polis stroked his beard, pursed his lips, shook his head and made notes on a long yellow legal pad.

He had already expressed his shock and sorrow at the reason for my visit. Harold and I had served on several civil-rights projects together and we knew and respected each other. He also had great admiration for Jean.

When I was through, Harold looked up and said flatly, without hesitation, "Jean has no grounds for divorce. She can't win one. The state of Connecticut does not recognize 'I do not love you' as a grounds for divorce."

I listened to his words gratefully. In the world of legal matters I had apparently at long last found some firm support. But I had plenty of questions. "What about the children? Could she take them away from me?"

"I don't see how," he answered. "If she can't win a divorce, she has to give up something in order to get one, and if she wants it bad enough, she'll have to agree to your terms." He paused, leaned back in his swivel chair, locked his hands behind his head, and said, "As a matter of fact, if you wanted to be hard-nosed and sue her for divorce, you'd have a much better chance of winning. We could subpoena this boyfriend of hers, the minister, and make him tell us what the real relationship is. Even if it's not sexual, not adultery in the technical sense, what they're doing is 'criminal conversation' in this state, jeopardizing the marriage. We could point to your intolerable suffering from sexual deprivation. We could point out her many and continued absences from the children. No, I'd rather have your case than hers."

Harold paused, picked up a pencil from his desk and began tapping it thoughtfully on his pad. "Why talk about divorce, though?" he went on. "You both have so much reason to try to work it out. Don't you think that's the best idea?"

"My God, yes, Harold, that's what I've said from the start. I'm never going to initiate divorce against her. I don't want that. From every standpoint, that can't be allowed to happen. From mine, from the children's, even from hers. We can't afford a divorce. Why, we barely make a go of it financially now, together, much less trying to do it in two households. No, I'm all for reconciliation and staying together."

"Why don't we try that for a while, then?" he said. "Why don't we just see what happens? Maybe no legal action will ever be necessary."

"I sure hope so!" I said. "That would be fine by me. Well, how much do I owe you for this visit?"

"Instead of charging you anything for our talk, I'd like you to put it toward the counseling. If we have to go into this thing legally later on, we can talk about that then. But let's hope you don't. And good luck to both of you."

I got to work late because of the lawyer's appointment and so was late getting home that night. Jean was out at a meeting, so after I got all the boys to bed I was alone. But I felt much more solid, more secure in this home and in this family. And I knew that the reason was my talk that morning with Harold Polis.

July 23, 1972

After dinner tonight Jean said she wanted to talk to me. That was an unusual request. It was only the third time in the almost six months of this ordeal that she had wanted to initiate a conversation. It was a hot, still July night and I was sweating from the heat anyway; when Jean made her request, I began to sweat even more. I thought, This is it. She is going to ask for the divorce, start the proceedings, try to kick me out.

Jean started out conversationally, almost cheerfully, so it didn't seem she was intending anything climactic. "Something very interesting came out in my private session with Sam yesterday." I remembered it had been her turn to go alone; then she told me Gloria wasn't there either. "Sam and I started off talking about my relationship with Daddy, but that didn't seem to be going anywhere. Then we started talking about Mother and me, and I felt we were hitting on something."

I listened with growing curiosity. Not only was it rare for Jean to begin a conversation of any substance, but she was revealing something about herself, and that was extremely unusual. I wanted her to—it was the kind of conversation I had been encouraging for months—but I was puzzled as to what had brought it about now and what she was getting

166

at. Nevertheless, I nodded and continued to listen intently.

"I think I had a poor relationship with Mother. She was a perfectionist, so I could never satisfy her completely. If I did something well, Mother would say I could do it better. She never gave me affirmation."

"Uh-huh, I see."

"What I think, after our session, is that I saw the same perfectionist in you and married you to get the affirmation from you that I never got from Mother."

"Well, I guess that could be," I said. "I never thought of it that way. If anything, I always imagined that you might have married me because your father and I are a lot alike, pipe-smoking, liberals, that sort of thing."

"Anyway, I think that a few years ago I began to say subconsciously, 'Fuck you, Mother,' and that's when we began to have trouble, or *I* began to have trouble. I didn't need, or wasn't getting, affirmation from you either. I think I married you for the wrong reasons," she said emphatically. "I'd like you to think about why you married me and let me know what you come up with."

I was drenched with sweat by that time, rivulets running down my neck onto my back, but at the same time I had a feeling of relief, almost of happiness. I had stared down the barrel at what I thought was going to be the final blast, and it hadn't happened. I hadn't panicked or lost control or come apart, although I was shaking inside. And what Jean had said indicated she had done some solid, substantial digging; beyond that, she was sharing the results with me in a way she had never done before throughout this whole process. Maybe, I thought wildly, this is the beginning of a real relationship—or a real attempt to form one, anyway—after all these months.

Later, in bed, Jean went off to sleep quickly, but I kept

thinking about her question. Why, indeed, had I married her? I suspected Sam had asked her to ask me that; it was the kind of question that would make me confront myself. My mind kept working nimbly and quickly; I was not in the least tired. Reasons tumbled out readily: she was a warm, genuine human being, more so than anyone I'd ever met; I thought she was beautiful; I was proud of her; she was deep and understanding and loving; we wanted the same things out of life, had the same values and priorities. And then I added to the list of reasons what Sam had once said, but which at the time I did not realize: Jean answered my need to be supported. Amid all the reasons, this last one clanked in most mechanically and unnaturally. Whatever the reasons, I knew one thing was certain: I loved her when we were courting, I loved her during all the years of our marriage, and I loved her still. I looked over at her sleeping form and wanted to hold her; my body ached with desire to express the affection I had within me. Thinking about how much and how long I had loved her, thinking about the happiness that love had brought me, I felt a glow of the same happiness returning. When I finally did get to sleep, a long while later, it was with an unfamiliar feeling of joy stirring within me.

The next Saturday it was my turn to go to the session alone. It turned out to be just Sam and I. Gloria was going to go back to graduate school for further courses and could not be with us.

I mentioned casually that I was still pained by not being able to share my bottled-up love with Jean, didn't know how to handle it, and could use some help in that regard if he could supply it.

No sooner had I made that statement than Sam exploded: "I will never be an accomplice in manipulating that girl, so don't come in here and ask me to do that," he thundered. His eyes were blazing; he jerked his angular arms about excitedly. "How could you be so cruel, so inhuman! In fifteen years I've never heard anything like this. How could you?"

"What do you mean 'how could I?'" I shouted back, startled and angry. "What the hell did you tell me on the telephone a little while back? I called you in terrible pain about my situation and you said, 'There's no need for masturbation. You shouldn't have to go through that. We'll do something about it.' You said it! And right here in front of all of us Gloria has said to Jean a couple of times: 'Sex doesn't have to crown this process, it can be a part of it.' So goddamn it, yes, I want the outcome somehow to be that Jean will let us make love again, but I didn't come in here without some encouragement that it could be worked out."

"Forget what Gloria said!" Sam shouted. "I'm talking about the cruelty and inhumanity you want me to be a part of. You could ruin sex forever for that girl. And for you. That's the worst thing you could do: force her to make love."

"That's not what I'm asking for, for Christ's sake," I said. "I only want to know what the 'something we can do about it' is that you spoke about."

"Look, Al," he said, somewhat calmer, "you've got only two alternatives. One is masturbation. The other is to get your sex somewhere else. Only be discreet about it. Not here—in New York. You know plenty of women there. That's the choice you've got to make."

"Okay, now I understand," I said. "As far as I'm concerned, my personal morality won't let me have any affairs.

Not even now. Not yet. You may not believe this, but I still love Jean. I've got to make this thing work before I go on to anything else."

"I believe you," he said, now almost tenderly. "And I think she still loves you, in her own way." I was shocked.

"Do you mean that? I can't believe it. She doesn't act like it. Do you think there's still hope?"

"There's hope until you're dead," he said.

"Well, where do we go from here?" I asked. "What should I be doing?"

"You know I'll be gone all of August," he said. "My wife and I are taking a trip to Japan. But there are others here you can consult. In the meantime just keep on with what you're doing." He paused, then very seriously and deliberately began outlining a proposal.

"What would you think about you and Jean joining a couples' group? I really think it's the best way to treat both of you now. In fact, I think we're kind of stymied the way we've been going. I strongly recommend the couples' group as the best way—maybe the only way—for you and Jean to make progress now."

"That sounds fine by me. I'll do anything you suggest. But how does a group work, and why do you want us in one now?"

"A couples' group puts you in contact with people going through the same thing you are now," he explained. "You expose yourself to others and they to you, and the insights you get help you see where you're at and what you are doing. Also, what you can do about it. This would give you and Jean an idea of how you stack up in comparison to others in the same fix. You find out you're not alone, and the people in the group help one another while they're helping themselves."

"God, that sounds great," I said. "But you'd better ask Jean. If I do, she won't want to do it."

"Okay, I'll talk to her," Sam said. "But I think you ought to let her know how you feel about it, too—then she'll make her own decision."

I left feeling excited about moving on to another stage of the counseling. When I came home, I told Jean—as casually as I could—that Sam had something new in mind for us, that he was suggesting we join a group of couples having problems similar to ours.

"No way!" she answered firmly. "I don't like that at all." Her outright rejection jolted me.

"Well, look, Sam is going to call and explain what it's all about and why he wants us in there now. Maybe after you've talked to him you'll look at it differently."

Our conversation then switched to the subject of our upcoming vacation, which caused a short, angry argument. I mentioned that the house we usually rented in Maine had gone up in price and now cost $150 a week instead of $125. "I don't like to pay that much," I said. "But we do have such a good time up there. I think two weeks is just about the right amount of time to unwind, really get a rest and feel like we're away."

"You think!" She snorted. "What about what I think? You always set the priorities."

"That's not true," I said. "You planned the whole last vacation—that camping trip—and you have never objected to the two weeks of Maine vacation before. As far as my money is concerned, over the years I've offered dozens of times to let you take over the spending. But you never wanted to do it."

"That's not what I'm talking about," Jean said. "Our kitchen is lousy, there are plenty of things that need fixing around here, and we ought to have a dishwasher. I think three hundred dollars for a vacation is too much when we could put it towards other things. Besides, I want some money left over so I can take a course later this summer at Union Theological."

"Dammit, that's three hundred dollars to spend on the whole family, six people, and that's not too much! We always set aside five hundred for our vacation; last year—the one you planned—ran closer to a thousand. There were family values involved then, and there don't seem to be any now on your part. You want to save half the money so you can spend it on one person, you, studying religion for a week. What the hell kind of thinking is that?"

"I'm beginning to think about me, and it's about time," Jean declared.

"Yes, so I've noticed," I shot back. Then a thought occurred to me. "Who says you couldn't take the course anyhow? How much does it cost?"

"Sixty-five dollars."

"Well, what's the problem? We can do both."

"Okay, if that's the way you want it, but you go up with the boys alone. Jim has to go to summer school to make up that F in French, so I'll stay here and see him through that."

"That doesn't make sense. Three of the boys want and expect you to be with them for a family vacation. I want you. Jim can stay at a neighbor's or with someone within the church community or with Grandma and Grandpa."

"No, I want it this way," she said firmly. "That's the way it's going to be."

"I think that's a helluva decision," I said, "but do what you want."

"I intend to spend the first week here with Jim, then

drive up to Maine for the second week. I've already reserved a car from Hertz to drive up."

"Really? Did you look around at Avis or National to see which had the best deal? Hertz is usually the most expensive."

"Don't tell me what to do! This is the way it's going to be!"

"Yes, but I wind up paying for it!" I snorted. She glared angrily, turned on her heel and walked away.

Maine. July 29, 1972

Dan, Charley, Mark and I arrived at our cottage around three-thirty in the afternoon. Driving down the narrow dirt road leading to the water's edge, I felt the same excitement and anticipation I had in other years. Before us the bay stretched blue and glistening under the midafternoon sun. The lighthouse across the way looking down on us, the rocks wet with spray, the beach, the lobster pots bobbing on the waves—all were just as beautiful as I remembered them. Before unloading the car, the boys had to run around to familiar places; then they spent a few minutes hopping over the rocks, checking the tidal pools and scaling flat rocks over the surface of the water. Within a short while Dan had a collection of shells, plants and sea life he'd picked up.

I had dreaded coming up without Jean. All the other visits—the last one two summers ago—had been times of immense joy and relaxation. Now, however, as we plunged into the routine of setting up our household, the mood of the place overcame the loneliness I thought I would feel. The cottage was exactly the same: potbellied stove in the living room; ancient toaster and waffle iron in the kitchen; rambling screen porch circling the front and side, overlooking the water. Upstairs, the magnificent sitting room we loved: nautical maps of the area on the walls; ancient Franklin stove in the corner; a huge picture window through which you could look out as far as the eye could see across the ocean. And there was the smell of salt water, the cawing of sea gulls, the openness of the view in all directions.

While I heated the spaghetti sauce we'd brought with us in the ice chest, Charley made a salad from the fresh lettuce and tomatoes we'd bought down the road. Mark set the table. Dan came back from the water in time to help serve; he brought with him more sea anemones, crabs, seaweed and shells for the tank he'd already started. After supper we went for a walk in the cool evening air. Along the water line we were dismayed to see heavy layers of oil, undoubtedly spilled from some tanker at sea.

Later, when we were settled in the upstairs parlor, beginning to put together the huge jigsaw puzzle which was a traditional pastime of our vacations, the foghorn started up. Right across the bay from us, the foghorn worked in tandem with the lighthouse—six stabbing rays, darkness, then six rays again, the foghorn punctuating the sweeps with its deep, penetrating blasts. I thought of Jean; she loved the sound of it. I thought of the times Nanna, Pap and Aunt Myra had been with us in this room on evenings like this, putting together a jigsaw puzzle, reading, talking, bound together in the peaceful snugness of the cottage, strangely comforted by the regular sounds of the foghorn. For the first time that day I felt lonesome.

Mark was the first to go to bed; he was nervous about being alone in a room in the strange house, so we put him just down the corridor, next to my room, and left the door open. Dan and Charley were set up in their sleeping bags on the screen porch downstairs. We were all tired from the trip and sleepy from the ocean air, so not long after ten we all were in bed. I thought of Jean, feeling incomplete without her. I realized with a shiver that I might have to endure nights like this, without her, for the rest of my life. I lost myself in the rhythm of the lighthouse sweeping across the night sky and the hypnotic belches of the foghorn and soon fell asleep.

Each day of that first week was gloriously the same as every other. In the morning we would eat breakfast out on the screen porch, watching Mr. O'Neill from down the street tending his lobster pots in the bay, and looking for tankers and cargo ships heading toward and leaving the harbor of Portland north of us. The boys straightened up their sleeping areas, took out the garbage, and then went across the road to the rocks and beach to play. After I cleaned up the kitchen, I would go upstairs to the parlor to read; I could look out and see their three blue-jean jackets' bobbing in and out of sight among the rocks. Dan's kite, red with a yellow body shaped like a bat, would soon begin to rise into the air. Charley's, yellow and black, would go up next. Soon the boys were staging dogfights, diving their kites at each other, pulling them out of steep dives just above the water, letting them soar far out at sea. Mark, frustrated, was crying because his little legs couldn't move fast enough to get or keep his kite up.

In the afternoon we drove a short distance to the beach and swam amidst the powerful, churning whitecaps smacking the beach. Sometimes we went on short trips—to the trolley museum near Kennebunk or to the amusement park at Saco. Suppertime meals were meat broiled over a driftwood fire on the beach across from our cottage, with fresh corn or peas cooked in the kitchen and brought over. For dessert there were marshmallows toasted over the open fire.

Almost no reference was made to Jean. I missed her terribly, but the boys seemed absorbed in their own activities and apparently had little thought for the world outside our cove. Frequently I'd suggest we hold off doing something "until Mom comes and do it with her," but the boys would insist—and I came to realize how true it was—that "Mom really doesn't like doing that." Jean loved the elements that made up the atmosphere of Maine—the foghorn, the solitude out on the rocks, the beauty of the shells and bits of polished glass and driftwood that could be gathered on the beach—but she did not enjoy the amusement park or surfing or any of the pick-up ball games we played. I thought, Maybe a daughter among our children might have made a difference. I wanted one desperately, though Jean always said it didn't matter to her; but perhaps it did.

Jean was coming up the next day, and I anticipated her arrival with both exhilaration and fear. Just having her there, where we had shared so many wonderful moments, was a delicious thought. I was sure the completeness of the mood, the totality of this world apart from any outside contacts, would bring us closer together. But at the same time I feared the coldness and imperviousness which she had brought to every event up until then. I didn't want my hopes dashed by the reality of her hardness.

The last night before her arrival I had a fine talk with Dan. He and I were working on the jigsaw puzzle, and as we held pieces up to examine them and worked together to fill in holes, Dan and I talked easily about the way teenagers react to authority, long hair, religion, rock music—topics we never got a chance to talk about back home due to the hectic pace of our lives. Mark had gone to bed by then, but

Charley was still up, and I could see he was absorbed in our conversation and pleased that he could participate marginally in it. During the evening I managed to put in seven puzzle pieces, an all-time high for me, and the boys acknowledged that was pretty sensational for Dad.

The next day we began looking for Jean right after lunch. Early afternoon became late afternoon and she still had not arrived. By six-thirty we had decided that we would eat by seven, even if Mom wasn't there by then, and save some supper for her. Just as we were about to begin, Jean drove up in her rented car. Mark and Charley went running to her excitedly, jumping all over her and giving her kisses and hugs. I felt just as they did. I went up and gave her a hug of welcome, but could feel in that brief contact that she was as stiff and cold as ever.

Almost immediately, there were little flicks of discord between us. I asked Jean if there was enough gas in her car to run a few errands after supper, and she said, "Well, I *think* so." Without thinking, I went over to the car, turned the key and checked the gauge. "You always have to question me!" she snapped angrily. I tried to explain I was only trying to clear up her uncertainty and mine, but she wouldn't accept that explanation.

Supper was a feast: lobsters from the bay, fresh corn, peas, lettuce and tomatoes from a nearby stand, chocolate pudding with real whipped cream for dessert. All three kids were chattering away, telling Jean what they had been doing for a week. She was animatedly filling them in on what had been happening back in the neighborhood: how Jim was living at the house—checking in regularly with his grandparents and neighbors—how the pets were, how the vegetable garden and the plants in Dan's room were doing. It was good just to have her with us.

With Jean there, however, the second week of the vacation was filled with suppressed pain for me. Every element was there for the pleasures we had known before: the informal, relaxed atmosphere of the cottage and the sea, the spontaneous way of life we led, and each of us to make what we would of our presence. But Jean was not the Jean I'd been with there before, and that reality hurt me a dozen times a day in as many different situations. We even slept together as we always did, in the bed where we had made love blissfully and eagerly, but none of the mood or substance of the past was reflected in Jean. The week generally followed the pattern of the first one, but doing the same things with a person who threw up a barrier against me was more painful than doing them alone and longing for her. As the vacation drew to its end, we came to the final Saturday night which Jean and I had always set aside to go out to an inn for dinner by ourselves. We agreed we would go out as usual, although Jean plainly indicated that for her it was a meaningless ritual.

A tanned teenage waitress, with hair streaked by the sun and salt water, seated us at an Early American table in the lovely inn by the sea. Bottles hung from rope loops; nautical knickknacks decorated the walls; the ceiling was low and the atmosphere subdued. We ordered drinks and talked easily about the marvelous food we had been eating, how much the boys enjoyed the visits to Maine, about how much fun it would be to have her parents and Aunt Myra with us again.

Dinner was excellent, the seafood exactly what we'd come to expect from the area. As I lit up my pipe and looked at Jean, I had the familiar feeling of incredibility about what was happening. Jean talked about a course in religious dance she was hoping to take in New York at some later date. Time flew by quickly and pleasantly. There were no flare-ups, no controversial differences, no bickering.

Next morning we packed up and got ready to go home. The aquarium with the starfish, jellyfish, crabs, eels and sea urchins was emptied back into the bay. Shells, driftwood and polished glass were put in bags to take back home as remembrances. Goodbyes were said to the year-round residents we had come to know over the summers. Suitcases were loaded in the station wagon, the kids got settled in back amid sleeping bags and pillows, we gave the cottage one last check, and we were on our way.

When we got home, eight hours later, tired and irritable and road-weary, Jean and I had a short, angry flareup. The mail that had accumulated was waiting in a stack on the dining-room table where Jim had deposited it each day. I began going through it to make sure nothing urgent was there. Near the top was the telephone bill; I opened it routinely, saw what it said and reacted in fury. On it were forty-five dollars' worth of toll calls to Marie Quinn in Westport—forty-five dollars' worth of supportive phone calls to a woman going through a divorce ahead of Jean, her closest confidante. I raged about spending that kind of money when she was criticizing me for spending it on things like a vacation for the family. Dan watched my anger for a few moments, then said, "Dad, don't rank on Mom too much. She's only trying to help. You know the trouble they're having up there."

His words brought me back to a shocking realization: these kids still didn't know what was happening between us! They still thought and assumed and took for granted our world was as intact as it had always been. They had ahead of them the shock, the hurt that such a revelation can cause children. I looked at Dan and all the other boys, now busily unloading their things and talking to Jim about what they'd done, and the terrible inevitability of what was in store for them came back to me. So far they were protected from that, but I knew the way things were going, that moment of dreadful truth couldn't be far away.

In the days following our return from Maine in mid-August, Jean was angry and impatient. She told me to stop calling her "Jeanie." She said she hated nicknames; her name, she said icily, was "Jean." When I reminded her that her father called her "Butch" and had done so since she was a little girl, she said, "Stop arguing with me and listen to what I say for a change."

In the face of constant hostility, I became depressed and frustrated. Somehow, I wanted Jean to know the sobering reality that the legal road to divorce might not be as easy as she imagined. We got into this one night when we were accusing each other of not facing the reality of the situation we were in.

"You may not even be aware of one major reality in what you want as the only answer," I said.

"Like what?" Jean demanded.

"Like getting a divorce isn't as easy as you may think it is . . . for you."

"How come?"

"For one thing, your relationship with Smothers leaves you vulnerable legally."

"Wait a minute, you're threatening me!" she snapped.

"Anytime anyone says anything you don't want to hear, it's threatening," I retorted.

"Well, what's there to prove about Leon and me?" she asked, just a little uncertainly.

"That you had some relationship, whatever it was, and it was and is important enough to threaten the preservation of our marriage and the continuation of our family. You'd have to perjure yourself to say that you didn't tell Sam and

Gloria and me and many other people that you were in love with Smothers—'in love with the wrong man,' to quote you."

"I don't know what you're going to prove. Lately I've thought a lot about Leon and me, and I recognize now I wasn't having a romance with him. I was just still doing things out of weakness, like needing his corroboration to act as I should. I wouldn't call that a love affair."

"Are you saying you weren't, or aren't, in love with Smothers?" I asked incredulously.

"Al, I'm telling you what I feel now, that's all."

"Then if you're not in love with Smothers—without that 'contamination' we can turn our attention to our relationship and make it work," I said earnestly.

"I can't be a whole person and do it with you, Al," she said wearily.

"But if we were working together, neither of us would feel the need to be defensive or hostile. We could say, 'Yes, I did that wrong back then,' and there could be a spirit of allowance, of understanding, of looking forward. We could approach self-examination and self-identity another way, through cooperation and helping one another. Why has this become after two decades an 'I must do it entirely alone' situation? That's what makes us two hostile armed camps, competing with one another."

"Al, you look into yourself. That's what the counseling's all about, that's what you're supposed to be doing. And I'll take care of me." With that, she cut off the conversation.

When she did this for the hundredth time, I thought of what Sam had said in front of both of us: Jean was terrified of me. Could that explain why she would have nothing to do with working with me? What else could explain her not even wanting to try?

According to her account, Smothers had fulfilled Jean to an extraordinary degree. He made her feel important, he freed her, he gave her the spontaneity she wanted in a relationship. But just now, moments ago, she had said the relationship was not what she once thought it was. Her "feelings," with which she was in touch, had apparently been wrong. Wasn't there anything objective and outside Jean that mattered any more? Were all the standards and judgments within her and her alone?

I remembered an article on marriage counseling I had read in *The New York Times* only recently. Jean and I had both read it, discussed it and taken different things away from it. But one point, which was statistical, we could not differ on: the number-one reason given to marriage counselors today as the cause for wanting a divorce was "the relationship does not fulfill my emotional needs." That seemed to be what was happening to us now; and I disagreed with that and objected to it, but it did me no good in preventing what was not a story in print but the real living of my life, my existence, and my world.

Occasionally Jean's whole attitude would change suddenly and dramatically, and this would be reflected in the way she looked. Her eyes were softer, her features relaxed; the whole girding inside which signaled to me her guarded defensiveness would disappear. I might step into the house one night and find that the shift in moods had taken place. I always hoped that it meant Jean had softened in her feelings toward me or was seeing us in the light that she used to, but each time up to now that had not proved true. I didn't always know what caused it or how to react, but I accepted the occasions gratefully and waited.

After we'd spent one entirely delightful evening without a clash or marring exchange, Jean provided a clue as to what lay behind her mood. "I went to see Faith this afternoon," she said casually. I perked up instantly, for Faith was one of the counselors Sam had said we could go to if we had something we wanted to talk over. "Really, how was she?" I asked.

"Really *something else*," Jean said sincerely. "We had a fine session." She paused for a moment and then said, "Faith suggested, too, that we join a couples' group. I'm thinking it over." That's all she said. Then she went back to discussing her plans for the dance course at the summer camp.

Jean's excellent mood continued all during the week. She didn't reach out with affection toward me, but she also didn't seem angry or displeased with me. She continued to make plans for her week of teaching, which was coming up in a few days. By Friday night, however, a few minor cracks in our smooth relations began to appear.

After supper that night I was listening to music in the living room. Mark called from upstairs, "Send Mom up to say good night, okay?"

"Jean, Mark wants you to come up," I yelled, and kept on listening. Some time later I couldn't remember if I'd seen Jean pass through the room and wasn't even sure that she'd heard me. I got up and found Jean in the bathroom rolling her hair up.

"Hi, have you gone up yet?" I asked.

"No, just a minute and I will," she answered.

I went back and listened again. Perhaps another ten minutes passed. Then, almost sure Jean hadn't passed through, I went back in to see what had happened. "Are you checking up on me?" she asked angrily.

"No," I sputtered, "but Mark's been waiting a long while, and he has to get to sleep."

"Are you saying I'm a bad mother again?" she asked

sharply, and the edge of hostility was back in her voice. "That's what you always do!"

"Look, Jean, I don't know what you're talking about. In recent months I've spoken up when I haven't thought you've been a very attentive mother, but that doesn't have anything to do with what's happening tonight."

"I hear you differently," she said, glaring at me.

"Why haven't you gone up?"

"Because I've had other important things to do."

"That's been the problem . . . the 'other important things' have usually pertained to you."

"I'm tired of that theme, that you and the boys can go on sweetly and serenely and wait for me to come to my senses and rejoin you." Suddenly what had been a small tiff was in danger of becoming a major argument. I thought of the progress we had been making lately and the senselessness of fighting over this trivial incident. "Mark is still waiting," I said, and went back into the living room. In a few moments Jean came stalking through angrily on her way upstairs.

Shortly afterwards, Jean left for a week's stay at the Methodist youth camp, where she was to teach religious dance.

By now the boys and I were set in a routine for taking care of ourselves while Jean was away. There were a number of revolving chores to do, and each boy took his turn: setting the table, feeding the dog and cats, peeling potatoes, making mashed potatoes, serving the meal. Each boy cleared his own place.

Jean had gone without even leaving a phone number or an address where she could be reached. She said if we needed her, the church office could get word to her. The boys might have thought it strange that Mom was gone so much, but they still had the security of knowing she was a part of us, only temporarily gone on projects. I felt a strong sense of purpose in keeping the home running just as it always did, with its constant flow of activities for the kids, the same spirit of open house reflected in the score of teenagers who came and went, the jam sessions in the basement, the friends staying over. Still, the lack of a mother could not be entirely concealed in the bustle of activity. Mark and Charley especially mentioned missing Jean. Her absence was felt in the hugs not given, the stories not read by her at bedtime.

Ours was a family tottering, carried on solely by its own momentum; I wasn't certain yet whether soon we might be a family permanently shattered and torn apart.

August 29, 1972

As August 29 approached, both Jean and I had felt increasingly uncertain about how to deal with it. It was our nineteenth wedding anniversary. If we did not celebrate it as we always had, the children would know something was wrong. What we did depended on what Jean wanted. Finally Jean decided that she and I would go out for dinner as we usually did after having our customary celebration with the boys.

Gathered in the kitchen, we all shared some of the sparkling burgundy I had brought home. The boys had all signed their names on a card, and I presented Jean with an Italian knit sweater and a playful card. Jean grimaced, seemed tense and unsure, and looked for a moment almost as if she might not accept it. Instead of thanking me or giving me a kiss as she usually did, she merely looked at it briefly, said "It's nice," and folded the sweater back carefully in its box. She had no gift or card for me.

In the fading summer twilight, we drove down the lovely back road to the restaurant we had chosen, a former private mansion with large white columns in front. The quiet of the place, the luxury of being waited on, the pleasantness of the evening—all helped ease the uncertainty of our contacts. Over cocktails, Jean relaxed her guardedness, and dinner went well. If anyone were looking at us from another table, if anyone overheard our conversation, wouldn't they think we were a normal and typical suburban couple?

When we got home around eleven, the children were all in bed. It had been hours since any sharp words or bad feelings had passed between Jean and me. She had even been tender in the way she shaded some of her inflections and called me "Al." My desire for her had not lessened over the months, and now, my hopes fed by the fine evening and recollections of our wedding day, I imagined that a relenting on her part could allow us to enjoy one another again.

When we were both in the bedroom, still relating smoothly and easily, I said, "Do you think, Jean, that on our anniversary night we could make a try to bring love back into our life?"

Quickly and curtly she said, "No!"

The rejection hit like cold water in my face. I groped for some words to express my hurt and disappointment. I couldn't think of anything to say to Jean that I hadn't said before, so I got angry. "How long does this madness go on?" I asked. "What's the point of it? What's the point of being together and talking together and enjoying things together if at any meaningful level I don't exist and I don't matter?"

"You don't seem to get the point, Al. I don't love you,"

Jean said. "I'm not getting any closer to liking you, and I still think divorce is the best solution for me."

"Divorce isn't the only and inevitable answer to problems like we've got," I said. "Ours have to be worked out 'down there,' not in a court somewhere. As far as I can see, that's what nights like tonight are for: to give us the setting; when the setting happens, to reach out, to break through to one another. If you're only in the counseling to mark time and only sticking around to get a clear conscience about leaving, then that's the best way to ensure that nothing positive can happen."

"I've learned more about myself, by myself, as the counseling has gone on," Jean said firmly, "and I'm more convinced than ever that divorce is the answer."

"How are you going to get a divorce?" I asked exasperatedly. "You have to have grounds. You just can't say, 'I don't love you any more,' and expect them to pop you out a divorce. That's too absurd. The religious sacrament, the legal document, the moral commitment is to marriage, not love. You say we can't make love—even though we're married and seeing if we can stay that way—because you're not 'in love' with me. An awful lot of people make love every day who aren't in love and for fewer reasons than we have. If that were the only reason for sexual relations, there'd be a helluva drop in the intercourse rate." We were beginning to go around in circles, so I asked pointedly, "Have you been to a lawyer?"

"No. Have you?"

"Yes."

"Who?"

"Why do you want to know? What's the difference?"

"So we won't go to the same one."

"Harold Polis."

"Okay."

"Harold says I have a better case for divorce than you do."

"How?"

"Because your involvement with Smothers was a factor in disrupting our marriage. Your refusal to consummate the marriage any longer constitutes pretty strong grounds, too. And the mental and physical cruelty you've been inflicting on me every day, the fact that you've slapped me three or four times now and I haven't touched you—those are pretty good reasons to start with."

Jean was frowning, clenching her hands, tightening her lips into a thin, hard line. "I told you," she said emphatically, "that I've figured out I was just using Leon to support my own views."

"But that's not what you said. You told me and Sam and Gloria and many other people that you loved him; you even told your parents."

She was glaring at me now, her eyes hard and blazing.

"Look," I continued, "I'm not going to sue you for divorce, now or at any other time, and you know that. I don't believe that's the answer for me or for us. So you can relax about any suit involving Smothers along those lines." She seemed visibly relieved.

"You keep saying, Jean, and you've said it for a long while now, that we shouldn't stay together just for the children. Maybe not. But they are a damn good reason to make every desperate effort to make a marriage work. If we didn't have them, it would be another story. But we do. They're ours . . . they're real. We're not unique in our problems. Most of the people you talk to our age are experiencing some upheavals or change in their relationships. But you don't run out and get a divorce because of it."

"Al, we've had seventeen years that were good, but they're not good for me any more. I had hoped the counseling would help you to see that."

"I see an awful lot I didn't before; I see the problems, at least as best as I can understand them, and I know what the realities are between us. But I also know where we stand in life, what commitments we have, and what's at stake in working for a reconciliation rather than a divorce."

"I had hoped you wouldn't fight, Al," she said.

"What do you mean, 'wouldn't fight'? What the hell do you want me to do? Say, 'Oh yes, it was fun while it lasted, but it's all over now,' and let it go at that? Walk away? Give up? Give up my whole life, my children, our home, everything? Is that what you mean by 'wouldn't fight'? That's crazy. I'm also a human being, you know. I have needs, desires, feelings. You're just one person. There are two of us involved in this marriage, and four other lives we're responsible for putting here. What do you mean? What do you want me to do? *I* had hoped the counseling would enable you to see these things more clearly!"

Jean heaved a sigh of hopeless resignation and began climbing into bed.

"Don't you have anything to say about what I just said?" I asked.

"No, nothing," she said.

On the same day nineteen years earlier, we had begun a commitment that was to have lasted the rest of our lives. Now we went to bed and stayed physically far from each other; we seemed to be even farther apart emotionally.

The next morning, without having made any further comment since she had told Faith and then me that she would seriously think it over, Jean announced without explanation that she would not agree to go to a couples' counseling group.

And she gave me back the anniversary present; she said she couldn't accept it.

Labor Day weekend

FLAMES LEAPED from the campfire, playing over the faces of the four of us gathered around it. Mark was sprawled on the ground, his elbows supporting his chin; Linda was sitting next to him, her dark hair in pigtails, her black eyes watching the fire intently; Karen was sitting in my lap, blond pigtails pushed back under my chin. Our lips were moving in unison and what was coming out was "I'm dreaming of a White Christmas."

It was a lovely, warm, star-filled night. The four of us were gathered in a clearing up in our woods; the three little kids planned to spend the night there. Beyond us, Charley and two of his friends were camped; we could barely see their small campfire through the foliage. It was now completely dark, around nine o'clock, and to fill the empty stillness, Linda had suggested we sing some songs. After searching for a few moments, we found that the only songs we all knew were Christmas carols; we had begun with

"Rudolph," and followed that with "Jingle Bells," and now we were on a quiet meditative one, "White Christmas." As we sang, Mark stirred himself, reached for a stick and the box nearby, and began toasting himself a marshmallow. The rest of us followed suit, never breaking the cadence of the song.

When we were through, there was another uncertain silence. What else did we know? Mark broke it by bursting out with "Hey-sanna, Ho-sanna" from *Jesus Christ Superstar*, a record he knew almost by heart. Punctuated by pauses for bites of charred, molten marshmallows, we sang as much of *Superstar* as we could remember. Then it was time to get ready for sleep. Each child reluctantly but sleepily got settled into a sleeping bag, and I heaped the remaining fire into one small glowing pile of embers. As a "night light" I lit a candle inside a glass lantern and set it inside the circle of rocks surrounding the fire. Then I went up to Charley's campsite and chatted with him and his two friends for a few minutes.

When I was walking across the starlit ball field, car headlights swept up the driveway and flashed around the bend to the house; Sara and Gene Nolting had said they might drop by. We talked for a few minutes standing on the patio. Then we decided that our voices carried too far in the stillness of the night and we might keep the children up, so we moved inside. Sara and Gene also were going to counseling with Sam and Gloria; they had started after we began going. Sara did not want a divorce, but she was feeling restless and was reevaluating her own life. They had six children. Gene was with IBM; the whole process of counseling seemed unnecessary to him, and he went with the greatest reluctance. As on other occasions I found that Sara and Gene talked to each other through me.

We had been talking for only about an hour when there was a thump on the front porch and a muffled banging on the door. Mark stood there wrapped in his sleeping bag, the two little girls behind him, encircled by theirs. "We thought we heard some thunder," Mark said solemnly. I looked up into the clear, starry sky. "Did you? Well, no sense staying outside and getting wet. You kids want to come inside and sleep?" The three smiled in relief, nodded in unison, and hurried up the stairs to Mark and Charley's room.

Before we could pick up the conversation again, Jean came home from an evening out. She was happy to see the Noltings. The direction of the conversation shifted now, because the Noltings could not play their remarks off me and it was too complicated to involve four people in a similar kind of by-play. Jean, however, was ready to take us off on a new tack; she enthusiastically began to tell Sara and Gene about her week of teaching religious dance at the Methodist youth camp and her plans to take courses in theology, sacred dance and perhaps dance therapy wherever she could find them. While she talked, I noticed she gave me more eye contact than she usually did, and I had the feeling that she was experiencing me as a human being, not as an abstract cipher. About midnight the Noltings left.

As I was picking up a few glasses and small dishes I remembered the three boys sleeping up in the woods, so I decided to check on them. Even in the middle of the night it was still comfortable outside, very little breeze stirring—a perfect night to be sleeping outdoors. Without a moon I had a little difficulty picking out the path, but I knew the way so well that with few missteps I reached their location. Everyone was sleeping, and the fire was out. I started back toward the big silhouette of the house; light was spilling from our bedroom in the left front downstairs, and the kitchen light in the rear illuminated a portion of the driveway. I looked at my watch; the luminous dial showed about twelve-fifteen. It had been a good fifteen minutes since the Noltings had left, so I wondered whether Jean was through with the bathroom. I walked around to the rear side of the house to see if she was.

The light was on, and through the slats of the Venetian blinds I could see Jean walking toward the chest in the corner where she kept cosmetics and other personal items. She had something in her left hand, and when she reached the chest and turned, I saw with a terrific jolt that it was her diaphragm! My heart pounded, and I could barely catch my breath, I was shaking so hard. Was I really seeing what I thought? I forced myself to focus, to calm down, to watch. She shook powder on what she held, and snapped it into a round case which she closed and put away.

My thoughts and emotions tumbled about in confusion. Had I been so naïve and trusting? I hurt with a new kind of anguish, a feeling that Jean had betrayed me—us—in the crudest kind of way. But that didn't go with her great religiosity, the whole church-oriented life she seemed to be following.

In confusion, I stepped back, returned to the kitchen door and came back in the house. I didn't know what to do. To rush in and confront Jean? Over what? She could have just been looking over the diaphragm to check it. Maybe—and my emotions momentarily leaped again—she planned to use it with me? I forced myself to sit in the bedroom while she puttered in the bathroom and tried to figure out how I could find an explanation for what I saw without blowing it all out of proportion or jumping destructively to wrong conclusions. At least I had to see how she reacted if I touched on something suggesting infidelity.

When she came out of the bathroom a few minutes later, I had thought of something to try. "Jean," I said, trying to control my voice, "earlier tonight, while you were out, I accidentally knocked your diaphragm case off the shelf, it popped open . . . and it was empty."

"You did that *accidentally?*" she answered coolly. I watched her face closely: there was no shock, no surprise, no fear of detection visible. She was looking at me calmly; her eyes held mine and stayed there.

"Are you having an affair with anyone?"

"Of course not," she scoffed. "Besides it's that time of month, and I wouldn't pick now anyway." She was precise and unhesitating in her answer. I was confused and unsure of what to do next. Any sign of guilt on her part would have given me the confidence to go ahead and tell her what I had seen. But there was nothing. I stood uncertainly; she waited for me to say something. When I didn't, she snapped off the light and climbed into bed. I gave up and got into bed also.

I lay for a long time, trying to collect my thoughts and make some sense out of what had happened. Even if it was a completely innocent incident, I decided, there was a physical possibility I was being completely naïve about. Just that possibility, the thought that she was carrying on with Smothers or someone else while I was desperately trying to save the marriage, filled me with grim determination. I had to be far more realistic, far less attuned to what had been and much more open to tough, unpalatable reality. There had to be a "new me," even if I didn't know who he was or how to be him yet.

The campers had come in for breakfast, the bright sun was already warm and the new day already well underway when Jean came in to join us. I could tell immediately by the way she looked at me that she was not hostile or angry. Instead, she seemed groping, uncertain; in her eyes was almost the same look she'd had the day we had rushed into each other's arms. Her voice, when she said good morning, was tiny and subdued; when she spoke, the tone was one of asking, not demanding. This time I was determined to respond from within me, to remain firm and controlled. Flitting from subject to subject, Jean made nervous conversation, most of it tentative leads shaped for me to take and go on with from there.

I listened to her approaches and responded noncommittally, but I knew I had to have space, to get away from her in order to settle myself better. A drive in the car would be the best way to be alone. Quickly excusing myself, I got up from the table and went to the bathroom to shave. Charley called after me, "Hey, Dad, can we have a catch?"

"No, not now," I said. "I have some things I have to do."

When I came back through the kitchen, Jean looked up at me anxiously, the question already in her eyes: "Where are you going?"

"Out. On personal business."

I went to a nearby park to try to pull myself together. Sulky dark clouds had been hanging low in the sky, and now a light rain was seeping from them. As I parked under the branches of a leafy tree, I could see tennis players scurrying for shelter, holding their rackets protectively under their shirts.

I had to take some action, do some things which were real and practical and apart from the probing of behavior we did in counseling and the hopes I always maintained for some day in the future. The first thing I decided was that there was no point in continuing the counseling if our real-life relationships were going to keep on this way.

Unless Jean really wanted to work with me to apply what we'd learned, it was senseless to go on in one world there and another in the lives we led each day. Then I would have to prepare myself to tell Jean that things could not go on this way. My heart sank at the very thought that I might have to initiate a break, but I quickly rallied my sinking spirits and told myself that doing otherwise wasn't helping get us back together anyway. I would have to give Jean a set period of time—a month perhaps—to make up her mind about what she wanted to do, then be prepared, without faking, without turning back, to do what I had to do. It was painfully obvious that all my begging, my beseeching and my offering to do whatever was needed were not saving the relationship. Somehow, I had to end my passive acceptance, my going along with whatever she decided, and take the initiative myself for a change.

Thinking the unthinkable, I began to feel a sense of strength and determination: I was at last moving to some kind of position to do something for myself. The rain was now falling more heavily; drops were sifting through the tree and splattering on the top of the car and off the windshield and hood. There was a lulling effect to it. My tense muscles began to relax, the hurry and press of my thoughts eased off. I slouched down in the seat and felt the tight, aching feeling drain out of my body.

I sat for more than two hours in the car. Then I drove home slowly, still lost in thought, not in any hurry to get back. When I came into the kitchen, Jean looked at me anxiously and said in a weak voice: "Would you share with me where you've been?"

"No," I said briskly, and kept going.

The rest of the afternoon Jean trailed after me. When I went into the living room to read, she came in and began straightening up the coffee table. When I sat outside on the patio, she came out and aimlessly began pulling weeds from a flower bed. Looking at her, seeing the pain she was suffering, my heart yearned to give in again, to reach out and console her and reassure her and try to begin working together in earnest. But each time I reminded myself of the short duration of those relapses, followed by even more painful and depressing periods for me. I was determined to reverse myself and be self-contained and self-assured, for my own good and perhaps for the good of both of us.

Before dinner Jean asked me if we weren't going to have a drink. "I'll make you one if you want, but I don't feel like any," I said firmly. I could see the visible effect on her of that unexpected answer. She said timidly that she would go ahead and have some beer "if you don't mind." After dinner I went into our bedroom, closed the door and began writing a long letter to Aunt Myra. I wanted to tell her how I felt at this point, what I had decided to do if Jean did not change; I asked her to share the information with Jean's mother and father if she felt it would not upset them too much. Three times Jean found excuses to come into the room to ask me questions that she could have asked later.

The next day, Sunday, Jean began to change again. Once more I watched the same process happen. Her voice became harder and her bearing more purposeful; she no longer reached out uncertainly but initiated her own moves, firmly and decisively. It seemed to me that there was no in-between in her moods. Either she was weak, dependent and a little girl, or she was hard, independent and uncompromising. Our relationship, it appeared, had to be like a seesaw—on an angle, one end up while the other is down. Unless we could get and keep it level and honest, I felt there could be no hope for a mature, healthy relationship.

One circumstance that worked against this and which I could do nothing about was that Jean now restricted her conversations almost entirely to women who were in the same frame of mind as she was. While we were having hamburgers and hot dogs outside on the grill, she disclosed that she was having lunch this coming week with Jill Stillman, a close friend who was going through a divorce; Marie Quinn, who was breaking up with her husband; and Noreen Antonelli, a fellow former ballet dancer, also in the same marital situation. How could she possibly get any perspective on husband and wife relationships from them other than to split, to walk away? Worse still, I felt she didn't want any other. She wouldn't expose herself to any counterbalancing views, she had refused to join the group counseling, and she refused to allow any intimacy between us to try to build new patterns together.

With these realities bearing down heavily on me, I went to Sam's the next Saturday. Unsurprisingly he mentioned that I looked gloomy. I told him I didn't think I had much to be optimistic about. "And besides, something else came up I can't figure out, but I'm afraid it's not good." I proceeded to tell him about the bathroom-window incident, Jean's changed behavior the next day, her change back again, and her almost exclusive involvement with women going through divorces.

When I finished, Sam said, "I'm flabbergasted. It just isn't like Jean to be committing adultery." I took his reaction to be an admission that in their private conversations she had not disclosed anything of that nature to him. "I just don't know, I just don't know," Sam said, shaking his head and puffing on a cigarette. He asked me about the women Jean was seeing, and after I described each one briefly he waved his hand and said, "Enough, I don't want to hear any more about them."

There was a pause, and I decided I had to tell Sam what I was determined to do. "Sam, after this incident, I've made a number of decisions. I can't keep on going like this, hoping you can bring us together again. It's a waste of your time and my money to keep on coming to counseling if nothing is going to change. I am going to give Jean a certain period of time, a month or so—whatever seems reasonable—either to go ahead with the divorce or to make a real effort to relate to me. If she hasn't done anything by the end of that time, I think I'll be ready to start a counter-suit against her. I don't want to do that, but it may be the only way to make her face reality."

Sam was listening to me with an intensity I had never seen before, his eyes sunk so deeply into the furrows of his brow that I could barely see them. After I finished, there were several moments of silence; then out of Sam there came a half-whispered response: "I'm stunned." Pause. "I cannot believe the distance you have traveled."

After a few more moments of silence Sam questioned the depth of my conviction. "Are you sure you want to do this? Some people stay in the same situation you're in indefinitely, living like boarders in the same house, no love, no sex, just together."

"No, I don't think I could do that," I said. "I couldn't survive."

"Good. I think that's best, that's healthy." Sam had uncoiled, had hooked one leg over the side of his chair, and was now waiting for me to say more.

"Sam, my basic question to you is this: Can you offer me any alternative to doing this? I can pull the trigger if I have to, but I don't want to. This is the absolute last resort if Jean won't do anything and we go on grinding away indefinitely. But, God, I would be doing it in the hope that the shock would accomplish what I couldn't any other way. I would do it because nothing else had worked and I wouldn't have anything to lose anyway. Do you know what

I mean? Is there any other way to avoid this? It would be like crucifying myself."

"Well, I can only say this: you and Jean have both been working all these months, but for different purposes. With you, it was the goal of saving the marriage. With Jean, it was the goal of finding out who she is. It's been hard getting you to do what she is doing because you are so intent on your goal. Gloria and I have been treating you both with basically the same approach: forcing you both to look inside yourselves, even going way back before the marriage, to get you to know yourselves better. I don't think you can look at that big a hunk of your lives without necessarily looking at your marriage and seeing how it fits into everything."

Sam was talking to me in a manner he had never used before in the counseling: he was talking *with* me, sharing with me his viewpoint and perspective, almost as if we had moved behind the scenes to see how the drama was unfolding. I thought to myself how much better I responded to this approach, how much it might have helped me earlier. I wondered about the change of approach, and I suddenly realized that now maybe the process was over, the ball game had been decided, and there was nothing to do except sit back and look at it.

"Sam," I asked solemnly, "are you telling me there is no hope?"

"Do you think there is?"

"You said once that there's always hope as long as we're alive."

"Do you see any hope?"

"In my ability and desire to change, yes. But I don't see any based on any changes in Jean or any indications that she wants to change."

"But there is hope . . . for you?"

"Yes."

"Okay, then, there *is* hope."

I asked him a question I would never have ventured in the previous way he handled our relations: "What about Smothers? Is he a factor any more?"

"Jean says he isn't," Sam said simply. "You know Gloria and I told her all along that her image of him was unreal, a fantasy. Jean says now she sees him differently."

"Why did she get into that relationship in the first place?"

"Well, Smothers offered her no threat. I've counseled many clergymen, in groups and individually, and I know them pretty well. Their world is quite small, their outlook is very restricted, and their scope is mostly narrow. You are very high-key compared to Smothers' low-key. The question Jean has to get at is, Why did she need him now? If she thinks she needed him supportively, for her own ideas about divorce and for her own growth, then she still needs support from someone else . . . but not, apparently, from you."

"Does that mean she's still weak, as you described her when we started all this?"

"Let me answer that for you this way. I don't mean this to be unflattering to Jean, but, Al, you never concentrated on her as a person. You really didn't know her strengths and weaknesses fully; you didn't know her as a human being. You certainly loved Jean, but you seemed to concentrate on her accomplishments, on what she did, rather than on what she was. You may even have loved the weakness."

I pushed even further into areas I would not have dared to go into with Sam before. "Well, can't you explore with her—and with me, too—what mature love really is, what a real relationship between her and me, on an even level, could be?"

"Al, I don't set the agenda," he said. "I can't set timetables. People move along at the pace they can handle. Sometimes they never get to the place I would want them to reach. About love, the best description I can give of it is what happened to me a little while ago. My daughter had to undergo an operation. I wanted to get in that hospital bed for her and undergo her pain. That's what love is."

I thought about what Sam had said, but the example he offered did not square with what we had been hearing in that very room. Sam's analogy was the way I would conceive love, as something selfless, other-directed. All that he had emphasized for more than half a year now was meeting *personal* needs, getting in touch with your own desires. I just didn't see that reflected or embodied at all in what Sam had described, but I did not want to get into a philosophical discussion of the meaning of love.

Besides, my relationship with Sam had just taken a completely new turn. Up until this hour I had felt Sam beating on me, pummeling me; I wasn't sure that some small part of it wasn't personal, although I recognized that a great deal of it was professional therapy. For the first time I felt a human empathy and concern reaching out from him to me; in return, I almost wanted to hug him instead of sitting across the room from him and exchanging words. When we came to the end of our time, I wasn't sure where or if we would go on from here. "Oh, yes, we'll keep going," Sam said. I was infinitely relieved to hear that.

That night the atmosphere between Jean and me was generally better. At the outset one flareup took place. I found Jean cooking dinner in a two-piece suit and asked why she was wearing it.

"Are you checking up on me?" she asked in annoyance. "What business is it of yours?" Then almost as quickly she said, "I had lunch with Jill Stillman, that's why, and I haven't had time to change." Somehow the irritation did not lead to more angry words or a continued bad mood.

Sitting in the living room after dinner, I told her that my session with Sam today had been a good one, that I could see better how she was trying to get inside herself and how this search related to the question of our marital relationship. As if in return, Jean told me some of the thinking she had been doing about just when it was she began to feel that something was wrong in her life with me. "I guess it was after Mark was born, five years ago, that I began changing," she said. She said she could not remember any incidents or situations which pinpointed how the change affected our everyday life, but she was sure it had happened about then.

Jean was making no attempt to end the conversation or turn it away from probing into our relationship. Sam had suggested a question which he said I might ask Jean if the right situation arose, a question which he thought would not threaten her, but which if answered would help both of us. I decided this was a good time to try it.

"Jean, I've been thinking about something I've wanted to ask you for some time, and I wonder if you would try to give me an answer." Her look was open and not angry, so I was encouraged. "What do you think *I've* been doing with these past seven months since we've been going to counseling?"

At first Jean answered my question with her own: "What do you mean, 'What was I doing?' I don't understand."

"I mean, how do you view my efforts to change, my reactions to you and to Sam. How do you see me?"

"Al," she said, "it's none of my business. It's not my job to analyze you." Anger flickered within me. I thought to myself, Here we go again; you're creeping back within your shell. But even more than an answer to my question I wanted Jean to keep talking, to keep communicating with me, so I remained silent and did not challenge her reply. For a moment we both sat quiet, an air not of anger or tension between us, but rather of expectant waiting. Then on her own initiative Jean began talking again, speaking in a low voice as if she really weren't talking to me directly, just indulging in a quiet soliloquy for which I was part of the audience.

"I think I've discovered that part of me is really my cousin, Billie Jo," she said softly. "You used to kid me a lot and say, 'Hey, you're not Billie Jo, you know,' but in reality I guess I am."

My thoughts ran back to Billie Jo: a simple, homespun Texas girl, a few years younger than Jean, who had done everything conventional that Jean had not done—married a local boy, stayed close to home, embodied the area's political, social and cultural conservatism. Billie Jo would never have gone to New York for a career, traveled to Europe or married a Yankee Catholic. In fact, she had dropped out of college when she met Larry, who was a printer, so that she would not outstrip him in education. Billie Jo was sweet and lovable, but she wouldn't have married me and I wouldn't have married her. Jean was continuing now in a detached, almost distant voice, and I strained closely to listen.

"Part of me was Billie, but part of me also was Martha." Martha was a childhood friend of Jean's and her maid of honor at our wedding. "When she came up to New York with me to study ballet, she was doing what her mother wanted her to do. Martha never really wanted to be a ballet dancer, but her mother was, of course, a well-known dance teacher, and Martha knew what was expected of her . . . and she was miserable. When she finally gave up and went back to go to college, she was at last doing what *she* wanted to do." Jean paused. All the time she'd been talking, she had been staring at the coffee table. Now she looked up at me, and the hardness wasn't there; instead, she seemed as gentle and reflective as she used to be. Then she focused her gaze once again on the tabletop and resumed her monologue.

"Mothers have that kind of influence over us. Mine certainly did. I did an awful lot of things because I knew they were expected of me . . . by Mother. Mother was very proper and very sure of what a daughter should do and should be. Nobody ever asked *me* if I liked to do them or not, and I never even thought to ask. So I just did them and felt that I was queer or wrong or something if I didn't feel the way I should've about them. In many ways I think my mother took me over just as she did Daddy." Jean said this not bitterly or unkindly, but simply as if it were a fact. "I got most of my feelings about sex, about marriage, about how a family should be from Mother, and I've been living with them ever since.

"The truth is that I'm not that 'sweet little Jean Singleton' any more, and that upsets people. But they're going to have to get used to that. I'm thinking for myself now."

Jean paused. I was almost afraid to breathe. It was as if a lid had been taken off the top of Jean and I could look into her for the first time. It was awesome. I began to see depths and dimensions and aspects of her I'd never known were there. I felt strangely frightened. Outside, the wind made small scratching and squeaking noises; the house was still, except when Jean shifted now and again in her chair.

She went on: "I don't come by my insights the same way you do; I don't read directly on the subject that interests or bothers me. I think about things almost constantly, but I do it by myself. I get a lot of help from religious sources, like the Harvey Cox book I'm reading now and the courses I take at Union Theological and other places. One day a man at Union was talking about the story of the Jewish people being a backdrop for understanding the Old Testament, and that rang bells in my mind. The story of me and my church and my family's involvement in it is the backdrop for us and for our marriage. I thought a lot about that after that day. I think I shouldn't have married you. I hadn't been around enough boys; I was too simple, too naïve. I've discovered now that I am really and truly a Methodist, and this doesn't jibe with Catholicism."

She paused, and very gently I asked her what she thought about the role she used to play: being a go-between between groups like our Modern Liturgy and her Methodist church. "It just isn't for me now," she said simply.

My question may have set off other mental trends; whatever the reason, Jean was now stirring, coming out of the strange, almost subconscious state she'd been in. She looked around, glanced at her watch and said it was getting late. She had been talking for pretty close to an hour, but I couldn't let her go without at least trying to connect her thinking to where we were at this point.

"Jean, I've really been fascinated and moved by what you've been saying. You have provided me with whole new perspectives on you that I haven't had, and couldn't have unless you'd shared them, and I'm deeply grateful. But what do you do about the fact that you aren't Billie Jo? You are Jean Singleton; you do have four children; we have given up more than twenty years of our lives to each other. What are you going to do about that? It won't go away. With awareness of what you feel comes understanding of the problem; then you have to do something about it. The best answer I can see is to be you, not try to be someone else, and work it out within the terms of you."

She had not interrupted me or given any sign that she was annoyed by what I was saying, so I kept going.

"Your father wrote to both of us the other day. We both got copies of the letter. Pap said we both sounded self-righteous to him, as if we both demanded a complete capitulation of the other person, and that neither of us was willing to make sacrifices and compromises to reach an understanding. I'm very much bothered by that letter because I respect Pap tremendously. He gives us a better perspective on the situation than either of us can have. I've wanted to make those sacrifices and compromises, and I'm asking why we can't. Must it be one answer and one only—divorce?"

Jean had listened closely to what I was saying; she was once again alert and completely part of what was happening. "I wasn't disturbed by Daddy's letter. He was angry when he wrote it. He used some pretty strong words, but that was his anger speaking. There are some things he just can't understand, and maybe you can't either. In his case I think there is just too much of a generation gap to overcome."

Then she got up and stretched. "I think it's time to be getting to bed." There was no point in trying to extend the conversation.

After she had gone to bed, I sat thinking for a long while. Many emotions were working within me. I was shaken by the extent of the change within herself that Jean had revealed. It showed how shockingly wide a gulf had opened up between us. I was troubled, too, by the way Jean looked upon these changes. From the first moment we met, we knew that we were very different people—different in our backgrounds, different in the way we responded to life. But these differences had caused us to be attracted to each other; they had provided the variety that made each of us interesting and made our individual contributions to the relationship that much more valuable. Now Jean was looking upon difference as a reason to part.

I thought about the obvious, genuine feeling she'd expressed about being in part Billie Jo. This struck me as a step backward for Jean, a retreat to something homey and simple, to a smaller, more restrictive, more cramped view of life and its potential. Maybe we all took that step backward at some point in middle age, but why Jean, and why at this time?

What troubled me most was her complete acceptance of the idea that simply to "feel" these emotions meant that they were now the governing principles of her life. I "felt" many times like I didn't want to go to work, but I couldn't just act on that feeling. The practical realities of life demanded that I go to work. But Jean was being urged to "feel" these needs passionately, and nothing was being said about going beyond that feeling to any action within the context of the life situation she was in. Supposing a year from now she felt she was Suzie Jones, who had gone off to become a high-priced prostitute; should she go off and respond to that feeling?

But above all I felt encouraged that Jean had shared such intimate thoughts with me. For the first time in seven months she had opened up the inner part of her life. And the only process we had for guiding us to such moments was the counseling. Whatever I thought about it, those hours were my solidest hope that out of these ups and downs, out of the turmoil and the anguish, something solid and substantial and whole for both of us could come. I went to bed better aware of the dimensions of our problem, but hopeful that more sharing and more understanding could lead us to a better relationship.

Over the next few days several other incidents provided me with more grounds for hope. The conversation with Jean had taken place Friday night. Saturday night Jean and I went out to dinner with the Robertsons and enjoyed a relaxed, easygoing evening, with fine conversation and no hostility. On Sunday my parents came to dinner—the first time in months they had been over when it wasn't a birthday celebration or special holiday—and Jean cooked a delicious meal and participated fully in an enjoyable family get-together.

On Monday the schools were closed for a holiday, and Mark and Charley came into New York to spend the day with me. We visited the Central Park Zoo, saw the new baby gorilla there, and ate lunch outside at the cafeteria, with the warm sun beating down on us; when we got home, we went for a swim in the lake. After supper Mark put on a puppet show for us in the living room, using the new monkey puppet we had bought at the zoo. To make a set on the coffee table, he fashioned the walls with three volumes of the encyclopedia, colored in trees and grass on sheets of paper and propped them up against the books, got some twigs and leaves from the yard to embellish the set, and then used the slide projector without any slides in it for the spotlight. In a tiny, squeaky voice, he carried on a conversation between the monkey puppet and a dog puppet he already had. The result was a charming, ingenious show, and we all applauded it enthusiastically.

Since the slide projector was already out, Charley wanted to look at some old slides, so he got a batch from our Colorado and Maine vacations. Jean only watched the slides for a few moments, then got up and left.

When we got into bed that night, it was raining, dripping steadily from the eaves outside our window. I put my hand between Jean's thighs, always a comforting, relaxing contact for me, and she did not push my hand away or pull away herself. Before I fell asleep, I had the good feeling that these had been a hopeful couple of days.

Whatever the fluctuations in Jean's moods and my expectations, and whatever the state of relations between us, the physical condition of the house kept going downhill.

The place was now unceasingly dirty. Linens remained unchanged for weeks until I organized the boys and we systematically changed them all. A beige rug in the TV room had been soiled repeatedly by the cats and the dog, who were now left alone in the house for long periods, and it stunk. Curtains in that room and in Jean's sewing room in the basement hung half finished for months. Stuffing hung out of an armchair clawed open by the cats, and Jean kept putting off having it fixed. The boys' underwear was in tatters and needed to be replaced. Meals were drab and usually late. All this was in striking contrast to the way we used to live; it was almost as if another family, a slovenly, indifferent one, had moved into our house.

Jean was gone most of the time. The boys said they didn't know where she was; I didn't. Jean's interests were now almost entirely outside the house and the family: her church, her few women friends, a part-time job at a dress shop in a nearby town—anything to get away from the house.

I tried to remember one family activity initiated by Jean since our whole upheaval had begun, and I couldn't. In the past we had taken trips with the boys to Mystic Seaport in Connecticut or Sturbridge Village in Massachusetts, or had spent weekends in the Pennsylvania Dutch area or in Washington, D.C. But now the whole thrust of her involvement was in the church and in herself. Sam said she was working on her new identity, her new value system and her new outlook on life.

There began to be some chaotic nights at home. The boys were increasingly rowdy and noisy at the supper table. Jim frequently got up to get things without bothering to say, "Excuse me." The confusion at meals bothered me tremendously, and I became angrier and angrier as Dan and Charley shouted back and forth at each other. Amidst it all, Jean sat serene and detached. She almost never reprimanded the boys. Anything went: Mark could and frequently did pinch her bosom and her behind; kids hopped up from the table without permission; the radio blared rock music. The new Jean was totally permissive, and was impervious to it all. She had taken to wearing aviator glasses now. She had cut her hair straight and severe. The total effect was in startling contrast to the soft, gentle look she used to have: now she seemed hard, tough and businesslike. She was "cool."

I was tired, discouraged and alienated from everybody. The job of trying to keep some order fell to me exclusively, and with it the unpopularity and resentment it caused. Being cut off from any emotional contact with Jean was by now normal, but being rejected and rebuffed by the children after I disciplined them was especially difficult to take.

One night I felt so completely wretched and miserable that I tried to reach out to Jean, who was reading the paper. "I just feel dreadful," I said. "I really love everyone here in this house, and tonight I almost feel just the opposite. I'm at odds with everyone; nothing is going right."

Jean scarcely looked up from her paper. "That's your problem, Al. You've got to wrestle with it."

"I know that, of course. But can't there be any reaching

out, any contact on a human level between us? Aren't there any basic human sympathies left?"

"I guess I don't have the same feelings I did before," Jean said. "I realize now how much I was role-playing, being the suburban housewife and retired ballet dancer. I'm not those things, really; at least I don't want to be. I'd like to go away somewhere and lead a simple life. I hate this way of life. I hate this house, too."

She was calm and methodical, ticking off the points as if they were items on a grocery list. "Aunt Myra wrote to me recently and said she didn't recognize me when I visited Texas in February. She said I was a completely different person. Well, they and you will have to get used to this new person, will have to accept me as I am now. Maybe this is what I should have been all along, and I'm only coming around to it now."

The finality in her voice and the flat assertion left no room for any discussion about or moderating of what she said. Jean seemed to have come to an important moment of declaration.

"Well, Jean," I asked, "what are you going to do about it?"

"I think we should talk to Sam together. He and I talked about divorce the last time I was there." That word brought a sharp stab of dread. "I know it isn't a good solution," she said, "but it's the best one possible for me."

"And what about the children? What's best for them?" I asked.

"Let's talk about that with Sam, too." Her tone was flat, unemotional and definite.

"Jean, I feel as if I've been taken. Since February I've done everything I know how, everything I could, to change, to find out what was wrong, to save the relationship. But it didn't matter. You had your mind made up then, and you still do. As Gloria said, you 'stacked the deck' and you've left it that way. I don't want this; I don't think it is the best solution."

"Let's discuss it with Sam," she said evenly.

"Everything we have here I love and want to keep going. I love this house, our way of life. So do the boys. You're going to smash that for people who don't want it smashed. How can you do that?"

"I'm sorry about the house because I know how much it means to you," she said matter-of-factly. "I wish there were something I could do to let you have it. I don't like it; I never have from the beginning." Months ago I would have been astonished by that remark; now anything Jean said didn't surprise me.

Then she turned calmly to discussing what she might do in the future. She talked about leaving and getting a job and beginning a new way of life. In a tone just as devoid of feeling, she finally said she thought she'd take a shower and go to bed. There was nothing more to say.

I went around closing up the house and turning off the lights. The dog didn't want to go out in the rain for her final airing, so I let her follow me and she hopped up on Charley's bed to make herself comfortable for the night. I covered all four boys and kissed them as they slept.

Jean was already in bed when I came down. As I slid into bed beside her, I realized the awesomeness of the events that lay ahead. At other points in our long years together— before Dan's operations or before a major decision—we had paused to pray silently together. "Jean, why don't we just say a little prayer to the God we both believe in for help in what lies ahead?" She didn't say anything, but she left her hand where it was close to mine. I grasped her hand

and held it tightly, but could feel only limpness in return. I had the feeling I was praying alone.

October 1972

Autumn was now upon us, the time of year I loved best. Our woods became one vast swath of color, starting with reds tinging the edges of leaves, then yellows as the leaves dried, then streaks of orange and gold. Around the lake the brilliant hues reflected off the blue waters, and the dark-green evergreens provided a striking contrast. The white clapboard Congregational church stood framed in its hillside of vibrant colors.

All my life I've loved the autumn. I love its *feel*, the chill briskness, the clean fresh snap in the air; I especially love the nights when the first fires of the year in the fireplace set the tone for a new season, foreshadow the wintry nights and snow ahead. Normally autumn was a part of me, filling me with good and familiar sensations. When Jean and I had lived in Texas, the one thing I'd missed most had been the autumn. In Texas there was no changing of the season, no cycle; everything stayed the same year-round, and that disoriented me. Jean, who had spent many autumns in the East, was bothered by this, too; she loved the Connecticut fall as I did. So when we came back, it was one of the first pleasures of nature we really enjoyed.

But this year, for the first time in my life, I could not be touched by the natural grandeur all around me. I saw it, I admired it objectively, but it could not get inside me. So complete was my absorption in the family's problems that no force, no distraction could break the total hold this impending catastrophe had upon me.

In the grip of this relentless reality, my moods varied. Some days I was furious at myself, seeing myself as a helpless drowning creature, letting things drift along without my active intervention while I floundered on my back. That picture would anger and disgust me, and I would determine to be firm, tough, just as unfeeling as she was about what was going on. But that mood would last only a short while because it kept running head-on into practicalities: if I was going to be that sharp, cold and indifferent, how could I foster cooperation and how was the household going to run? If I became other-directed and tried to show I could become just as disinterested as she was, what would become of the children?

Friction between the children and Jean, even though the boys didn't know the seriousness of our problem, flared up frequently. She was on the phone making plans to go out one night and Jim said in a loud, sarcastic voice, "Atta boy, Mom, make it three nights out of three." She ignored him and went out.

I discovered little circles on the calendar and found out Jim and Dan were keeping a log of the days she wasn't home when they got home from school; the calendar was covered with little circles. The three big boys also resented the way Jean never disciplined Mark; he seemed to be able to do whatever he wanted. One day he refused to do what I asked and ignored my warning that he would be punished if he didn't, so I spanked him, to a chorus of "Holy smokes, it's about time! Chalk one up for Dad!" Once while Jean and I were exchanging angry words—something the children had never seen before in all our married life—Mark happened to walk in; he clapped his hands and said, "Oh boy, a boss fight between Mom and Dad!"

All of this depressed me horribly. The last thing in the

world I wanted to have happen was the breakdown of relations within the family. I could begin to see the family coming apart before my eyes. I couldn't prevent my marriage from falling apart if Jean chose to allow it; and now I was helpless to stop the deterioration of the other relationships that was taking place. What a dreadfully wasteful and destructive direction for our efforts to be taking!

One night toward the end of October an incident occurred that shook me profoundly.

Jean and I were in the kitchen before supper, having a beer and chatting about the ordinary events of that day. It had been a calm and quiet day; at least I couldn't remember any incidents which might have led up to what happened. Jim and Charley were playing cards on the dining-room table, within sight of us; Dan was doing his homework on another part of the table; and Mark was in the den watching TV.

Suddenly Charley got up, came hurrying into the kitchen and started mumbling or babbling something. He was uttering sounds, but they didn't make sense. Lots of times Charley would clown around, his exuberance bursting out in loud shouts or a leap to touch the ceiling, but this time he just stood there. Then I looked into Charley's eyes: they were wide with terror. He had fallen back against the refrigerator, still uttering the same nonsense syllables. The noises sounded like "Uh kahn taw . . . Uh kahn taw." The sound was pleading, desperate. I froze in terror. He was paralyzed, unable to speak.

Jean and I both moved to him and were trying to calm him down. Even in our frightened instinctive concern for him, however, we were not working together. Each seemed to counteract what the other was doing, and we were getting in each other's way. Jean suddenly became absolutely calm. It flashed through my mind how she had always been annoyed when I became calm in an emergency (through my newspaperman's training and experience in difficult situations). Now she was doing that and I was becoming panicky.

We both walked Charley into the living room—she guiding him by one arm, I by the other—past the older boys, who had gotten up in curiosity and some concern.

Charley was still mumbling the same phrase. His eyes were just as wide as they had been before. We sat him down on the gold sofa and began to ask him questions.

"Who am I?"

"D–Dad."

"What's your name?"

"Ch–Charley." His answers were stammering, struggling. But when he answered correctly, we both said to him, "Yes, see, you can talk! You are talking. Don't worry about it; you can talk."

Gradually he began to relax. His gaze became less fixed. He looked around the room, at us, at where he was sitting. The effects of the spell, the attack, whatever it was, seemed to be disappearing. In a few more minutes he was talking normally and responding to questions at a regular speed and tone of voice. We hugged him and reassured him that he was okay, but that we would take him to the family doctor just to check up on things.

When Jean and I were alone again, my frayed nerves snapped. "My God, don't you see what's happening? We're killing the children in this whole horrifying process. Don't you care? Don't you feel *anything* any more? Does a child have to have a nervous breakdown before you'll stop saying, 'They're resilient. They can survive'? Do you have any emotions, any heart, any feelings left?"

Jean looked at me calmly and squarely and said, "I hear you, Al. I just don't happen to agree with you." Then she walked away and busied herself in another part of the house.

At one of my sessions with Sam, I learned that as a reason for wanting a divorce Jean had offered the statement that during eighteen years of marriage I had constantly imposed my will on her and she had acquiesced. I wanted to explore this matter further, so one night after supper as we were sitting in the living room, I asked Jean if she had any idea of why I had "imposed my will" or why she had allowed me to do it without protest.

"I guess you imposed your will because I let you, or because we both thought men were supposed to do that. I don't know. I let you do it because I never thought that I was important enough to have my way, that what I wanted counted. Now I've changed."

Her answer surprised me because I might have said the same thing. It was a response I could agree with and understand. But why did this add up to a divorce? I asked her that.

"Al, you're trying to argue me out of what I feel, not understand it," she said.

I said I didn't think I was imposing on her any more— at least not in any way I was aware of.

"Oh, yes you are in certain ways," she said.

"*How?*" I asked, surprised.

"In your raising hell over my phone bills to Marie Quinn in Westport. In your questioning why I contributed fifteen dollars to the Humane Society last week to have them put away the little kitten."

"Is that imposing my will?" I asked incredulously.

"In a way, yes," Jean said.

"Well, what's the difference between that and having honest differences of opinion? Do we always have to think the same? Can't we differ and express ourselves without it being my imposing my will?"

"Yes, but you always make the final decisions. You pay the bills."

I started to say that I had offered many times over the years to turn that chore over to her, and gladly so, but Jean broke in to say I was "getting picayune." The conversation was ended.

When I came home a few nights later, I was thoroughly delighted to see that Jean had finally finished the curtains in the den. In fact, everything in there had been cleaned up. The easy chair with the stuffing hanging out had been taken away and another one from the downstairs room brought up in its place. The room had been vacuumed and it looked like its old self, a real pleasure now to be in. I thought with satisfaction, This may be a sign Jean is taking an interest in the house again.

As we were getting ready for bed, Jean came to the bedroom door and announced, "Al, I'm not sleeping with you any more. From now on I'd like to use the den as my bedroom." I was stunned speechless by her statement. Then my anger rose and I said, "Jean, that's typical of what the problem is. You left that room crummy and horrible for the rest of the family for almost a year. Then when you found a use for that room to suit yourself, you fixed it up. Go ahead; no one can stop you. But that's just the way you've acted toward this family since February."

For the first time in more than nineteen years, we slept in the same house in separate beds.

November 19, 1972

THE DAY had unfolded like any typical Sunday in the late fall: attend church in the morning, return home about noon to change clothes and get a snack, check in with Jean to see about anything she wanted done and when she thought we'd have dinner. Then Charley, Mark and I, along with four of their friends, took off for Mianus Gorge across the New York State line, not far away, for a two-hour hike along unspoiled trails.

Jean normally came home from her church about noon, got supper ready and left instructions when to put it in the oven, then went back down to the church for the afternoon and perhaps the evening. This day, however, she was home when we got back from the hike around four. Everyone was thirsty from the walking, so we had something to drink; the boys then went back outside to play. I went to the bathroom to freshen up before going outside to do some chores in the yard.

When I came out of the bathroom, Jean was standing in the corridor waiting for me. "Al, can we have a talk?" she asked. I was surprised because usually she wanted to talk only after some flareup or important development, but things had been relatively calm for some weeks now.

"Sure, if you want to."

"Would you rather do it now or tonight?"

"I guess now is a pretty good time." Mark had come back into the house and was playing on the living-room floor with some toy soldiers, tanks, artillery pieces and airplanes. Jean shut the door to the living room, led me into the den, and shut that door behind her.

Then she turned to me and in a very calm and sure voice said, "I've told my lawyer to go ahead and start the divorce proceedings."

Those were the words I had dreaded and struggled to avoid for nine months, but Jean said them so calmly that to react to them in any extreme way would seem to be interjecting drama where there was no place for it. I looked at her for a few moments; she was entirely in control of herself, not a hint of any nervousness. It was obvious no words of objection or argument were possible.

The first question that came to my mind was, How was she going to do it? "What grounds are you going to use?" I asked. My voice surprised me by coming out calm and even; inside I was empty and hollow.

"Mental cruelty."

"What does that mean?"

"It's just a category; it's what my lawyer chose."

"But how are you going to prove it? It doesn't exist, it's not true."

"Al, let's leave that to the lawyers to decide."

Her calm, cool detachment was stirring anger in the void

which had existed inside me. "Why in God's name do you have to do this now with all that lies ahead for us? Why do you have to ruin the holidays and Jim's birthday for everyone?"

Without hesitating an instant, she said, "Al, there's never a good time."

"Yes," I replied angrily, "but some times are worse than others, and this one couldn't be worse. Why couldn't you wait till after New Year's? You've waited this long already."

She never flinched, batted an eye or faltered. "No, this is it. I'll talk to the three older boys so they'll know. I'll take the responsibility for taking this action."

"I want to be there when you do it," I said.

"Why?"

"Because it involves both of us, not just you, and our children."

She shrugged her shoulders as if it didn't matter either way.

The rest of the day continued to be like any other Sunday. The boys all drifted in for supper; I read the Sunday papers after dinner; and then Dan and I got interested in watching *Patton* on TV. Jim had gone off to a religious-education meeting of his teenage group, so obviously our family discussion was not going to take place that night. Jean stopped to take a look at the movie for a few minutes, got absorbed and watched with us until it was over, after midnight. Tomorrow was a work and school day; we would all be tired in the morning.

After I made my rounds of the boys' bedrooms, I slumped down on my knees beside my bed and rested my head in my hands. I was in the right position to pray, but no prayers came out; instead, all of my weariness, all the weight of my feelings drained out of me. For several minutes I remained there, numb. Then I roused myself, said if there was a God would he please help us, and fell into bed, exhausted.

Next morning I woke up and immediately felt shaky and uneasy. I had a powerful urge to stay in bed. This was not like me; I was always ready to get up as soon as I awoke. The day ahead of me seemed a physical hurdle I could never get over. A heavy, depressed feeling dragged me down. I forced myself to shave and get dressed, but it was a tremendous effort to do anything. In the cold light of day I now faced the hard, harsh reality that Jean was going to go through with her divorce after all.

On the train I tried to lose myself in the *Times* but something powerful and relentless gripped me and would not let me go. My palms were wet, I began to sweat all over, I writhed in unbearable tension. I remembered anxiety attacks I'd had as a freshman in college a quarter-century before; the symptoms were exactly the same. I felt like something inside me was trying to escape from the prison of my being and the sentence I faced. When I got off the train, I was confused; I could not focus on the route to the advertising agency where I had a meeting scheduled. I'd been there scores of times, and it was only a few blocks away, but I couldn't think how to get there. I struggled to stop the panic, to make myself calm down, think clearly and not come apart. My hands trembled; my mouth was dry. I told myself I had to be strong and had to keep going, and somehow I got my thoughts clear enough to reach my destination.

At the agency meeting I managed to shove my chaotic feelings under a surface of calm and control. When I got back to my office, however, the same unbearable tension stalked me. I tried to turn my attention to work, to get things done, but I couldn't do it. I gave up and walked up to Central Park. Stark stripped trees were swaying in a stiff breeze, and dark clouds scurried over the tops of buildings. In the zoo area a few old people sat huddled on benches; mothers pushed bundled children hurriedly along the paths. I started to walk up paths, across grass, over rock ledges, my arms and legs responding stiffly and mechanically. At times I couldn't remember where I was or how I got there. I was terrified by the thought that I might be losing my mind.

Suddenly I emerged from the park on Fifth Avenue, at a point in the Sixties where I knew exactly where I was. I headed back to the office immediately. I called Sam and told him I had to see him right away; he paused only a moment, then said, "Okay, six tonight." The anxiety that I had wrestled with for nine months was now in control of me, robbing me of my strength and resources. I fought it, but I couldn't break the grip. All afternoon I kept the door to my office shut, pacing the floor, trying to get control of my turbulent emotions.

Why was I so completely demolished? What was happening? I couldn't give myself an answer that would break me out of the anxiety. The afternoon stretched on endlessly; finally, a little while before I usually left, I couldn't stand it any more and took off for the train.

When the train arrived in Connecticut I went straight from the railroad station to Sam's office, even though I was forty-five minutes early for our appointment. Being there gave me a feeling of relief. By now, the secretary had gone home, the final appointments for the afternoon were underway, and the waiting room was empty. My emotions began to settle down; I got some control over myself. I relaxed enough to concentrate on a magazine, and I read to make the time pass more quickly.

At a little after six a woman emerged from Sam's office and passed by me; then Sam came out, nodded to me to come in, and went in himself. I sat down and immediately began pouring out to him what Jean had said and what had happened since then. Sam let me finish, then he said, "You're suffering a death reaction, a classic bereavement ordeal. You're grieving for Jean just as if she had died. Only she hasn't, and the frustration is that you can't mourn her leaving like a real death. You realize that you've lost her, she's gone. But she's still alive, still there, although to you, she's dead. And there's nothing you can do about it."

"Sam, I went back twenty-five years in my life today," I said. "I had the same feelings, the same reactions I had when I was a freshman in college. Same sweats, same panic, same confusion."

"That can happen. You've pushed aside everything you've learned since then and gone back to that time. Twenty-five years ago those reactions got you through a crisis somehow, so you're trying them again. Only you aren't the same person you were then, Al. Your biggest problem now is hope; you've never given up hope. And that's what's whipsawing you. If hope were dead, you'd be numb to the pain you're feeling. You wouldn't care, you'd be resigned, you'd accept. Hope feeds expectations, and those then intensify your frustration and pain when they aren't realized. You've got to kill hope if you want to survive."

"How can I do that?"

"By facing reality. By living with the reality that it seems obvious Jean doesn't love you any more. She's been saying that for nine months. You've got to start letting off some of that frustration you're feeling. In your case the best way is to deal directly with Jean. She's the cause. The same with anger. You don't want to let out something jarring or explosive toward her for fear you'll wreck something, so you keep the anger in. You've got to start letting it out. Look at the blacks in Watts. Frustration and anger built up over the years. Then explosion. Now maybe they can do something about it."

"Yes, I can see what you mean."

"Al, you're the kind of guy who needs someone to come home to," he said. "You've got to start some new relationships."

"But that isn't what I've been in here for. I wanted to save this one. I just don't feel like starting new ones; I don't even have anyone in mind. It would be strictly mechanical, strictly forcing myself."

"Well, you've got to start sometime, and this is as good as any."

"I can't see complicating my life now with another female relationship. What I have now is more than I can handle."

"You don't have to get laid to have a relationship. But if you do, as I've said before, don't make it here. Do it in New York. Be discreet."

I felt much better after the hour with Sam. When I got home, Jean was on the way out; we barely had time for a greeting. Everyone had eaten, so I had supper alone. As I sat thinking, I realized how right Sam was: I had walked on eggs with Jean, afraid to crack the thin surface of the relationship that remained. It wasn't enough for me to say that I loved her and couldn't be hard on someone I loved. There was something in between mushiness and hardness: a firmness I hadn't known how to achieve. For my welfare and hers, I had to learn this, no matter how late my resolution was.

November 22, 1972

After nine months of having the true situation kept from them, the children found out this night the actual state of the relations between their mother and father.

Only rarely did the entire family watch television together, but the movie *Brian's Song*, about the football player who died of cancer, was one which appealed to all of us. We had missed it the first time it was shown, and now it was being repeated. As we watched, I was very moved by the story. My emotions were already raw and near the surface, and the power of the drama and the human feelings it conveyed made my eyes fill with tears regularly. I looked over at Jean several times; she was very near outright crying, too. The boys were riveted to the set; while they weren't crying, they had unusually solemn looks on their faces. When it was over, we all felt that we had seen something extremely touching and worthwhile.

Mark had been put to bed and Jim and Dan were doing something in their rooms; Charley was still with us in the living room, talking about some of the things we'd seen in the drama. Suddenly Jean interrupted Charley, saying, "Would you please go upstairs and get your big brothers? Tell them I'd like them to come downstairs."

My stomach knotted. I felt my heart beat faster. I knew what was coming.

Jim and Dan came down looking curious, wondering what Mom wanted. She told them to sit down; Jim and Dan both stationed themselves on the blue sofa to my left,

Charley took a seat next to me on the gold sofa, and Jean faced all of us, seated on the other blue sofa to my right. She had been fiddling with her cuticles while Charley went to get the boys, and we had said nothing. When they were seated, she began.

"Boys, I want to say something which is very important. The way Dad and I have been living the past nine or ten months is no good." I watched the boys' faces; they showed some interest, but no apprehensiveness or special concern. Curiosity still seemed the main factor in their responses. Jean was in complete control of herself—no nervousness showing, no wavering in her voice. She did not rush her words, but spaced them out precisely.

"This just can't go on this way." She paused, then without breaking the cadence of her speech or adding any special emphasis, she said, "So I've asked Dad for a divorce."

My eyes turned to the three faces looking at her. A surprised expression was beginning to form on them.

She went right on: "I'm not proud of what I'm doing, but I'm not ashamed of it either. There are some reasons only I can understand. Most people don't understand what I am doing, but some do. But I feel this is the right thing and the only thing I can do."

Still no one had said anything. The three were looking at Jean, absorbing what she had said. She was sitting perfectly upright on the edge of the sofa opposite them. Only a slight movement of her hands betrayed her tension. I waited for someone to say something.

The first words came from Jim: "Instigators ought to get out!" Jean blinked. Her face flushed. But she did not break; there were no tears or words of protest.

In the few moments since Jean had begun talking, I had grown absolutely calm. This was a scene which I had wanted to avoid more than anything in my life. But I felt strength and determination building as it began to unfold. Jim's words gave me even more support.

Jean did not say anything. The boys were silent. I wanted them to know how I felt.

"Boys, I want to say something," I began. The evenness of my voice surprised me. "I never wanted this to happen. This is not my idea. Right from when this all began, last spring, I've said that this is not the answer for Mom and me and for our family. I still love Mom, I still want our marriage to continue. Mom, you boys, our home—all of this is everything that means life to me. I don't know why she insists on doing this, but I know I am not getting out. I intend to stay here." As I said this, I realized the difficulty I faced in carrying this out, and anger began to stir within me. "You seem to be the only one who wants this, Jean. It's for your benefit and no one else's."

Jim spoke up again. "I just didn't know things were anywhere near this bad. I had no idea. I thought we were a happy family."

"Yeah, me too," Dan said. Charley just watched his big brothers and said nothing.

Jim continued, "The normal thing you always hear about is for the father to go, but no way do I see it should be Dad. That's not fair. It's your idea. It ought to be you."

Jean listened to what he said without losing any of her control. "Well, we'll see. That will be up to us and to our lawyers."

"To hell it will," I said angrily. "It *isn't* up to any lawyers. They don't live here, and they don't know what's going on. This is between you and me. The door has been open for you to stay or go. Nobody's pushing you. No one wants you to leave. We all love you. But if your answer is that you've got to go, then go. Just don't tear me from this family in the process."

"How would you get along without me?" she asked. Her question startled me. It seemed to be directed to the practicality of running the house, a minor consideration in the immense human consequences that were at stake.

"There's no question that we can get along without you," I said. "Unfortunately, we've had plenty of practice this past six months."

She was still waiting, looking at me as if I hadn't answered the practical part of her question, so I began all over again. "As for how we would get along, that can be worked out. I can arrange my own schedule at work. Grandma and Grandpa can help out. So can Jim and Dan. We can manage it all right."

Having received my answer, Jean did not comment on it, but instead began to explain to the boys that "things change between grownups, and we have to work them out somehow."

"Sure, but working them out doesn't have to mean divorce," I said. "Besides, it's not just between you and me. There are four children involved, and they count tremendously. And your parents and mine, all of whom love us dearly."

Jean had gotten up while I was talking and had walked to in front of the fireplace. "I think we ought to end this. It's getting destructive," she said.

"If you want to end it, you can," I said. "But I want to make how I feel absolutely clear. I love you, I love these children. I know you've said many times that we don't stay married for the sake of kids or grandparents or anyone else. But I also know that from my standpoint we can work this out if we both want to."

"I guess it comes down to I don't really believe you love me, Al."

"You've also been saying all along that 'we can only speak for ourselves.' Okay, that's all I'm doing, speaking for myself, and I say, 'I love you.' "

"Okay, so I'll only say that I don't feel you do," she replied. And with that she said good night and went into her bedroom.

The whole thing had taken about twenty minutes. The three boys got up and went to their rooms without saying anything further. I remained seated right where I had been sitting. This was a moment no man ever wanted to go through; it was now over, and I felt only sadness and determination.

I took my shower and went through my normal routine of checking the boys. Charley was awake, lying in the dark on his back, his arms behind his head. With his long, golden hair illuminated by the light from the hallway he looked delicate and handsome. I sat down on his bed and pushed his hair back from his forehead. He smiled softly at me. "Charley, I'm terribly sorry this night had to happen. I wish to God it never had. But Mom and I love you kids. Don't worry. Everything will work out all right." He nodded, but said nothing. I went over to Mark's bed and pulled the blankets up around his tiny, sleeping form. I thought about how securely and innocently he had been sleeping while his big brothers were downstairs.

Dan was about to turn his light out when I came into his room. He flipped over on his stomach and asked me to scratch his back. I told him the same thing I told Charley. He, too, merely acknowledged that he heard me but said nothing in reply.

Jim pulled off the pair of stereo earphones he had on

and leaned back on his elbows. "No way does it make sense for you to have to go, Dad," he repeated.

"I don't want to, Jim, you know that. I don't want anyone to go if we can help it. Maybe now that you kids know what's going on Mom will feel differently about it. I'm sure she'll listen to you when she won't listen to me."

When I got to my own bed, I was strangely drained and unfeeling. I seemed beyond emotion.

The Thanksgiving holidays were the first major event we went through as a family with everybody knowing how things stood. Jean was as much a part of our activity as she always had been. For the first time in our married life we did not go to one of our parents' homes for the holiday: Sara and Gene Nolting invited us to join them and their six kids that day, and after talking it over, we decided to do it.

The day went as pleasantly as any Thanksgiving gathering is supposed to. In the clear, brisk afternoon sunshine, the Nolting boys and Gene played my boys and me a game of touch football. Jean and Sara busied themselves getting the huge dinner ready. Before dinner late in the afternoon, we drank wine around a crackling fire in their den fireplace; the children sprawled on the floor and played games or watched football on TV. Jean and I fit into the conversations as we always had; in fact, there was an absence of any sharpness or hostility between us. Not until we returned home that night and went our separate ways to bed was I reminded that we were not the couple we had been.

The day after Thanksgiving we went over to Grandma and Grandpa's to help them eat leftover turkey. Ralph and Carla had come down for the weekend from Vermont, so that added a holiday touch to the dinner. The pain which

I had carried with me from the other night was diluted in the warm spirits of the gathering. Jean talked normally with all the members of the family and hardly seemed like a woman who had just committed us and our children to an inevitable wrenching separation. As the glow of the companionship grew on me, I felt that the actuality had not yet happened and the immediate moment held only happiness. I was proud to have my children there talking to their aunt and uncle, comfortable with these people who were the links to the essence of my life. Everything about the day had a reassuringly familiar feeling about it. I began to feel that maybe Jean had relented in the face of the reaction led by Jim.

When dinner was over, I was surprised at Jean's insistence that I take the boys home to play so she and Carla could clean up the dishes. Jean did not come home until after ten, when the boys were already in bed.

Next morning the reason for her long delay became apparent when Carla called me. She was on her way back to Vermont, but she wanted me to know the grim reality: Jean wasn't going to change. The two women had talked at great length while they did the dishes. The news was disheartening enough in itself, but Jean had mentioned something else which hurt and puzzled me further.

"I asked her specifically if a third person was still involved," Carla said, "and Jean said yes." Carla recounted this as though I should know, but of course that was not what Sam or I or others had gathered. She said Jean didn't mind her sharing the conversation with Ralph or me.

I called Harold Polis, my lawyer. He listened to what I reported and said how terribly sorry he was to hear it; because he hadn't heard anything from me in some time he'd hoped that meant good news.

"Al, I'd suggest you get right down to the bank in the morning and check on your joint savings account. That's the first thing her lawyer is going to tell her . . . to get out what her lawyer thinks is hers." When I went down the next day it was too late. A few days before, Jean had withdrawn half of our two thousand dollars' worth of savings; five hundred of the remaining amount was tied up with a car-payment note, so I had five hundred dollars to my name.

Over the next few days the children's awareness of the trouble between us began to show up. Sometimes it was strong and open. At dinner one night Jim was about to get up from the table and serve himself something from the stove. He stood up, paused and said, "We'll have to ask you for permission, Dad, when you're the one here." Jean kept on eating as if she hadn't heard.

At one meal the little boys were talking about a cute new dog in the neighborhood which had a black eye. Charley said, "Mom needs a black eye for what she's doing." When I was putting Mark to bed after we'd had a good time together all evening, he burst out: "Dad, I don't want to leave this house. This is where I want to stay. All my friends are here. I want to stay here with you and Mom!"

None of the digs at Jean or the cutting remarks gave me satisfaction. Jean seemed not to be bothered by them or concerned enough to deal with the matter. She just brushed them aside and kept on going.

Almost two weeks had passed since Jean had told the boys she wanted a divorce. When I asked her again what she intended to do she said she wasn't sure just now, but that we would have ample time to talk things out with Sam and that there would be no paper-serving or legal unpleasantness. So we went on, all of us, suspended between an unreal, uneventful daily existence and the harsh reality of a blow which was going to fall sometime, somehow.

November 29, 1972

Just as on any weekday night, life was going on full-blast in all parts of our home. Jim had finished his homework and was watching TV in the den. Dan was up in his room working on his fresh-water aquarium. Charley was wandering around, undecided as to whether he wanted to watch TV or play records. Mark had gotten out of the bathtub and was almost ready to listen to a story before going to bed. Jean was at a church meeting and I was just finishing up the dishes in the kitchen.

As I was sponging off a counter, the back doorbell rang abruptly. I thought it was strange that anyone would be at that door; they usually came around to the front. As I walked over to open the door, I suddenly felt uneasy. When I switched on the porch light and looked out, I got a cold chill. A beefy man with heavyset features was standing there, holding a piece of paper in his hand.

I opened the door and he asked gruffly, "You Albert Martin?" When I said yes, he thrust the paper at me. He flipped open his wallet, showed a badge and said, "I'm Deputy Sheriff———." I didn't catch the name. "This here is a summons for you to appear in court next Tuesday." He turned the paper over and stuck a stubby finger at a word halfway down the side: "divorce." Then he said, not unkindly, but as if he had said this countless times, "Good luck."

I stood there stunned, holding the paper in my hand. My

legs began to shake and I felt as if the wind had been knocked out of me. In stark legal language it said: "Jean S. Martin vs. Albert M. Martin . . . Superior Court . . . you are hereby summoned . . . "

I remembered Jean's promise that there would be no papers served, no crude legal arm-twisting, plenty of time to work things out. And, appropriately, I remembered that she was down at her church when the thing was done.

Outrage and disbelief rose within me. I scanned the paper quickly: "intolerable cruelty" was the grounds. She wanted custody of the children, possession of all property, removal of me, temporary alimony and child support, payment of all legal fees.

I walked through the house, not knowing what to do with or about the summons. I wandered into the den and said angrily to Jim, "Mom had a sheriff deliver this to me a few minutes ago." Jim jumped as if he'd been touched with an electric wire. "No kidding!" He snatched the summons and read it quickly. "This is crazy. She wants everything. What does she think she's doing?"

"I don't know," I replied, "but I sure as hell am not going to let her do it if I can help it." Jim handed the paper back to me, shaking his head in disbelief.

Dan was drying his aquarium when I walked into his room. "What's that?" he asked.

"Read it!"

"Holy smokes!" he said. "How can she ask for all that? That isn't fair." I was pacing his room, shaken, angry, trying to think what I should do.

From his room Mark called, "Ready, Dad." He had gotten himself into bed and now wanted me to read him his good-night story. The little freckle-faced boy snuggled into my lap as I began to read. My thoughts were elsewhere;

Mark looked up after a few minutes and said, "Dad, you're reading like this . . . " and imitated me making low, muttering sounds. "Gosh, Mark, I'm sorry," I said. "I'll try to read better." It was a tremendous effort, but I managed to control my voice and to read more slowly and distinctly for him.

Charley was downstairs; he must have been talking to Jim about what had happened because he was excited and upset when he came upstairs to bed. A little later I heard Mark crying and I went up to his side. In a tiny, pleading voice he cried, "Dad, I don't want you and Mom to split apart."

I hugged the little bundle of reddish hair and kissed him. "Mark, I don't want that to happen either. None of us do. Don't worry, though, we all love you. Nobody is going to leave you alone."

"I'm going to live with Grandma," Mark said tearfully.

"You won't have to do that, Mark. Mom and I will take good care of you. Don't worry."

Charley had been watching us both with serious, troubled eyes. "Dad, I love you both. But I don't want to leave this house. This is where I live, this is where I want to live."

"I know that, Charley," I said, "and I want you to live here, too. Mom and I will work that out. Now turn over and let me scratch your backs." When I left, they were whispering back and forth in the dark.

I went downstairs and decided to call Harold Polis. My voice was nervous and excited. He took the information I gave him calmly, assured me nothing was going to happen right away, and said we should meet soon. I asked him anxiously if he still thought we could win the case, and he replied, "I haven't seen or heard anything to make me change my mind." Then I asked him if he saw any way

Jean could conceivably prove intolerable cruelty on my part and he answered, "I don't see how."

I felt better after making the call, but my thoughts were still turbulent and my emotions still careening wildly. When I thought about Jean's demands contained in the legal summons and the reasons for her wanting to break up our marriage—"Al, I don't love you any more"—the whole incident seemed an outrageous nightmare. And when I added to that the continued presence of the Reverend Smothers, when Jean had told me she no longer thought she was in love with him, I got even more furious. The future lives of all of our children were being upset and directly influenced by this relationship between Jean and Smothers, and I was being victimized by it while helpless to break it up. The boys had to know that Smothers might eventually be their guardian or foster father if Jean kept up the way she was going; that was an important factor in how the kids should look at what lay ahead.

While I was angrily considering what to do about Smothers, I heard the cellar door slam downstairs: Jean was home. It was ten-fifteen. The older two were up in their bedrooms, but not yet in bed. They too were still upset and disturbed by events of an hour and a half ago. They knew everything that was taking place and were big enough to form their own opinions; indeed, at some point they were probably going to have to make a choice as to where they would live. I was torn about whether to involve them in any part of any showdown with Jean. But my anger obscured any objective judgment I might have made at that moment—in retrospect, I think I did the wrong thing—and I called Jim and Dan downstairs.

Then I went to the top of the stairs and shouted for Jean to come up because there were some things we had to talk about.

"Why? What do you mean?" she called back.

"Because I got your love letter, that's why." She did not answer. A few minutes went by. I went back to the stairs and shouted, "Are you coming up or are we going down?" In a moment Jean did come up and we went into the living room. Jean stood while the rest of us sat.

"First of all, I am outraged that a man bangs on my door and out of the blue hands me this, telling me to be in court next week. That's brutal. And you said there would be none of this."

"Al, I don't know anything about it. My lawyer must have done that. I'll call him in the morning."

"Since you're saying one thing and something else is happening, I think there is another factor the boys ought to know about. It directly involves their future and how they look at it.

"Boys, you know now that Mom said many months ago that she didn't love me any more and wanted a divorce. What you don't know—but many people do and you'd probably find out anyway—is that Mom also told me then that she was in love with another man. It's someone you both know—especially you, Jim—and since Mom may marry him, it's important you're aware of him." Both Jim and Dan were listening with intense interest and curiosity. Jean was standing impassively, no emotions visible, her arms crossed.

"Mom has told me and others, and she's right here to deny or explain it, that she loves the Reverend Smothers and maybe will marry him." Both boys looked at her in disbelief. Jim's reaction was mocking criticism: "That clown! Remember what all the kids thought of him when I was in that youth group with him? You must be kidding!"

"I wouldn't have brought this out except that as recently as a few days ago Mom told someone in our family that

Smothers was a 'very important' person in her thinking, and tonight, of course, this legal paper begins to clear the way for her to go to him."

Instead of anger or indignation at what I had told them, the boys were reacting with absolute incredulity. Jim stated firmly, "Mom, in no way would I ever think of living with that clod. You've got to be crazy to be serious about him." Dan chimed in: "What could you possibly see in him?" Jean didn't answer, just listened calmly.

Then Jim remembered the legal summons sitting before us on the coffee table. "How can you ask for everything in the world that's on that piece of paper?" he asked. Then he went on: "Look, I want to stay here; this is my house. You don't seem to care about us, Dad or anyone. All you care about in this paper is yourself."

Dan said, "I just don't see how you could do such a thing."

Jean waited until the boys had finished. She did not try to outshout them or cut them off. Then she said matter-of-factly, "I don't know what I'll be doing about Leon, marrying him or not. I want to try a number of things in my future. Religious dance, some more courses in religion, lots of things—"

Jim suddenly remembered something and burst in on her: "Hey, Mom, you wouldn't want me to say this in court, but I just remembered finding Smothers either here or just leaving plenty of times last winter when I came home from school."

I flew off the couch in a rage. "Smothers, here? In my house? My God, you've got one helluva nerve!"

Jean was not ruffled. "We were counseling," she said.

"Counseling? Is that what you call it? Is that what leads to that paper and divorce? If I ever caught him here . . . "

Dan had not said much up to this point, but now he

asked earnestly, "Mom, right now I favor Dad. This just doesn't make any sense. What's your reason? I mean, I didn't even know that you were unhappy. We all seemed happy. It's nice around here. What do you mean by 'mental cruelty' or 'intolerable cruelty' or whatever it is?"

Jean thought for a minute; then she said, "That's just a legal term, Dan. It's a grounds you use if you can't say it any other way. I really didn't know the paper was going to be served. Yes, I think it's cruel and shocking, too, and I'm going to ask my lawyer in the morning why it happened. As I understand it, those demands on there are just starting points."

Jim and Dan both began talking at the same time, anxiously asking questions, trying to find out why Jean was doing this. "Why? Why? That's the thing. You've got to have a reason. Tell us."

Jean did not answer. They kept pressing her with the same question. Finally, she said, "Boys, I'm afraid I need more time to think about how to tell you properly. I can't give you an answer right this minute. You know I think best when I'm scrubbing a john or baking a cake. Let me think about it some more."

"My God, what are you saying?" I said angrily. "You've served me with a legal paper and now you're going to figure out why you did it? That's ridiculous! You've had nine months to come up with an answer. That's preposterous!"

For the first time Jean seemed a bit unsure of herself. Hesitantly, she said, "Any answer I could give you now . . . would . . . would only be prejudicial."

"Prejudicial? What does that mean? To whom? I don't mind having it all out in the open about Smothers and any other aspect of what has been going on. I've got nothing to hide."

Dan said, "Dad, you're shouting."

"You're right, Dan, but I've got plenty to shout about. Mom has just threatened to shatter the whole existence of all of us, and when you ask her for a reason she doesn't even have one."

"I think it's time to wind up this discussion," Jean said, and she started to turn away.

"Wait a minute, Jean," I said. "When you decide what you're going to tell the boys as your reason, I'd like to be there, too. I'd like to hear what the 'why' is myself. Then we'll all know."

She ignored the comment and kept walking.

The boys and I sat there for a few moments. "Dad, if you've known about Smothers all along, you've let Mom tromp all over you. You shouldn't have taken it," Jim said.

"Jim, you don't turn off the love you've had for a person for more than twenty years that easily. I do love Mom and I'll take an awful lot of crap if I think it will help straighten things out. Now she's filed the paper, though, and I don't think anything can stop her."

Dan said, "The thing that gets me is that Mom asks for all those things, wants everything and can't tell us why she's doing it."

"Dan, I'm not saying we don't have problems—we do —but everyone has. You boys reacted as I did: I thought we were perfectly happy. I still think we can be that way again, but Mom insists she doesn't love me and doesn't want to try. I don't know what anyone can do about that."

Worry, concern, fear, pain kept me up until late. Around five-thirty I woke up cold, got up and pushed the thermostat higher. I heard Jim turning over several times in his bed above me. I never did get back to sleep. When we came in for breakfast, Jim said he'd been awake since four-thirty. Dan said he hadn't been able to get to sleep last night for more than an hour. Jean seemed to be the only one who had slept soundly.

There was a new presence which joined the six of us in our house now, which sat with us at the dinner table, which influenced what we said and even how we heard one another. It was the open awareness of the split between parents. I wondered how a family could find more horrifying circumstances under which to try to continue normal living.

Reactions to the situation varied. The older boys mostly were biting and caustic in their remarks to her. Mark became wild and undisciplined, taking advantage of the fact that Jean did not curb him. Charley was in the middle, beautifully absorbed in his Little League, Scouting, school orchestra and other activities, only now and then reflecting the resentment of his older brothers.

Jean seemed determined to ride out all the reactions and criticisms untouched. She simply did not respond to any of it. If the older boys criticized her, she ignored it. If Mark pulled on her bosom or snapped her fanny, she showed no reaction. It was as if none of this existed; the only reality was the course she had set toward a divorce.

Jean became even more uncommunicative with me; she pulled into a more tightly closed shell. My only relations of any substance were with the boys. After dinner we often played ping-pong. Jim and I had a keen, even competition. Our games were very similar and we went at it intently; the winner depended on who had the slight edge that day. Dan's left-handed game was more erratic: when he was good, he was the winner. At other times, he was terrible. Charley was coming along okay and Mark was just beginning to be able to hit the ball back.

Jim was the Monopoly champ. He beat everyone he played.

Then there were the Rummy 500 games, the spin-and-see-where-you-land games with Mark, the stories read to the little kids at bedtime.

Without my involvement in the family, I don't see how I would have survived. A huge void existed in me which Jean had once filled. The boys could never completely fill this up, but the degree of companionship and human response they gave me enabled me to keep going.

December 1, 1972

The Christmas season began in earnest. Around our house December 1 was the day to start marking off the days until Christmas and to begin seriously thinking about shopping. Normally there would be a quickening of the excitement, an intensifying of the Christmas spirit, but on this first day of December Jean and I were going to see the lawyers for the first time.

This was a meeting both attorneys had set up before Jean gave the go-ahead to file the papers; its purpose was to see if she could be persuaded to reconsider and come up with any answer other than divorce. Even after the summons was delivered, Harold had wanted to go ahead with the meeting. "Look, lots of times women file these papers and never carry through," he said hopefully. I grasped at the suggestion of hope, although I didn't see a single sign of backing down in any of Jean's behavior.

We met in Jean's lawyer's office. Harold had not yet arrived, so we chatted easily—after a little initial awkwardness—about what she had done that afternoon. She told me about helping give eye tests at the younger boys' school and what an interesting experience it had been. We both remarked that it was extraordinary none of our children wore glasses because I wore them constantly and Jean was relying on hers more and more.

Harold arrived in a few minutes, excused himself and went in to talk privately to Jean's lawyer. I had not met Jean's lawyer, but I had heard about him and I feared his reputation. When I told Harold who Jean had retained, he said, "Bad, tough luck, a difficult, irascible man." His name was Vic Podell and he had a reputation for being ruthless about getting what he thought was best for his client. After about five minutes Harold came out, accompanied by a youngish-looking, smooth-skinned, dark-haired man wearing round silver-rimmed glasses. "This is Vic Podell," he said. We shook hands and the four of us went into his office.

Harold began, with the obvious prior agreement of Podell. "I've known you and Al for quite some time, admired what you both have done in the community and personally liked you very much. I feel every effort should be made to avert what could be a tragedy, and that's really the purpose of our being here today. To see if something can't be done to avert legal action."

Jean was listening closely. Podell was cleaning his nails with a letter opener.

"Both Vic and I are family men. We know that people have their differences, but that marriage is something special, something sacred, and that a marriage should be saved if at all possible, especially when there are children involved, as there are, with four of them in this situation."

Podell was beginning to look slightly bored, as if he considered the remarks a necessary formality. He was now working on his cuticles. Jean looked a little impatient, as if she were wondering about the ultimate point of Harold's remarks. I lit up my pipe and felt a telltale stiffness about my neck and shoulders. I felt as Podell looked; I expected nothing to come of this, but I was glad Harold was making such a genuine and passionate try.

Harold then pointed out that nothing had been done legally that could not be undone and that speaking for himself and for Podell as well—with a glance in Podell's direction for his approval, which Podell gave with a nod after a momentary pause—he was asking Jean if she would make one last try for a reconciliation. Her answer was brief and immediate: "No."

Harold then said, "Supposing the marriage counselors say there is some hope, that there are things which have not been tried. Would you be willing to go back for more counseling?"

Jean said, "I don't know what you mean."

"For instance, Al has said," Harold continued, "that couples' group therapy was suggested as something that would be helpful to you two, but you turned it down. Something like that. If the counselor emphasized how important it was . . . and how it might save the marriage, would you consider doing it?"

"You can ask Sam whatever you like and tell me what he says," she said, "but I'm not bound by it. I'll decide then myself."

Harold then began to sum up where we stood, in a lawyerly tone. I felt these words were directed more at Podell, to let him know officially how we felt.

"I want it plainly understood," Harold said, "that Mr. Martin does not want this divorce. He does not want it because he still loves his wife, he wants his marriage and family to continue, and as a Catholic he is naturally not in favor of divorce." That last point surprised me. Harold and I had never discussed it. I figured he threw that in for some legal purpose, too. I wasn't against *all* divorce, just this one.

There was a pause. I didn't know whether I was *supposed* to say anything or not, but there was something I *wanted* to say. "I have not undergone any profound reversal or emotional change in my life. I still think I married the right person. None of the difficulties I've discovered in these past nine months of counseling have convinced me that I made a mistake in marrying Jean or that our marriage couldn't be saved if we tried. For the sake of our children and for the marriage itself, I'm willing at any time to make that effort. Divorce is not the answer for us."

Harold said, "Therefore, because of these reasons Mr. Martin will oppose Mrs. Martin's motion for a divorce. He does not intend to leave his residence and he will seek to keep the family intact in that home."

Podell cut in caustically, "Never in my lifetime have I seen an outcome like that, and I don't expect to see it here. I think Mr. Martin should know he is just making matters more difficult for everyone by the stand he is taking."

I got angry at the arrogant manner Podell displayed and at the content of what he was saying: don't get tough, roll over and play dead, we're going to win anyway. I controlled an impulse to lash out at him with my own angry rebuttal.

Jean looked intently down at her hands in her lap. Podell scanned everyone like a professor examining his class to see if anyone had any questions. Then he said briskly, "Well, I don't think we can accomplish anything more today."

We got up—we did not shake hands—and left.

As Harold and I walked back in a cold, biting wind to his office, I told him I was furious at Podell's arrogance and cockiness. "Well, he thinks he's got things going for him because of the woman angle," Harold said. "Nine times out of ten, he's right. But I think we've got a good chance of being that number ten."

Jean had stopped off to pick up some groceries and was later than I returning home. She came in and began hastily throwing together some supper. Her whole body projected intense anger. She moved sharply, quickly, forcefully around the kitchen, slamming drawers, snatching towels, cursing slow-heating burners.

When the kids had cleared out for a few moments, she snarled at me, "I hate you! I hate this house! I hate this whole goddamn mess!" She was swearing and crying, spewing emotions with every movement she made. She closed the kitchen door and with us alone muttered savagely under her breath, "Goddamn it all, goddamn you!"

In a few minutes she had put supper on the table. The boys came in, saw what it was—canned soup and hot dogs—and complained loudly. Nobody enjoyed it. Jean ate a few bites, got up in tears and stalked out of the room. "What's the matter with Mom?" Mark asked. A few seconds later she brushed through the kitchen with her coat on, her face red with rage and tears, and went out, slamming the door behind her. There was silence for a few minutes. Nobody seemed to know what to say; nothing seemed appropriate. Finally I said, "C'mon, guys, eat your supper. You've got to have some food in you. We'll save some for Mom for later." Then the routine of the evening fell into place once more: dishes to clean up, round-robin ping-pong with all the boys downstairs, some games in the living room, then boys to bed, little ones first. By eleven I was exhausted and went right to sleep. About twelve-thirty I heard someone in the living room; Jean had come home.

The next morning at breakfast she was more upset than I had ever seen her. Distorted in a livid mask, her face was a shocking contrast to the soft and gentle Jean she had once been. "You bastard! I hate you!" she raged. The boys had not yet come down for breakfast.

"Jean, nobody's holding you here. You can leave anytime you want!" She screamed, slammed the door and went downstairs. I could hear her choking with tears and rage.

When I came home at suppertime, she had pushed her anger beneath the surface; it showed in sharp, bitter digs, but it was not exploding out of her. The tension crackled between us. In the midst of that atmosphere at the supper table, Mark said in a tiny voice, "I had a dream last night. I dreamed that our family was in a war and everyone was killed." When I heard the words, my heart was wrung with anguish.

Afterwards I said with tears reflecting the depths of my feeling, "For God's sake, Jean, we can't do this to the children! We've got to do something better. Everything that means anything in life is in this house and in these people."

She pounced viciously on "this house" and snapped, "That's all you think of, the house ... the kids."

"I don't mean wood and cement, but the spirit and the human feelings that exist here, the vitality all around us." Jean stalked out of the kitchen and out of the house again.

Jim came through the kitchen and asked: "Where's Mom?"

"Gone out."

"Where?"

"I don't know. Same place as last night, I guess. Wherever that is. Maybe Marie Quinn's."

Jim shook his head in disbelief. "If it's up to us, Dad, you know you'll get the support of the kids."

For the first few days of December, Jean remained in the same furious mood, but by the end of another week she had worked her way through her extreme anger and was in better control of her emotions. She became crisp, cool in her reactions. All the factors falling into place as a result of her decision were lining up against her: the boys were hostile and critical; her parents continued to write, hoping that Jean would change her mind; the legal reality was that she could not throw me out of the house because she had no grounds. But in spite of all the adverse circumstances, Jean continued determined and undaunted.

In direct contrast I was riddled by anxiety and despondency, filled with pain, dismayed at what was happening. No matter how I tried to look at the situation, I came to the same conclusion: I didn't want this to happen. Not ever, but surely not at Christmas time. The only other choice was to leave myself, but I couldn't for two reasons: I couldn't have survived tearing myself away from my loved ones; and I was convinced there would be no Christmas at all if I didn't take the major steps to provide one. So I stumbled on.

Christmas was such a part of me from my earliest childhood recollections and such a part of our life as a family that I reacted instinctively and was swept along by moods before I realized they had happened or could prepare to deal with them.

Christmas was made up of so many rituals: with the boys searching the shelves in the cellar to find the boxes of Christmas-tree lights, brushing off the year's accumulation of dust, bringing the strings upstairs, untangling them, testing the lights, taking the big outdoor bulbs and hanging them across some of the evergreens facing the road. It had meant detailed conversations with each of the boys when they were younger about what they wanted from Santa Claus, now a process involving only Mark; it meant deciding what each of the boys would get for the others and for Jean, figuring out how they were going to pay for it; it meant working with Jean to arrange her shopping trips and sneaking the gifts into the house to be hidden under the eaves or in some other place where the boys would not think to look. It meant reading Christmas stories to Mark, with Charley eavesdropping casually and pretending he really wasn't interested and was too old for Santa stuff; it meant the lighting of the advent wreath candles at the dinner table on the four Sundays before Christmas.

This year each observance was a jagged, painful reminder of the sharply contrasting reality between what existed and what had been before. I hoped that the Christmas mood, which was such a powerful and deep-rooted force in all of us, would help in reaching Jean so the bitterness and tension between us could give way to softness and conciliation. Instead, each event in the Christmas sequence brought a firm and decisive reaction from Jean to deflate that hope.

About ten days before Christmas, Charley, Mark and I went and bought the Christmas tree. Jim and Dan said they definitely wanted one but left the actual selection to the little kids after giving them detailed descriptions of what kind of tree to look for. Jean was out when we bought the tree, passed through the living room after we'd set it up, said, "Oh, you've got one. Good," and kept right on going. In previous years she'd been the supervisor of the tree-trimming ritual, coming in periodically to squint at it and say, "A little more tinsel over here . . . some more lights over there," often taking ornaments and bulbs herself and joining in.

That same night we had a brief, nasty argument. She had been gone so much that I wondered if she would be with us Christmas Eve and Christmas Day. When I asked her, she said angrily, "Of course I will!"

I said, "I don't think I can take that for granted. Besides, you told me that last year you wanted to be with Smothers so badly that you could hardly stay here. Now it seems you're free to go."

"That's not true!" she said. "You're misinterpreting what I said."

"How can you misinterpret 'I wanted to be with Leon'? A lot of things you said before now seem subject to misinterpretation." We were both angry now.

She walked away, then turned and said, "For your information, I've asked Vic Podell to hold off all proceedings during Christmas so that won't interfere with us."

"Hold off!" I shouted. "What do you mean, 'hold off'? Nothing's going to happen now for a few weeks anyway. You've already ruined the holidays and Jim's birthday. Thanks for nothing!"

Jean seemed to respond to the grimness and tenseness that filled our house in the days before Christmas by staying away. She was working more at the dress shop during the daytime and had begun to do some Christmas shopping. On the fifteenth, a Friday, she was out all day, and the next day she spent at her church, rehearsing a Christmas liturgy she was helping to put on. That set up an argument between her and Jim.

Jim's sixteenth birthday was on Sunday, December 17, but we had agreed to celebrate it on Saturday, with the birthday dinner set for five-thirty. When Jean got ready to leave for her church that afternoon, she said she thought she'd be home for dinner, but if not, we should look for her a little later on. Jim snapped angrily, "You don't have to come at all. You're never here anyway!" Jean ignored the remark, said, "See you later," and went on her way. We had our party in the living room, and she came home about an hour after it started, just in time to catch the end of it.

The big boys became more and more rebellious. At dinner one night, with Jean absent again, Dan commented that "maybe we ought to tell Mom that if she wants to go, she should just go. That might wake her up." He suggested a timetable: wait until after Christmas, then tell Mom she's got to change and stay home more often, or tell her she was free to go. The season was marked by the horror of that kind of conversation, rather than by the spirit of Christmas joy we had once enjoyed.

Christmas records went unplayed. We sang no Christmas carols because they seemed hollow and inappropriate. What joy to the world? What good will on earth? What good will to men? God and sinners might be reconciled, but our family was not.

Yet so deeply was the ritual of Christmas ingrained in us that it provided enough substance for us to fashion our own degree of happiness. Relationships in all directions, except between Jean and me, could survive disappointments and anger and still be renewed.

On the Friday of Christmas weekend I walked to get my train. In years gone by, I had enjoyed a wonderful feeling of relief as I looked forward to our annual Christmas vacation. But that night as I remembered that 1972 was slipping away, I thought of what this year had held and what lay ahead in this holiday time. Every night since the decorations had gone up along Park Avenue I had tried to ignore them, to hurry along without noticing, to block them from reaching my consciousness as I walked to my train. But tonight, the last working day before Christmas, which was Monday, it was impossible to walk through the surging tide of Christmas color and spirit and not be touched by it.

People poured out of offices, leaving annual parties behind them and clutching the effects of the good times. Everyone was carrying gaily decorated packages. Christmas music floated out of glittering lobbies, mixed with the confusion of people bustling along and greetings being shouted back and forth. I felt as though I were walking through a tunnel of confetti, through a ticker-tape parade of sound, spirit and festivity, and I hurt deeply.

I thought of the home situation I had to go back to and of Jean: unyielding, unchanged, a drastic contrast to this spirit of fun and good feelings. The spirit of the season hadn't made a dent in her or produced even the slightest thaw. Before, going home on a night like this had always meant a feeling of exuberance and happy anticipation: tonight it meant dread and anguish.

Inside Grand Central a huge choir of schoolchildren in white and red gowns stood on the balcony overlooking the cavernous terminal and filled its expanse with amplified sounds of Christmas glory. On the train, commuters who paid no attention to one another all year long beamed and chatted good-naturedly.

On the way home I drove past outdoor Christmas lights twinkling brightly on lawns, past homes with smoke pouring out of chimneys and curling up into the star-filled night, past batches of last-minute shoppers, past families bunched together carrying Christmas trees. I drove up to our home; the outdoor lights had not been turned on, and the house was in semidarkness. When I went inside, the little boys were playing with the tiny cars, houses and trees in the miniature village under the Christmas tree. Jean was not home. The boys thought she was Christmas-shopping, but they weren't sure. The Christmas vacation lay ahead of us, normally a time bursting with good feelings and good things for us to do; tonight, it seemed hollow and empty, a draining, demoralizing period. I switched on the Christmas-tree lights and sat down to play with Mark and Charley.

Jean and I moved on parallel paths during the weekend, not touching, not relating, doing the basic things that touched on our own family Christmas and ignoring some of the other customs. We did not send out any Christmas cards. Our card list had grown to more than two hundred friends all over the United States and in several foreign countries. To a handful of our closest, dearest friends, I sent a short note of explanation, saying that the situation was at least not final at that point.

On Saturday night Jean went out for the evening after working in the dress shop all day. Jim and Dan went to parties that their friends were giving. Mark, Charley and I played Monopoly in front of the Christmas tree, its lights shining down on us and a fire going in the fireplace. Mark wondered if Santa Claus was going to come to our house this year because we had spent so little time preparing for him. Charley said he hoped Mom hadn't been too busy to help Santa out by getting some of the things they had said they wanted for Christmas.

On Christmas Eve the entire family went to our Christmas liturgy. Rather than hold it in the high school cafeteria where we normally met, we had borrowed an Episcopal church in our area that had a lovely, open, in-the-round worship area. The service was simple and traditional. Throughout it I felt as I had at Charley's recital: trapped, overwhelmed.

Christmas morning finally came. When Mark and Charley burst in on me about six-thirty, I thought of what lay ahead: the beautiful exuberance and innocence of the children as they opened their presents; and the grim awareness that I would probably be watching the last Christmas celebration in which my whole family would be together.

Next the little boys bounced in to get Jean and then they ran upstairs to wake up their big brothers. When everyone had drifted sleepily into the living room, Charley and Mark had already begun their explorations amidst the packages.

"Hey, Santa ate the cookies and drank the milk we left him," Mark shouted excitedly, pointing to the empty glass and the crumbs alongside the fireplace. "And there's his footprint in the papers we put for him to land on," Charley said, turning to us with a wink.

I instinctively looked across at Jean for the pleasure we shared at moments like this, but she did not return the look.

Presents were opened after the younger boys delivered gifts to all members of the family. Jean and I did not exchange any; she did not feel we should. Charley was looking for the ones from us to each other; then in sudden realization he looked up with a dark frown: "Oh, I forgot."

The pleasure of the moment swept aside any further reaction by the kids; they plunged into playing with their toys, trying on their clothes, looking over what each one had gotten. Once again the momentum of what we were as a family carried us past the harsh implications of the moment.

We sat as little islands of emotion: the smaller boys lost

in the pleasure of their gifts; the bigger boys, now past the joyful moment of seeing what they had gotten, slipping back into their own feelings about the overall situation we were in; Jean now briskly turning her attention to getting ready for the worship service at her church that she had helped plan; and I wanting desperately to bring to this Christmas the spirit that we had felt all the other Christmases of our lives, and wracked by the impossibility of this.

As the day wore on, nothing pulled us together into a whole and meaningful unit; Jean and I together did not lead the family in joint, unified celebration of Christmas. Instead, we went off in our own directions: Jean to her church, the little fellows around the neighborhood to inspect what the other kids got, the older boys to their own interests outside the home.

Splintered, ununified, we passed through the day and on in our inevitable drift towards separation.

THE NEW YEAR, 1973, arrived, and I faced the bleakest year of my life.

Nineteen hundred and seventy-two had turned out to be a nightmare, but in the first weeks of that new year I was happy and unaware of what lay ahead. The whispered "I love you" on New Year's Eve was a month old before the troubles began.

But 1973 was beginning with no such illusions. I could scarcely believe that we were the same people or that so much change had taken place. And ahead lay only more painful realities.

There was not even now for me the weekly hope of the counseling sessions, either with Jean or alone. All her time was directed towards church activities. The only flickering, lingering hope I could cling to was the fact that we were both still in the same house, both still open to daily contact.

I came home each dark and wintry night to the same unyielding, unhappy relationship, but each night I gleaned enough scraps of what used to be to pull me through another twenty-four hours. On rare, isolated and totally unexpected days, Jean would suddenly change, and it would be like a ray of sunshine bursting through a stormy sky.

One Saturday afternoon in January Jean came home late in the afternoon and was gay, bubbly and eager to talk. She had been at the Cloisters, a branch of the Metropolitan Museum overlooking the Hudson River in New York. We both remembered the last time we had been there, during our courtship days some twenty years before. I asked her if they still had the marvelous tapestries hanging from the walls and the baroque music piped in softly and soothingly wherever you went. She picked up the excitement of my question and told me animatedly, "Yes, yes, just as it used to be"; then she described the lovely view of the river down below, the tranquillity the museum had inspired in her. She described in great detail, with much feeling, the hours she had spent there. Our words and sentences, questions and answers, tumbled good-naturedly into one another. The scene was so devoid of any problem between us that I could envision myself saying, "Yes, hon, that's interesting. Hey, wait just a minute. Can I fix you another drink? How about going out to dinner later?" And that it would be perfectly normal and in stride with the evening for her to respond: "Sure, let's. That's a great idea!"

Which Jean was she: the one who was trying to devastate me in court? Or the one who sat there cozily and charmingly, chatting away in the kitchen of our suburban home? How could she be both? I didn't know.

Because the boys and I were together so much and such a marked rearrangement of our living habits was taking place, the boys discussed Jean's conduct openly and frequently. Dan was the most frequent and outspoken speculator about what was happening. "It's crazy," he said. "Mom seems to have a split personality. She says she wants us kids, but she doesn't act like it. She's away most of the time, and she's always on the phone when she is here. She thinks that cooking and washing clothes make her a mother."

I knew I could get no explanation from Jean about where she went or why she was away, but when I asked the boys they said they didn't know either. I asked them if she ever sat down and explained how she felt about what she was doing or why she felt she had to do it. "Nope, never," Dan said. "Jim and I have really given her a hard time some days, trying to get her to tell us, but she won't. We told her she was 'acting crazy,' but that didn't bother her. I just don't understand. She's trying to wreck everything we have here, and she never shows any concern about it, never says where she's going, just always acts carefree."

I realized, too, that I was falling into a kind of competition I really didn't like, but I was powerless to stop myself. As soon as I came home, I immediately sensed myself gauging the boys' reactions. Were they angry and surly at me? Were they relating better to Jean? Were they joining her in rejecting me, too? I tried to prepare myself before I came home not to succumb to that kind of sensitivity, but the boys were the only thing in my life that had any meaning now and I couldn't get rid of the fear that they might be lost, too.

Instead of continuing private counseling with Sam, I had joined another group which he himself conducted: it was for men and women actually going through divorces right at that point. I found the men's reactions—when their wives had left or were initiating the action—were very much like my own. How long the couple had been married and how many children were involved were also factors in the amount of difficulty each pair was having. Eric, a very distinguished-looking man with a pencil-thin mustache, and I were the two who received the most prodding from Sam and some members of the group. The other men and women had initiated the divorces and were getting help with the adjustments this required. Their reasons were standard and understandable: another person, fighting, alcoholism, years of hell in "bad" marriages. None of these could help me too much to understand "I don't love you any more."

The members of Sam's group were tougher, much more purposeful, much more biting and direct than I. The members saw me as flinching from facing the practical options available, which they enumerated: try to kick Jean out, leave her myself and start a new life, demand that she take action and do it right away. I was seen as a man who was drowning but who would not swim to shore. I knew what they were saying, I knew the rightness of it from the points of view they held, but that wasn't "me." Somehow I would have to develop a new Albert Martin, but those options didn't provide answers I could live with right now. I had resolved many months before to give Jean only a certain amount of time before I acted on my own, but I had endured this long, Jean seemed on the verge of acting herself, and I was determined to wait it out that much time longer. That was the solution that I could live with and that I felt suited me, so I hung on.

Early in February I had lunch with Stu Robertson. He listened to me talk about my continual fear of losing the children; about my competition with Jean for them and her lack of interest in competing with me; and about my anxiety-ridden, deadlocked situation, trying to accept an inevitability I didn't want and waiting for Jean to act.

"Al, it sounds to me like you're drawing your Maginot line around you, pulling in your defense perimeter and waiting grimly," Stu said. "That's a tough spot to be in. But it seems to me you have to do something better than that."

There was a pause; then Stu looked at me and said, "Jean's not doing too well herself."

"What do you mean by that?" I asked, my interest immediately sharpened.

"She made a phone call late the other night."

"Yes, I know." I told Stu the circumstances that led up to it. Jean had come home late—sometime around midnight—and I was having a few people over: Sara and Gene Nolting and George Herman. Jean fit right in, chatted easily and comfortably, and turned quite a few remarks and her attention toward me. I was quite surprised.

When the people left, Jean and I had a conversation we'd had before: I said that if we could do the same thing harmoniously and were able to relate together to people, to get along with each other, what were we doing getting a divorce? And I asked her why she hadn't told the boys her reasons, even though she'd said she would four months ago. Jean got furious and screamed that I didn't understand her; before we were through it was a pretty bad shouting match. We went to bed. Then about two-thirty I heard her go pounding into the kitchen to use the telephone.

When I looked across the lunch table at Stu there were tears in his eyes. "The person who received that call told me about it. The person is worried about Jean and the way she sounded. The person is afraid Jean is cracking up and heading for a breakdown."

As I heard Stu's words, my eyes filled with tears, too, and

I wanted to cry. We both sat for several minutes in the crowded restaurant, tears streaming down our cheeks.

"Stu, what are we going to do? I don't want her to be hurt. God, I love her. What can I do?"

We sat for several more minutes, not saying anything, both lost in our own thoughts. Then Stu got up and we walked outside.

Wasn't there something someone could do to help two suffering people? As we were walking along, Stu suddenly stopped and turned to me; he looked at me with a face etched in pain and said, "I'd like to try to talk to Jean."

I grabbed him by both arms and hugged him close. "Stu, please do. Whatever you can do to help her helps all of us—me, the kids, Jean, everyone."

As I headed back to work, concern for Jean ran through my mind. That and hope, hope that still wouldn't die.

February passed into March. Jean was still working a few days a week at the dress shop and keeping up the same round of church activities. By late March I was seriously concerned about the effects of our situation on all the children. I asked Jean if she would come with me to a child psychologist, but she saw no need. I made an appointment at the Child Counseling Center in town.

The psychologist was a warm, intensely human person named Mrs. Meyers; she was about my age. I told her about the status of my relationship with Jean and the tense situations that were taking place around the children. She agreed that the situation was loaded with potential damage for the children, the extent depending on how it was handled. I had been in an anguishing dilemma, and I brought this up next with Mrs. Meyers.

For months I had been considering the alternative of

leaving home myself. One Saturday morning I had even taken the list of classified ads from the night before's paper and tracked down a number of furnished rooms in the area that I could afford. The experience was so ghastly and it was so horrifying to consider the squalid drabness of what was available that it shocked me for days. Harold Polis had warned me, too, that if I left I might as well give up any legal claim to having the boys. And I could not imagine a worse fate for me than living alone in a room somewhere away from my family. But I hadn't tested that idea from the psychological standpoint: whether after all it would not be better for the boys. If there had been strong psychological advice that I leave for their benefit, I would somehow have found the strength to do it. I put this whole possibility in front of Mrs. Meyers.

She doodled with a pencil for a few moments, then looked up and said, "I don't see it. First of all, it's not what you feel you ought to do. You have your rights and your feelings, and your life is important, too. But from the standpoint of the boys, it seems to me they would be hurt even more if they saw their father leave, either willingly or unwillingly, when they know he doesn't want to and that his heart is with them there in that house. No, indeed. From a psychological viewpoint, I think it best for the boys to see a strong father, determined to stand up for what he thinks is best and what he has clearly explained to them and with which they seem to agree."

This support relieved my doubts and made me feel much more positive about what I was trying to do.

April came, and Jean said she now needed to find a better-paying job and a place to live before she could consider leaving. I told her how concerned I was over the effects on the children of the indefinite situation; she declared firmly, "I'll go when *I* think the time is right!" In that light I asked her to join me in going to the Child Counseling Center to find out what steps were best for the kids. "No, you've been there already. They're prejudiced by your story," she said.

"Okay, you pick a place and let's go there," I suggested.

Jean said, "I'll think about it."

A few weeks later I read an article in the paper on the work being done with emotionally troubled children at the Gesell Institute in New Haven. I showed it to Jean and suggested that this might be a "neutral" place we could both agree upon. She thought about my proposal for several days, then said I could set up an appointment there and we would go together.

On April 23, 1973, Jean picked me up at the railroad station in midday and we drove up to a two o'clock appointment with Dr. Lois Stark, director of the institute which the famed child psychologist and author Dr. Arnold Gesell had founded.

Dr. Stark, a small, bustling, cheerful woman of middle age, greeted us and led us into her office. She began by asking us several questions: who wanted the divorce, what were the reasons, how we felt about it, how many children were involved, what ages they were. Then she rechecked Jean, asking her if there was any slight possibility that she would reconsider and would want to try for a reconciliation. Jean sat calmly with her hands folded in her lap and answered no.

Then Dr. Stark questioned us further about why we each wanted to keep the children, what plans we had for their care, how we would work it out if we got them. Jean and I had been talking between us for some time about the possibility of a rotating-parent arrangement; the children would stay in the house and we would rotate every six months being in charge of them. We put this idea to Dr. Stark.

Dr. Stark reacted quickly and negatively to our scheme. "It would be no solution for anybody. The children would be confused and would have no sense of permanence. And you both have lives of your own to lead; you can't spend the rest of them rotating as child-sitters."

Then she went on. "First, it is the general feeling here at the institute that in a situation like this—neither parent wanting to give up the children—they do best by staying with the parent of the same sex. Since Mr. Martin does want them and does seem able to care for them, we would recommend all four stay with him."

Jean turned angrily to me and charged that I had led her into a trap. "You knew that was how they felt or you wouldn't have come here," she snapped. I began to protest when Dr. Stark interrupted.

"I say that's how we *feel* from a *psychological* standpoint. But we know that that isn't very likely to happen. The courts are not yet to the point where they take psychological factors into consideration very heavily when they make decisions like this. They still almost invariably favor the mother. But you are both concerned about the emotional well-being of your children; that's why you are here. As a *practical* solution, therefore, it might be best for Mr. Martin to keep the older two boys, since teenagers very badly need a father's influence, and Mrs. Martin keep the two younger ones, since the younger ones still have a strong sense of need of the mother."

I was appalled. Splitting up our boys? My God, what a horrifying thought. I blurted out my objection to the idea:

brothers shouldn't be torn apart, for how could they have any sense of family that way?

"Mr. Martin, it's not a good solution," Dr. Stark said. "The best thing, of course, is for them to have both of you. But if that's not possible, what can you do? There are no good solutions in this kind of situation. It's just the best you can do."

We asked more questions and expressed our concerns over how such an arrangement might work. As the hour wore on, Jean perked up and became more and more excited by the idea, more positive and accepting of the approach. Her anger had disappeared, and she was now turning to more practical matters—how to tell the children, when to make the break. By the time the meeting was drawing to a close, Jean was soaring with enthusiasm.

As we drove away, a tremendous sorrow overpowered me and I began sobbing bitterly, my face buried in my hands. "Jean, Jean, oh God, do we have to do this to them?" I cried. Jean drove on in silence, not answering my anguished question. I cried most of the way home. Gradually my tears stopped, but I could still feel the pain within me.

When she saw that I was somewhat recovered, Jean began talking in practical, matter-of-fact terms, listing the things she needed and would take from our home. She said briskly that we could work out visiting hours and other details later. She seemed happier and more animated than I'd seen her in a year. When I came close to breaking down again, she said crisply, "Al, you've got to face realities."

As we got almost home, the thought of what the day meant and what was going to happen overwhelmed me again, and I again burst into tears. Jean turned on the car radio, found some lively music and hummed along with it as she quickly and resolutely drove the rest of the way home.

 *Epilogue*

It is now more than two years since Jean spoke the words that shattered our world. There is not much recognizable beyond the shell of the life we once led.

Jean remained in the house for almost a year after our visit to the Gesell Institute. Her indecisiveness, the very fact that we were still together, gave me passing hope that she was going through a phase and might someday emerge from it. But one day she put a load of wash in the dryer, punched the "start" button, told us we could find plenty of food for dinner in the freezer, and went out the door.

She lives in a small apartment downtown in our community. Mark lives with her. Jim and Dan had their choice because they were legally old enough, and decided to stay with me in the house. Charley was not old enough to exercise a choice, but he said he wanted to stay, too. After a court investigation, he was awarded to me.

The legal realities that Harold Polis told me would weaken or even eliminate Jean's case for a divorce never became relevant. Connecticut adopted a no-fault divorce law; all Jean had to do was apply for a divorce and wait a few months, and she received it.

Leon Smothers resigned from the ministry, divorced his wife and left our area. I heard he got a job counseling at a boys' rehabilitation institute in New York State. Jean says she has no contact with him.

Jack Connors left the Catholic priesthood for good. He is finishing up a doctoral program in counseling on the West Coast.

We learned midway through 1973 that Jean's father was incurably ill with cancer. Pap faced death as he had faced life: with humor, courage and integrity. Incredibly, he remained open and fair to both Jean and me until the end. He loyally supported Jean in whatever she chose to do. Yet the last time we were together, he said that he and his wife still prayed that Jean would change her mind, although they had little hope she would.

Jim, Dan, Charley and I now keep this ten-room house and the yard going, but it isn't easy. I have compressed my working hours in New York so that I can get all the kids off to school each morning and be home right after five at night to make dinner. Each boy chips in his bit to help: cleaning bathrooms, using the washer and dryer, vacuuming, cooking when necessary.

For me the working day stretches from six-fifteen in the morning until almost one at night; I do some of my best cooking after midnight. I am totally exhausted by day's end, but I would not want to be anywhere else.

In many ways—superficial ways—we are the same family we were before. Teenagers still gather here to vibrate the walls with jam sessions in the basement. Charley and his friends now use the ball field to practice for their Little League games. And Mark and his little pals are edging into those workouts occasionally, too. Mark comes to visit us on Wednesdays and on weekends; he keeps up with all his old activities in the neighborhood. We all still swim in the lake, play tennis on the neighbor's court down the street, and go for walks in the woods nearby. But I know it is all a shell, and beneath it something very important is missing.

I know that this is true as far as my own feelings are concerned. There are moments of such emptiness and loneliness in this house that they almost shatter me. Photographs I have not yet taken down from the walls remind me of our days as a happy family. There are memories and reminders everywhere, so I know just how much is missing.

I also know it as I hear Charley's voice when he telephones his mother. I see it in the growing toughness and callousness toward close family relationships that Jim and Dan show more frequently. I can see it in Mark's confusion when he visits us and isn't sure at first how he fits in and which is his home and who is his family.

I know we are not what we once were, too, because of the picnics we do not get invited to, the neighborhood gatherings we are not part of any more, the nights and weekends we do not spend with other families. We are some kind of amputated, truncated, mutilated thing, and for us that is an incredible change.

I still try to sift among the pain and debris of two years and come up with answers that will finally let the hurt out of my gut and release me from the tension that grips me from early morning until late at night. About a year ago I wrote an article for the Op-Ed Page of *The New York Times* about what I was going through and how I felt about it. The responses from scores upon scores of people all over the country told me that I was not unique, I was not alone, and others were hurting, too, and searching for answers as I was. So I began to search in a larger way and started to write this book.

Yet today I still have not come up with good answers, final answers, real, satisfying, enlightening answers. I know there were many faults with the world Jean and I lived in, and it was not exactly as I thought it was back then. I know I certainly contributed my share to our problems and that the rest of a lifetime can be spent trying to piece together all the reasons, causes and blame. Beyond that, there is one thing I know for certain: I can't imagine a worse person for this to have happened to. I loved my wife, I loved my family, I loved being married, I loved the life we led, I loved having Jean to share it with, to give to, to be loved by; I loved everything there was about it completely and unquestioningly.

I think of all we had and where we are at now. During those moments I get furious at Jean, so outraged that I could burst my lungs screaming and smash things in my fury. I think of the hopeless, futile struggle I carry on: making more money than I ever have in my life, but falling deeper and deeper into debt. There is not enough money to keep up two households; nothing left with which to send the boys to college, for unexpected needs, for vacations or pleasures of any kind. Pretty soon, at the rate we are going, there will be no money, period, and I won't be able to borrow any more and we will be forced to sell the house and complete the shattering of this family and all that it was. And I am outraged.

Amidst all this, more and more lately, I think about something Sara Nolting said to me early on. Sara said, "I wouldn't want to be you for anything in this world."

I agreed with her then and thought about those words countless times over the months. But now I am becoming convinced that there is one other person I'd even *less* rather be: Jean. When I think of the horrifying price she has paid for whatever it is she has obtained, my rage turns to sorrow.

I am not thinking about the tangible things she gave up: like our house, this lovely area, our evenings out on the patio. She said all along she didn't want these any longer, and I can understand that, because it is possible to give up the physical things of life.

But I am thinking of her turning her back on the weekends jammed with the vitality and exuberance of young people that we still have around here; the humanity that radiates from Mark and his small pals all the way up to Jim and Dan and their teenage friends. She gave up the visible growth of personalities, attitudes and viewpoints around the supper table every night; the delicious moments of the waning day when you're rubbing a kid's back and saying goodnight to him; the noisy rough-and-tumble between kids that almost drives you out of your mind, followed suddenly by the glorious calm, the healing peace. How could she willingly give these up?

How could she? How could she? How could she?

I asked myself that question for two years, and I was sustained by the belief that she never could. But now I am left with the reality that she did. And I still ask myself: How *could* she?

I guess the fact that she *did* and I never could *understand* it says a lot about what happened to both of us. Something made Jean change profoundly. After scores of hours of counseling, dozens of hours in therapy groups, dawn to night thinking about it, shelves of books hungrily read and thousands of dollars spent, I still do not have the real answer even to that.

About all that I do have are some dim outlines of how this could be possible and an intellectual grasp of the needs of self-fulfillment and self-identification. But deep down inside me there is a certainty that *I* couldn't have done what Jean did and that the Jean who was could not have done it either.

This, I believe, is part of the tragedy of Jean and me. We became two different people with two different value systems. Compounding the tragedy was the fact that the counseling itself pulled us further apart rather than bringing us closer together. Yes, it did put us in touch with ourselves, it did enable us to see our needs better, and it did encourage us to fulfill them. But that is what is dreadfully, cataclysmically wrong with the process. An extraordinary emphasis on self is happening today across our nation, and this is why we continue to tear our marriages apart, splinter our families and raise our divorce rates to new heights every year. The very core of what Sam Glazier practiced—and what the counseling establishment preaches—is the enshrinement of individuality, the freedom of self, at the expense of marital union and social compromise.

By concentrating so overwhelmingly on the individual and his freeing of himself, the consequences of relationship are almost entirely overlooked. And the tragic result is that people caught up in the emotional chaos and upheaval of a marital crisis can seldom look beyond their recently perceived individual needs in order to choose the tough, unpalatable, excruciating steps of rebuilding the relationship. It is easier to say that no basis for the rebuilding exists, or that it's not his or her need. This is especially true when the whole counseling process, the overwhelming climate of the therapy, involves telling the individual to do only what he wants. When the counseling validates the following of personal needs and desires wherever they may lead, when no counterbalancing values or objective restrictions or convincing alternatives are put forward forcefully enough, the inevitable result is a huge rush *en masse* for the exits. Why should anyone stay? As Jean said during one argument in the car, "Do you realize how much pain and effort it would take to work out this goddamn mess?" No one in the counseling seemed to suggest it was worth it.

I made a false presumption when we began the marital counseling. I think it is the one popularly held until you actually go through the process yourself. I clearly remember telling myself on the train going home that first night to meet Sam that a marriage counselor was in the business of saving marriages. That isn't true. Sam told me so that night: "We are in the business of saving individuals, not marriages."

The fatal flaw in that approach is that *individuals* are also what make up marriages; so when you don't save marriages, you also very often don't save individuals. Not all the time, true. But frequently enough, and discernibly enough as you look around, to see that this is truly a fault. I am an individual; my children are individuals; who cared about saving us? Marriage counseling can't continue to follow the unreal premise that you treat married persons the same way as you treat individuals who have no connections, no relationships, no responsibilities.

There is a specialness about married people that has to be recognized and responded to. A marriage relationship calls for some degree of selflessness and other-directedness, and a willingness and disposal toward compromise in order to work. I don't mean the destructive distortions that often meant surrender or capitulation or domination of one person by another. But I do mean the voluntary relinquishing of *total* individuality and the surrender of some vital self-interests to make possible a common good greater than simply the sum of each individual's needs.

The simple fact is that *marriage* counseling isn't working in terms of treating marriages. It *is* working in terms of *individual* counseling. You don't have to be a social scientist to find this out; all you have to do is look around: divorce rates are soaring. They have climbed over 80 percent in the last few years alone. One out of every three marriages now winds up in divorce. The highest failure rate of all is in the bracket of marriages fifteen years old and older, the bracket Jean and I were in and the group that supposedly has the most firmly established roots, the deepest family patterns. The expectation is that this trend of marital distress will get worse.

The stampede for divorce parallels the radical shift in technique and objectives that marriage counselors made seven or eight years ago when they moved from the preservation of marriages to the liberation of individuals. At present, only one out of every ten marriages coming before counselors emerges intact at the end of the process. Heart-transplant operations had about the same survival rate, and they were abandoned as an unsound risk. I cannot believe that somewhere in the 90 percent of the marriages that are *not* saved by counselors there are not some couples who wouldn't have been made better by some approach other than "do your own thing, identify your needs, fulfill your own identity." The human wreckage and the individual misery we are strewing over our society and casting into our next generations demand that we reassess what we are doing.

I don't know if a different, broader, more relationship-oriented type of marital counseling would have made a change in what eventually happened to Jean and me. When I see the profound personality change that has happened in her, I think competent psychiatric care could have made a difference. If it had been indicated for me, I would have willingly undergone it. Marriage counseling has wandered into an area of therapy previously considered beyond its competence; it begins processes it cannot healthily complete. I'll never know if anything else would have worked for us. But I would like to have given it a try, to have struggled in an atmosphere that cared more about whether a marriage of twenty years' duration ended.

I think there are bad times to be certain things in history. It was bad to be a witch in Salem in the 1700s, bad to be a Negro in America before May 1954, bad to be a "pinko" during the frightened days of McCarthyism, bad to be a polio victim the year before they discovered the vaccine. And I know it is bad to be in marital trouble in America today because the times have never been worse for getting effective help.

I know I do not want to see my four sons face the same misery I did or to encounter—either in society at large or, God help them, in counseling—the same values and perspectives that affected the outcome of my marital crisis. I do not want them to grow up with an overriding concept that marriage is only a vehicle for personal fulfillment. I do not want my boys, in their marriages and in their lives, to shove aside a sense of commitment, responsibility and sacrifice. Nor do I want them to lose the notion that being a good, decent person, a loving and caring husband, a concerned and dedicated parent are unimportant or irrelevant or in any way not worth being. I know what the lack of these values can do to human lives.

I grieve for my son Charley, who has wanted nothing more these past two years than his mother's care and interest. His longing is even deeper now when he does not have Jean there to greet him after school and to tuck him in bed at day's end with a good-night kiss. Those are *his* needs, his birthright, and he did not ask to become the victim of an adult's self-fulfillment; nor did anyone seem to care, along the line, what *his* own identity would become.

I grieve for Jim and Dan, who, as they are going through the teenage experiences of dating and establishing their first grown-up relationships, are deprived of a mother's understanding and perspective. I grieve at the hardening and cynicism toward women that I already see in them.

I grieve for Mark, who cannot come running up to me in the driveway each night, as he used to, to tell me what happened at school that day, or to practice that mean cowtail swing of his at a baseball I throw his way, or to respond with a loud "yeeaahhh!" to an invitation for a quick dip in the lake before supper. He and I cannot ever take back those moments.

I grieve for myself, too, for the love I once knew and the fearsome new beginnings I must make in midlife.

And I grieve for a woman I knew who was warm, gentle, outgoing, compassionate; who related so vibrantly to me, to her children, to people, to the community, to religion; who was an attentive, concerned mother, giving of herself to the job of helping four young human beings grow to their own maturity. I grieve for that woman, who now seems to me hard, austere, angry, her whole existence centered on her independence and her own church.

I grieve because in the context of Sam's counseling Jean must be considered a success: she is in touch with herself and her own needs, and she is fulfilling them. The tragedy is we are all the losers as a consequence.

There must be a better way; there have to be better answers.

For the sake of those who are coming after us—and they seem to be legion—I hope and pray we find them soon.